Additional Acclaim for *Greenback*

"Engaging . . . The dollar generates amusing characters and anecdotes, and Goodwin deftly weaves a tale of unbroken faith from the lives of men who often broke theirs."

—*The New York Times Book Review*

"Engaging . . . Goodwin rolls through American history, stopping wherever there's something to be said about the dollar. . . . This breezy book will no doubt entertain you."

—*The Wall Street Journal*

"Fascinating anecdotes and facts about the dollar, as well as the politicians and bankers who guided its odyssey, are woven together."

—*Businessweek*

"Vivid . . . Goodwin's thoughtful meditation on what Americans have made of the dollar, and what it has made of us, rings as true as the silver we've banished."

—*The New York Observer*

"[Goodwin's] book is as crisp as a brand-new dollar bill."

—*St. Louis Post-Dispatch*

"Goodwin is a flat-out marvelous writer. He has a wonderful eye for humor, fashions memorable sentences, and is an artist at clever turns of phrase. Who knew economic history could be this interesting?"

—*Flint Journal*

"Immediately and surprisingly engaging . . . He approaches his subjects as if they're exotic new places to be explored and enjoyed. He revels in their idiosyncrasies and inconsistencies. And he skips the chamber of commerce to spend as much time as possible with town cranks and eccentrics."

—*The Boston Globe*

"Goodwin possesses a fine eye for the telling anecdote and the picturesque detail. . . . [A] surprisingly engaging popular history about a subject that should be as boring as watching paint dry. Not a bad investment of your time and hard-earned greenbacks."

—*Denver Post*

W9-CBS-174

Also by Jason Goodwin

─────────

On Foot to the Golden Horn

Lords of the Horizons

A Time for Tea

GREENBACK

THE ALMIGHTY DOLLAR AND THE INVENTION OF AMERICA

JASON GOODWIN

Picador
A John Macrae Book
Henry Holt and Company
New York

www.picadorusa.com

Picador® is a U.S. registered trademark and is used by Henry Holt and Company under license from Pan Books Limited.

For information on Picador Reading Group Guides, as well as ordering, please contact the Trade Marketing department at St. Martin's Press.
Phone: 1-800-221-7945 extension 763
Fax: 212-677-7456
E-mail: trademarketing@stmartins.com

Designed by Victoria Hartman

Library of Congress Cataloging-in-Publication Data

Goodwin, Jason, 1964–
    Greenback : the almighty dollar and the invention of America / Jason Goodwin.
        p. cm.
    Includes bibliographical references and index.
    ISBN 0-312-42212-1
    1. Dollar. I. Title.

HG591.G64 2003
332.4'973—dc21   2002068805

First published in the United States by John Macrae Books, an imprint of Henry Holt and Company

First Picador Edition: January 2004

10 9 8 7 6 5 4 3 2 1

To Tabby and Jay, pioneers;
their son Felix, born in the U.S.A.;
and in memory of Esme.

"I wasn't worth a cent two years ago,
and now I owe two millions of dollars."

Overheard by Mark Twain

Contents

GREENBACK

INTRODUCTION: AMERICAN DREAM

This is how I spent my first dollar.

When I was seventeen I took sick on a bus going toward the railway at Ahmādābad. The guidebook called Ahmādābad India's Birmingham. I had been traveling in India for a month. On the back of the bus it said Horn Please and OK Tata. The driver burnt joss before a postcard of Kali on the dash. I found a commercial traveler's hotel where nobody spoke English, and spent the night sweating in a cold room.

In the morning I gritted my teeth, got dressed, and tried to find a way out of Ahmādābad. The railway terminus was Victorian Gothic, with pinnacles and Venetian windows. It was full of people in pajamas. The queues stretched for yards and moved slowly. After a long wait I asked for a ticket to Bombay. The ticket clerk consulted a piece of card and shook his head. In two days. Maybe. The people behind me were losing patience, starting to thrust themselves into the gap between me and the grille, their hands full of money. I felt too ill to give way. I eased a green banknote out of my money belt and put it under a pile of dirty pink rupees. I slid the pile across to the clerk. First-class sleeping berth to Bombay, I said.

The clerk no more examined the dollar than I had. He made it disappear, and gave me a small cardboard ticket with a berth number written on it. Soon afterward I watched Ahmādābād slide away through the carriage window, and the next day I reached Bombay.

So that was how my dollar bill went: on a bribe. I was impressed by the dollar's power to bend the rules, even miles from its home. I haven't bribed anyone else since, but I've spent dollars and earned dollars. A decade ago in Eastern Europe I got to enjoy the Cold War buzz of a dollar bill. I like the words nickel and dime. Sometimes I take a dollar check into the bank in England, and pay it in across the counter, and then I have a Mitty-ish moment as a day trader, or a Hollywood consultant, or an art expert or a drug baron. It's quite different from banking a thousand quid, or fifteen hundred euros, or two hundred and forty thousand lire: handling dollars puts me figuratively closer to the money. The cashier always crosses out the printed £ sign on the paying-in slip and puts in a $ sign with two downstrokes, just like a cartoonist indicating a swag bag. In English cartoons, burglars' bags are marked SWAG. In American cartoons, people even get $$ in their eyes.

The swag, globally speaking, is set at $7 trillion. The great majority of these dollars exist electronically, but around $666 billion's worth, in denominations from $1 to $10,000, is printed, on 22 billion paper bills or notes, of which almost a third are held outside the U.S. This means that there are more dollar bills in existence than any other branded object, including Coke cans. Yet two centuries ago there were supposedly only $10 million in the U.S. And that was a lot: 10 million was a lot of anything in 1776. They've been breeding.

So it's no wonder that dollar bills are suspected of having a secret life. U.S. Customs researchers recently analyzed dollar bills from suburban Chicago, Houston, and Miami. They found that 78 percent of them were contaminated with cocaine. Old bills generally, and the bills from Houston and Miami in particular, yielded a heavier dose than bills from Chicago.

Cocaine may not be the only hitchhiker on a dollar bill. The oil man Howard Hughes, who had more dollars than most of us will ever see, couldn't touch them for fear of catching germs; like King Midas, who turned everything he touched into gold, Hughes wound up battling with his riches. Staff at one old San Francisco country club actually wash the change they give to members. Other people pop money briefly in the oven.

Sinister messages may be hidden in the Great Seal of the United States, which appears on the back of the dollar bill. A popular theory fingers a Masonic sect called the Illuminati whose aim is to overthrow governments. They are so secret and ruthless that nothing more is known about them. The first American to get frightened about the Illuminati was a Boston preacher called Jedediah Morse, whose more famous son was the telegraph king and inventor of the Morse code. Another obscure belief of occultists is that a mysterious man in black appeared one day at Thomas Jefferson's elbow and told him how to reproduce the symbols on the Great Seal. Anyone with a ruler, compass, and a taste for voodoo can use a dollar bill to design a nine-pointed star traditionally associated with calling up the Devil himself.

It is legal to add your own mark to a dollar bill, if the intention is not criminal. So a web site called Wheresgeorge.com invites people to buy a small rubber stamp for $4.95 and use it on their dollar bills: the stamp says Wheresgeorge.com and allows people to track that particular dollar's progress by its serial number on the web. Curiously enough, the best performer on Wheresgeorge.com to date is a dollar bill that has traveled a miserable 375 miles—as if these bills know someone's onto them and are giving out false signals. For undeniably 3 billion dollar bills, of various denominations, have gone in for serious travel. They have gone to South America and the Golden Triangle in Southeast Asia. They live under mattresses in remote Russian villages. They club together to enjoy the expat life in Europe (Eurodollars) and the Middle East (petrodollars). They never go home. "Would it be giving away a trade secret," I asked my bank in Hampshire, England, "to tell me how many dollars you have on hand, right now?" The teller, rather mysteriously, thought so.

Every dollar bill issued by the Treasury or the Fed since 1863 is as good today as it ever was. You can even use one today to pay your tax. (Try taking a ten-shilling note or fifty thousand old French francs to the bank and see how far you get.) America's social security system isn't all it might be, but dollar bills get cared for cradle to grave: veterans of the household washing machine, crippled notes, shattered fragments—all, provided the serial number is still intact, can be tenderly nursed back into circulation one way or another. As for the old bills, a scripophile, a paper-money collector, will obviously pay more than the IRS.

I read in the paper recently that a priest was detained trying to smuggle three counterfeit hundred-thousand-dollar bills into the U.S. The paper pointed out that hundred-thousand-dollar bills do not exist. But they do: they are just no longer made. Hundred-thousand-dollar bills show Woodrow Wilson and were produced for internal use at the Federal Reserve.

I also read that an old lady had tried to pay for her shopping in Bloomingdales with a million-dollar note. The judge said gently:

"Million-dollar notes are not legal tender."

She had made the note herself, by cutting the zeroes from ten-dollar bills and fitting them together. She said to the judge:

"In this case, sir, they are."

But no. Money is a belief that has to be shared with other people, even judges. Otherwise money's useless: you can't eat or wear it,[1] buy love with it (though you may broaden your chances), and you don't get to take it with you when you die. Money can be anything you like—gold or silver, peas or paper, tiny shells or massive stones, or nothing at all but surf on the electronic highway. But everyone must agree on what it is: we accept money because we believe others in turn will accept it too. It works because it works.

Laws—sometimes draconian laws—exist to buttress a belief in money. The issuing powers defend their copyright ferociously, even against confused old ladies. But her "economic crime," as the Chinese put it, was to get caught: economists don't (and can't) distinguish between legitimate and counterfeit money. "From the economist's standpoint counterfeit notes and coins, so long as they are accepted, carry the same power as their legal counterparts," says Gavin Davies in his *History of Money.* The old lady was caught because her million dollars weren't really a million dollars at all: but the only reason they weren't was because she was caught. Otherwise she might have turned the bill into a million dollars' worth of cat food. Then the cat food manufacturer could have paid the butchers, the butchers would have propped up their favorite restaurants, the chef would have paid the truckers, truckers the farmers, farmers the seed companies, seed companies the truckers, and so on. The woman was in spending mode, and the greatest danger she posed to society was the outside possibility that her million-dollar note, being considered legitimate, might never actually be broken at all. Mark Twain wrote up this possibility in his 1889 story "The Million Pound Note."

History gives few instances of old ladies defining what money ought to be, but men have done it time and again, and the dispute

---

1. Cases I will cite later of quite ordinary Americans both eating and wearing money do not contradict this statement. Americans have also smoked money and used it to fix planks. At each moment, though, it stopped being money.

about what is and isn't real money runs like a silver seam through the bedrock of American history.

I can't help seeing this doughty forger as an American type, as she stands there in court with her own unacceptable but seemingly unshakable views on money. Europeans are trained to think differently about what money is and where it comes from. For them, money is an attribute of power, a symbol of authority, a sign of legitimacy. The bad king debases the coin and robs his people of full value; the good one keeps with tradition and maintains the standards. The subject people make the best of both.

"In this case, sir, they are" is a patently absurd reply; but in other circumstances it would be a noble claim. Special pleading is, after all, the essence of liberty: it's assuming the right to be different, not to toe the line, not to surrender one's sovereignty to force or fashion. In 1776 the British government declares that colonial grumbles and resentments aren't a warrant for colonists to disobey the law. "In this case they are" sums up the Americans' revolutionary response. Liberty is noble, it is dangerous. "In this case," says the slave owner, the gunman, or the terrorist, by way of justification, and free society must be forever negotiating the boundaries of its liberty.

Enter, then, the hero of the piece.

ON THE FACE of the dollar bill there is of course another face. The dark background points up his fleecy white curls, white cravat binding his neck, white ruffles on his shirtfront. He has a mutton jaw. He's looking at you through tired little eyes, a stubborn commander who won his war by refusing the possibility of defeat. He kept his army together for eight hard years until the enemy's army—one of the world's best-trained, most-experienced, and well-paid fighting forces—gave up first. General Washington ground them down.

He's appeared on the bill in a thin, lyre-shaped frame for almost eighty years: before World War II, before the Great Depression, the same George Washington on the same dollar, same color—black—same tufts of laurel leaves, the numeral 1 in each corner, the same scrolls and cobwebs.

It was produced in the roaring twenties, the age of streamlined artifacts, skyscrapers, mass production, and design consultancies: an eighteenth-century portrait among the laurel leaves and table mirrors of a fancy whorehouse. Even then it looked like a shrine.

For the U.S. had only just emerged from an exhausting cycle of theological debate that rivaled in its way the acrimonious religious conflicts that battered Europe in the sixteenth century, and produced the nation state. America's theology was a secular one. It revolved around money and liberty, promise and return, profit and loss.

It revolved, in fact, around the miracle of money.

The money religion is known as the worship of Mammon, and the Almighty Dollar is the supreme being. With devotees even in Indian railway stations, it's an institution bigger and tougher than the Catholic Church; there are Catholics who disagree all the time with the pope, but in a bull market the chairman of the Federal Reserve is considered infallible. In the last fifty years several countries have converted en masse to the dollar, while in others, where the process has been officially discouraged, individuals have enthusiastically converted their pesos, pounds, or rubles; wild scenes ensue around the globe as people scramble to buy dollars as a hedge against inflation, deflation, devaluation, or the bitterness of persistent poverty.

New York is the Holy City, where bankers native and foreign move from one boardroom sacrament to the next in hushed limousines like cardinals attending curiae. Across the world the faith is sustained by financial advisers, banks, stockbrokers, and currency dealers, while corporation lawyers, tax accountants, and the IRS debate the rules with all the vigor of medieval theologians arguing over the number of angels who might dance on the point of a pin. Media pundits operate like old-time preachers in their pulpits. Money is touched incessantly by the miraculous, and the lottery wins, the successful share flotations create a moment when the magic of the dollar touches people like a straight draft of grace.

The dollar has been called spondulicks, bucks, dough, wad, ready, boodle, beans, and simoleon, which is perhaps done to make it more acceptable: call it money and it's serious; call it a C-note or a sawbuck and it's part of the game, part of what Dante (while reserving a peculiar hell for the moneymakers) called *La divina commedia,* and in which we are all included.

When people think about money, it is generally to wish they had more of it. Americans made this their starting point, and experimented with money as no other nation ever had the chance to: wampum, paper currency, private banknotes, gold and silver, government money, bank money. On the way, the people learned to strike a deal, fix a price, watch their interests. They learned how to conjure money not out of the thin air exactly, but out of the natural riches of the land and the ingenuity of their own minds, and fell to arguing how much, relatively speaking, it was worth. Settling that dispute, over the years, defined them as a nation. To get where we are today has meant ironing out a lot of differences, or ironing them, at least, deceptively flat.

A PROMISE TO PAY

On Spanish Silver—Bohemian Mines— Alchemy—Surprising Gifts

Rome was founded by two boys raised by a she-wolf; Britain by Trojans; Poland by the sons of a river goddess. In China the worm of creation crept out of the egg of eternity: the egg was probably laid in India; and when God decided to create man, according to the Basques of northern Spain, He took the parts from a Basque grave-yard. Only America was born in the love of money.

"Oh, most excellent gold!" Columbus exclaimed, on his first voyage. "Who has gold has a treasure [that] even helps souls to paradise." Ferdinand and Isabella of Spain sent the first American gold to the pope, who used it to gild the new ceiling of Santa Maria Maggiore. The rest was made into doubloons. These were entirely new coins that bore a double portrait, and they signaled the creation of Spain out of Ferdinand's Aragón and Isabella's Castile.

The Spaniards accordingly succumbed to gold fever. Gold that had taken the Aztecs and the Incas hundreds of years to collect was stripped from their temples and palaces in the space of a generation, and shipped to Spain. Later, every rumor pointed farther inland, over the next ridge. Cibola, the Seven Cities of Gold, did not exist. The Spaniards struggled north—into modern Kansas—on the scent of another golden city, Quivira. Soon afterward, the French would hear of Saguenay, a land in the far north where men studded with rubies flew through the air like bats. The French king, Francis I, sent Jacques Cartier, a Saint-Malo navigator, to find it.

Science taught that the fiercer rays of the sun drew precious metals toward the equator. Over time, the sun's influence transformed even base metals underground: veins of lead matured into silver, and silver into gold. It was no accident, people said, that the Incas who worshiped the sun had yielded the conquistadors wealth beyond measure.

But it turned out that there wasn't really that much gold. There was no golden man, El Dorado, dusted in gold dust, who dipped his body and washed the gold away in the waters of a hidden lake; his legend was only the best of the stories everyone wanted to believe. Perhaps the world was too young for the sun to have completed its transmutation for there was plenty of silver instead, and by 1600, locked away in the high Andes of modern Bolivia, there was Potosí, the loveliest city in Spanish America, larger than Paris, London, or Madrid, with twelve churches, baroque *palacios,* paved streets, and public drinking fountains: "Rich Potosí," its motto ran, "the treasure of the world, the King of Mountains, and the envy of kings!" People of the city considered honor more precious than life, and food cost more than anywhere else in the whole Spanish empire. Above the town rose the silver mountain, La Montana de Plata, where thousands of Indians dredged the hill of its ores, packed the earth into barrels, and took it to the refinery at its foot. Hundreds more labored to draw the precious metal from the dirt. The mercury technique of extracting silver from the ore reached America in 1557.

Mercury boosted output from Potosí tenfold, and sent the Indians deaf and blind and mad. The molten silver was poured into dies. Indians struck the image of the king of Spain onto the discs. Still rough at the edges, the coins were placed in sacks and the journey to the coast began.

Nothing in Potosí could prepare you for the shock of leaving it. A searching wind blew across the valley, disturbing only flakes of shale. For hundreds of miles on either hand nothing grew but gray tufts of spiky merino grass. The caravans of silver plodded through to Arica, where Spain's Pacific fleet, the Armada del Sur, fetched the treasure up the western coast of South America to Panama. Pack mules then bore it across the isthmus to join the main treasure fleet, bound for Seville. In the forty-six years from 1580, eleven thousand metric tons of silver and gold were laden in the transports, flanked by warships on the watch for French and English pirates lurking in the West Indies. The money followed the sea trail blazed first by Montezuma's gold; Pocapetls' Aztec riches, amassed over hundreds of years; metalwork of such intricate skill that the great engraver Albrecht Dürer declared himself in mourning for what the Spaniards had already melted down; thousands of tons of silver, and some gold still: the riches of a continent, rifled to fill the war chest of a Spanish king.

Spain, paradoxically, refused to grow rich. González de Cellorigo pondered this melancholy lesson in *Memorial de la politica necesasaria y util a la republica de Espana* of 1600: "Riches that ride on the wind are the ruin of Spain . . . the reason for the lack of gold and silver money in Spain is that there is too much of it and Spain is poor because she is rich." He was right. So recently united under Ferdinand and Isabella, so urgently cleansed of its Jews and its Moors, so rigidly policed by the agents of the Inquisition, Catholic, statist, noble Spain saw almost nothing of all this wealth but palaces, fountains, and faraway wars, while its Moorish schemes of irrigation fell into decay, and its Jews, who had understood money, rebuilt Thessaloníki, in modern Greece. As prices in Spain rose, Spanish silver leaked abroad, to buy things cheaper, until the kingdoms of Spain were called "the Indies of other foreign kingdoms," and the flood of silver that hit the coast of Spain, as a percipient Venetian remarked, was shed as lightly as rainwater spouting from a roof.

Today the Silver Mountain is still worked. The miners work in a cooperative. They come from Potosí and have nothing else to do. They work long hours and do not live long. They show the tunnels to visitors who bring them gifts of gunpowder.

AT THE SAME time as the conquistadors were riding into South America, a central European nobleman, the count of Slik, was starting to mint his own coins using silver dredged from the wooded mountains of Bohemia, in what is now the Czech Republic. The hills are dotted with dilapidated spa towns, equipped with joyless proletarian hotels, and they are also riddled with shafts and tunnels that were dug between the fifteenth and the eighteenth centuries, when most European silver was mined from Bohemia. One of the gloomier spa towns is Jachymov.

Known in the count of Slik's day as Joachimsthal, the place was far from gloomy. It was raucous, ugly, and rich, a boomtown feeding on the terrific output of its mines. When in 1519 the count of Slik, who owned the land, turned his portion of silver into coins, nothing quite like them had ever been seen before. The new coin from Joachimsthal was called a thaler, meaning from the valley, *thal*,[1] and in a world where merchants dealt in old, worn, underweight coins of

---

1. Whence the English *dale,* and *dell.*

dubious value and near-illegible provenance, the bright new coins were accepted with pleasure. They showed the count seated in full regalia, so majestic that his crown stuck out and jostled with the inscription around the rim, and they weighed a Saxon ounce.

Their size appealed to merchants participating in a European economic renaissance: a big silver coin was more useful when deals were getting bigger, too. Other central European rulers started to follow the count's lead, remodeling their own coinage on the thalers of Joachimsthal, and before long there were some fifteen hundred imitations circulating among the tiny, tightly packed statelets of the Holy Roman Empire. The weightiest imitator, though, was their overlord, the Holy Roman Emperor himself, the Habsburg Charles V, king of Spain, emperor of Germany, duke of Burgundy, ruler of the Netherlands, Bohemia, much of Italy, and the whole of America, who adopted the thaler as a model for his own standard coin, a coin that sifted out across the world—the Italian tallero, the Dutch daalder, the Ethiopian talari, the Samoan tala, and the English dollar.

IN 1527, Joachimsthal got itself a mine physician, Georgius Agricola. When he was sixteen years old and still known as plain Georg Bauer, Agricola formed a resolution to discover the elixir that would give him seven hundred years of life, and the stone that would turn everything it touched to gold. His studies led him to a string of universities in north Italy and undermined his confidence in alchemy. At Leipzig, Erasmus showed him how to reason. "Seeing so many writers assure us with all earnestness that they have reached that goal for which they aimed, it would seem that faith might be placed in them," Agricola reflected; "yet also seeing that we do not read of any of them ever having become rich by this art, nor do we now see them growing rich, although so many nations everywhere have produced, and are producing, alchemists, and all of them are straining every nerve night and day to the end that they might heap up a great quantity of gold and silver, I should say the matter is dubious."

But in Joachimsthal, working among the miners, he saw something more interesting: incontrovertible proof that men could turn dross into silver. He bought mining shares, and they paid out handsomely.

For all the hundreds of books that scholars and wizards had written on alchemy, miners' more useful knowledge of their craft had been gleaned in obscurity and handed down the generations in relative secrecy before Agricola took an interest. He became the first scholar to explore the hidden life and lore of the silver mines. His first book, with a preface by Erasmus, dealt with mining terms and traditions in the form of a dialogue. Agricola saw the subterranean world as a distinct entity, and in his next book, *De Amantibus,* he made a heroic attempt to classify and describe creatures who lived underground. He began with worms and rabbits, and worked his way up to the boggarts and goblins miners frequently encountered in their work. Some were malicious; but the kind called *cobalos* in Greek and German were gentle. They stood about two feet high, and looked fantastically old, laughing a lot and always busy with something.

Finally Agricola reached the object of his studies: *De Re Metallica* was the first detailed exposition of mining technique ever published. Agricola was dead by the time it reached the printer, but it made his name and remained the standard textbook for almost two centuries, running to ten editions in three languages. To those who said that mining polluted rivers so that fish died, destroyed forests and game, disfigured landscapes, and brought to light what God had left invisible, Agricola had a reply. He tackled even Ovid, who had written: "And not only was the rich earth required to furnish corn and due sustenance, but men even descended into the entrails of the earth, and they dug up riches, those incentives to vice, which the earth had hidden and had removed to the Stygian shades. Then destructive iron came forth, and gold, more destructive than iron; then war came forth."

JOACHIMSTHAL'S LINKS to modern America weren't exhausted by supplying the country with a name for its currency. *De Re Metallica* did not appear in an English translation until 1912. Handsomely published by the Mining Society, it was translated and edited by an American classicist, Lou Hoover, and her husband, Herbert, a wealthy mining engineer. They dealt with Agricola's methods and beliefs with cautious respect. "Neither the sea nor the forest so lends itself to the substantiation of the supernatural as does the mine," they wrote. "The dead darkness, in which the miners' lamps serve only to distort every shape, the uncanny noises of restless rocks whose support has been undermined, the approach of danger and death without warning, the sudden vanishing or discovery of good fortune, all yield a thousand corroborations to minds long steeped in ignorance and prepared for the miraculous through religious teaching."

Herbert Hoover went on to become the thirty-first president of the United States in 1929, the last year of America's golden age when ordinary citizens could convert their paper dollars into gold on demand. Then came the Wall Street crash and the onset of the Great Depression.

JOACHIMSTHAL'S SILVER was worked out long before then, and the town had become a minor spa specializing in diseases of the liver and the heart. But in 1904 Madame Curie rifled through the ore of Joachimsthal's abandoned mines, brought to her in Paris on railway boxcars. From the ores that had produced the first thalers, or dollars, she managed to isolate and identify two new elements, radium and polonium, whose discovery shriveled her hands and then killed her, but breathed ghastly new life into the declining town, soon to be known by its Czech name, Jachymov. The Nazis began their experiments on an atom bomb here, which the Russians completed. In communist times as labor heroes took their cure, political prisoners were mining uranium from the hills.

In the early morning of Monday, July 16, 1945, the United States exploded the first atomic bomb made with weapons-grade uranium in the desert of New Mexico; three weeks later, shortly before midnight on August 5, Washington D.C., time, American airmen dropped one A-bomb on Hiroshima and, a few days later, one on Nagasaki, destroying both cities and ending World War II. Perhaps Ovid was right. Either way uranium and the dollar, the purest symbols of power in the modern world, are gifts of a shabby little spa town in the Bohemian hills.

MANY ARE THE tales of miners striking it rich, and the next minute losing the whole lot, and the count of Slik did not enjoy his new wealth for long. In 1528, just nine years after he struck his first thalers, the Habsburgs took over. The imperial reichsthaler, dubbed a rix dollar in English, was valued at eight Spanish reals. These "pieces of eight" bore on their face a scroll in the form of an S, possibly signifying the Seville mint through which all Spanish American silver had to pass, and the two pillars that Hercules had set up to guard the mouth of the Mediterranean. Ancient navigators thought it impossible to sail beyond these pillars, but Charles V's American wealth visibly disproved that, and he had his coiners add the legend *Plus Ultra:* There Is More Beyond.

This Habsburg king has every reason to smile: made of Mexican silver, this eight-real piece, or Spanish dollar, was the most popular trade coin in the world. The reverse shows the Pillars of Hercules at the mouth of the Mediterranean, draped with the motto *Plus Ultra.* Some have thought that the left-hand pillar established the $ sign.

Spanish silver dollars were the mainstay of world trade right up to the middle of the nineteenth century, and stuffed the treasuries of every monarch in the world, sealed the eyes of the Chinese dead, lured Polynesian kings into the Christian fold, weighted the skirts of Balkan gypsies, oiled palms in the Levant. The Spanish called them onzas de plata, silver ounces, peso, peso duro, or piastre. In the East Indies they were known as gourdes. Pirates in the West Indies—all buckle, swash, and frisky plank—killed for them. Some became charms. Some were buried in the ground. And now and then they still turn up all along the Florida coast and around the shores of Central America, pieces of eight fused into jagged lumps by the action of the sea, where canny divers who chart old wrecks still claw a fortune from another's watery loss.

· 2 ·

THE TREASURE HUNTER

The Wilderness—Wampum—Pirate Coins—
Treasure Hunting—Witchcraft—
Coined Land—An Open Invitation

On November 16, 1643, sixteen treasure ships and their escorts sailed from Puerto Plata in Central America to carry the year's production of silver back to Spain. The fleet took a northerly course to bring it out into the Atlantic beyond the Bahamas, where it would pick up the westerly wind and currents. Two days into the voyage, however, a hurricane blew up and orders were given to reef sails and run under bare poles until the storm blew itself out. During the night the *Nuestra Senora de la Concepcion* lost her bearings, and in the morning her crew found themselves on an empty sea, racing toward the "boilers" of the Bahamas, where coral reefs clamber erratically to the surface of the sea.

The boilers are ticklish to navigate, and the *Nuestra Senora,* laden with silver and tossed by impetuous winds, foundered at last. Her bottom was probably ripped out on the saw-toothed coral; the shock may have dislodged her masts, too, and her end would have been quick. Probably a portion of her crew fell to prayer; others were immobilized by dread; some found anything that would float and tossed themselves into the sea. In an hour or two, maybe less, they would be dead, while the shattered hulk and its cargo of silver slid unmoved below the raging wind-whipped ocean. A great deal of effort and ingenuity had been expended on this ship, many hopes and expectations, all suddenly gobbled by the hungry sea, as if it had never been.

But it wasn't over. The *Nuestra Senora*'s cargo would come to life again, through the efforts of a man whose near-incredible success would transform much more than his own fortune, and drive him headlong toward a failure that gave birth to modern money in America.

IN 1651, some two thousand miles farther to the north, in a big log cabin on the banks of the Kennebec River in Massachusetts, Mary Phips gave birth to her twenty-first child, William.[1] Old Mr. Phips found the strain too much and died; his widow certainly remarried, and produced another eight children—a big, rumbustious, illiterate family who lived by trapping and hunting, farming and fishing. Their house was built of wooden posts, and there was no glass in the windows.

"In the beginning," wrote the contemporary English philosopher John Locke, "all the world was America," by which he meant wild and thinly populated; a country without connections or conveniences. The Phips homestead perfectly fitted the description. Standing on a rocky coast it was surrounded to landward by Waba-

---

1. Modern researchers have turned up only six junior Phipses, but they have to work with records that are scarcely more reliable than legend.

naki Indians, with hostile Frenchmen further to the north; it lay well beyond the reach—or the protection—of what passed for government in Boston. It belonged to a watery empire of beaches and cliffs, riverbanks and ports; an empire which never in two hundred years moved more than a hundred miles from the sea. Even at the pinnacle of their Atlantic power, when the British controlled eleven hundred miles of land, from Newfoundland down to Florida, colonial America remained just a skinny bight of land, banked up against the woods and staring hungrily out to the ocean and beyond. All trade and all travel, the passage of news and the circulation of money, was by the coast: in all those years you took a ship to go, say, from Boston to Philadelphia. And even though London was far away, three thousand miles across the ocean, it was closer to many colonists than they were to each other, or to the unknown lands and rivers that lay beyond the Appalachian Mountains to the west.

Instinct kept the colonists hugging the shore. As the sun rose out of the sea each morning, the shadows of men and spires and ships leaned toward the woods as if to point out the purpose of the day. As the sun moved, the shadows slowly turned, until by evening, when the time comes to be home, they lengthened eastward toward the Atlantic, and only the shadows of the trees slid nearer, bleeding into dusk across the new-made fields.

The Phips family tract was huge, for in land colonists were rich on a scale unimaginable in the Old World. Only the labor to work it—labor that was so cheap and abundant back in England—was fantastically scarce: the Phipses had to breed their own. Tobacco farmers in the south turned to African slaves to work their fields. But slaves cost money. Cash was very scarce. Farther north, high wages for labor helped the poor, and undermined the pretensions of the well-to-do. John Winthrop, the first governor of Massachusetts, described an argument said to have occurred in the 1630s between a certain Howley and his servant:

"The master being forced to sell a pair of his oxen to pay his servant his wages, told his servant he could keep him no longer, not knowing how to pay him next year. The servant answered him, he could serve him for more cattle. 'But what shall I do,' said the master, 'when my cattle are all gone?'

"The servant replied, 'You shall then serve me, and so you shall have your cattle again.' "

No one in the Old World spoke like this.

WINTHROP, HOWLEY, AND the servant came from England; so did the cattle. So did the grass that cattle ate, the ax heads that cleared the forest, the nails that fixed the houses. In 1620 tobacco growers even bought themselves English wives—billed as "young and uncorrupted girls"—for 100 pounds of good leaf. Next year a wife cost 150 pounds: the value of tobacco was tumbling.

But timber, the casual treasure of North America, held up. It wasn't gold but the depthless forest of America that was the basis of the colonists' simple fortune: straight, clean, malleable timber taken from forests undisturbed for thousands of years. Barns and houses went up with simple spans of forty feet or more in what William Allen called the "best poor man's country in the world," where paupers could live like princes did at home. "All Europe is not able to make so great fires as New England," wrote a pamphleteer in the 1630s. "A poor servant here that is to possess fifty acres of land may afford to give more wood for . . . fire . . . than many noblemen in England." A £300 shipload of timber could be sold in southern Europe for £1600[2]: sawmills pressed farther up the rivers: by 1665

2. John Perlin, *A Forest Journey, The Role of Wood in the Development of Civilization* (New York: 1989).

more than twenty were at work on the Piscataqua River, each doing twenty times the work of a couple of sawyers, preparing around fourteen massive pines a day.

The thwack of the steel-headed ax and the rasp of saws sounded the bass note of white American civilization. Up into the days of blue jeans and mail order, up to the day in 1890 when the census declared that the frontier was finally closed, generations of frontiersmen were to perform the old productive ritual of ringing, felling, and planting between the stumps. Corn flourished on the old leaf mold. The surrounding forest fed their half-wild hogs. The timber they cleared was split into rails, perhaps, to stake their claim, and used to raise a cabin. What they couldn't use they burned in the fields, for fertilizer. Chopping logs was the quintessential American activity for so many years that nineteenth-century Americans called a ten-dollar bill, marked with a big Roman X, a sawbuck, because it looked like one.

But while the ax nibbled at the forest's edge, money stole into its heart, silent as any native hunter. Money transformed the life of the forest, valued and devalued, and prepared it for the coming of the white men's farms.

Money came in with the fur trade, the oil industry of the seventeenth century. Keeping northern Europeans warm stimulated a demand that brought Russia and America simultaneously into the European orbit. The Phips family joined in. Young William Phips "Hunted and Fished many a weary Day in his Childhood," for beaver, moose, otter, and even bearskins, but white trappers alone could not keep up with the demand: some idea of its scale can be drawn from the ten thousand beaver pelts Connecticut sent to Europe every year. Settlers brought guns to the native Americans. They introduced money. The natives succumbed, at a deadly and unforeseen cost, yoked to one end of a commercial chain that stretched to Piccadilly out of the wilderness.

The chain at the American end was made of little shells, looped on a single thread of misunderstanding. Every summer, for hundreds, maybe thousands, of years, native Americans had been collecting these shells on the sandy beaches of New England, from Long Island to Rhode Island. Come the idle winter months, they used stone drills to manufacture "wampum": "white" wampum from the column and inner whorls of periwinkles, "black" wampum from the stem of the common round clam, or quahog. They vigorously polished the ¼-inch-long cylinders on smooth hard stones, and strung them tightly together on hemp or animal tendons in strings of 360 beads, which the colonists called fathoms.

Modern economists would call wampum a primitive money: perhaps they mean it wasn't managed by economists. The colonists also saw it as primitive money, and that meant they could make it work better. They set a wampum exchange rate into shillings and pence, according to the furs it bought, and adopted what they took to be Indian reckoning, by which one black bead was worth six white. From an Indian perspective wampum wasn't primitive money at all: it wasn't exactly money, and it took some skill to produce. Wampum had considerable value in native society, but not for what it could buy or sell. Woven into patterned belts, wampum bore witness to a variety of exchanges. Dutch and English colonists instinctively focused on the number of shells in a belt, but the Indians gave consideration to the patterns, the feel and presence of the belts themselves, as they were given and received in ceremonies to mark treaties, signify valor, or to display the rewards of high status. The patterns formed a kind of mnemonic, suggestive of old agreements and encounters. On the proper occasions the stories on the tribes' belts were told by the elders. Powerful men took them to the grave. The loss of a wampum belt was a wound to the identity of the tribe.

The coastal Indians were under continual pressure to deliver wampum in tribute to their more powerful neighbors farther inland, so in that way wampum was like money. Now the whites joined in. In 1644 the settlers "fined" the Narragansetts two thousand fathoms of wampum, in annual installments: a fathom from every Pequot man, a half fathom from every youth, and a handsbreadth from every child in the tribe. Production had to be stepped up, and skirmishes and bad blood marked the beaches. Meanwhile the whites sent the wampum into the forest where, for its imperceptibly fading resonance in native American society, it delivered the furs.

London ladies (then as now) did not live in harmony with the forest three thousand miles across the ocean. The result was a wildlife massacre. Too late, tribes found themselves hunting in an empty forest. Twenty thousand years before, in a dazzlingly short time, their ancestors had wiped out the lumbering giants of North America. Now buck and beaver, wolf and raccoon were headed the way of the giant sloth, the mammoth, and the mastodon. Searching for fresh game, Indians began shifting west, poaching on the territory of other tribes.

While the stability of native American society was being undermined, and the ecology of the forest overturned, colonists discovered that they could use wampum as a currency themselves, as long as the Indians, unwittingly cast in the role of central bankers, were prepared to redeem wampum in furs. But slowly the game drew away. The colonists were greedy, using their quick steel drills to produce a glut of wampum that undermined its value. The English accused the Dutch of cheating them; both blamed the Indians. A fathom of wampum was conventionally an arm's length, and the Dutch complained that the Indians used very tall men when receiving payment, and almost dwarves when paying out.

The Indians spotted fakes easily, and all the forged wampum "of Stone, Bone, Glass, Muscle-Shells, Horn, yea even of Wood and broken Beads" sidled back into the white men's pockets, while "the good, polished wampum, commonly called Manhattan Wampum," disappeared into the forest. In 1648 the general court in Connecticut ordered that no wampum "be paid or received, but what is strung and in some measure strung suitably, and not small and great, uncomely and disorderly mixt, as formerly it hath beene." In forty years the colonists had slashed and burned their way through the native currency. In 1649 Massachusetts stopped using it, although it apparently lingered on as money for the whites in upstate New York until 1701. For treaty making with the Indians it was used right up to the nineteenth century, in vivid demonstration of its essentially ritual, nonmonetary importance. It was last presented and received in Prairie du Chien in 1825, when one thousand tribal leaders assembled to hear the white man's ultimatum—a scene beautifully rendered twenty years afterward by an engraving on the Bank of Wisconsin's five-, ten-, twenty-, and fifty-dollar bills.

WILLIAM PHIPS, STRONG, well-built, and illiterate at eighteen, set his face in the direction of the sea, where the Kennebec River ran into the broad current of the Anglo-American empire. He served an apprenticeship at a local shipyard, and in 1673 he walked to Boston to work as a shipwright in a bigger yard. The industry was booming: the first American ship had been launched in 1631, and by the end of the century a third of Britain's shipping was built in America. The country was a chandler's dream, a vast storehouse of masts and spars, pitch and twine.

"For his *Exterior,* he was one *Tall,* beyond the common Set of Men, and *Thick* as well as *Tall,* and *Strong* as well as *Thick:* He was, in all respects, exceedingly *Robust,* and able to Conquer such Diffi-

culties of *Diet* and *Travel,* as would have kill'd most Men alive." He
fell in with a young widow, Mary Spencer Hull, and courted her
father, a sea captain and land speculator. Both were ready to believe
his promise that one day he would command a king's ship, so rich
that he could build a fine brick house on Green Lane for his wife.

He began by contracting with a ring of Boston merchants to
build a ship on the family homestead, to be delivered complete with
cargo, probably timber and victuals. But relations with the Wabanaki were worsening. On August 14, 1676, a nearby settlement was
destroyed in a surprise attack, and some fifty settlers were killed.
Phips's ship had just been launched, but its cargo was still waiting on
the shore when the smoke began to drift upward across the bay.
Phips lost not another moment. Leaving the lumber and the homestead to the Wabanaki fire-raisers, he gathered up his family and
neighbors and swept them all to the safety of Boston.

IF BOSTON WAS safe, it was also stony broke. Merchants in
Boston as elsewhere found it hard to lay their hands on the coin—
the so-called specie—that turned the wheels of foreign trade. To
make the most of their silver, almost all the colonies at one time
or another settled on a local substitute for transactions at home.
Wampum was "lawful money" for a while, good for paying debts
and taxes; peas, rum, nails, and corn followed. An admirer called
them "an abiding Cash."

This knack for substitution came as second nature to men dealing with novelties every day, but the concept of "lawful money" was
a smoking fuse laid against the ancient right of kings to regulate the
currency, a small but ultimately significant declaration of colonial
America's aims and purposes. What began as an expedient would

little by little come to frame an alternative pattern of experience, until relations between Britain and her colonies grew clouded by an atmosphere of mutual exasperation.

The search for specie continued: silver and gold had obvious advantages as currency, as a Springfield constable discovered when his skiff capsized, hurling a year's tax revenue in dried peas into the water. In Virginia, where nails formed a legal currency, the authorities had to intervene to stop people burning down their barns to get them out every time they shifted ground.

Since silver was not to be found in North America by conquest or by digging, it would have to be secured by manipulation and enterprise.[3] A colony would post lists of exchange for silver coins that seriously overvalued them. In England, anyone with a Spanish dollar could get four shillings and sixpence, the rate calculated for silver by no less a mathematician than Isaac Newton, in 1717. The colonies, though, were ready to offer special rates—five shillings in Virginia money, six in Massachusetts. Despite the occasional windfall, the policy drove merchants giddy with confusion, for the valuations changed from year to year, and from coin to coin, as colonies competed for the cash: silver in the colonies was governed by strange tides. At one moment all the Spanish coins in Massachusetts might prick up their ears and head south, like migrating birds, to spend their winter in Virginia; or all the Dutch dollars on the continent would suddenly vanish, zombielike, and come homing in on New York. It wasn't just merchants who were peeved. In 1679 the governor of Virginia set about hoarding pieces of eight, which were valued

---

3. Alchemy still offered possibilities. An interest in botany, chemistry, metallurgy, astronomy, and medicine led an earlier governor of Massachusetts, John Winthrop Jr., to become the first American Fellow of the Royal Society, Britain's leading scientific association. He also sold a secret medicinal compound called *rubila*. He used to go off to a mountain in Massachusetts, the Governor's Ring, to spend "three weeks in the woods . . . roasting ores and assaying metals and casting gold rings."

officially at five shillings. When the shortage had grown sufficiently acute, he arbitrarily declared them to be worth six shillings each, and used them to pay off his troops.

The New York merchants wanted all the foreign coin melted down and recast in English shillings, but the English preferred a cheaper Royal Proclamation, which forbade anyone to offer more than six shillings for a Spanish dollar. Like much British legislation in the colonies, it was unwelcome and ineffective.

THE SILVER MONEY that sloshed through the ports and the plantations of America was fabulously diverse. It was brought in by men like William Phips, who, now married and prospering in command of a ship, had joined the colonial cavalcade running down to the Caribbean. Sugar was so profitable to the West Indies that planters devoted every acre to cane, and for a century to come enterprising New Englanders victualed the West Indies like ships at sea, supplying barrels of salt pork and beef, broken fish for slaves, salt fish, seasoned timber, honey and horses and chickens in return for their molasses and pieces of eight. Most of that coin—or the shadow of it, a bill drawn on London—went to buy English hoes and English axes, English petticoats, perhaps, or books.

Colonists were generally a prim, provincial, self-righteous people, with simple clothes, reserved manners, plain homes, and a reading scheme largely confined to the King James Bible; but they were clamped like mollusks to the shore, and not ashamed to strain the silt of piracy for Spanish silver. They could build ships, fix tackle, and serve rum, and asked few questions. In 1646 a lucky storm drove the buccaneering Captain Cromwell into Plymouth with three shiploads of Spanish silver and eighty crewmen who "did so distemper them with drinke as they became like madde-men." Nobody cared.

The town was dying on its feet. "They spente and scattered a greate deale of money among the people."

The good, bright coins seldom lingered in the colonies before they were turned around and sent back into the byways of Atlantic trade: only the dregs of the world's mints stayed to circulate, in this end-of-the-world, edge-of-the-map place America. Even the Spanish dollars they commonly used had lost roughly a quarter of their original weight. Many were already very old, rubbed and shaved by countless hands across the years, their inscriptions barely legible. Nobody, it seems, scrupled to prematurely wizen the rest. Steady hands could split a Spanish dollar in two, scoop out its silver innards, and clap them together with a blob of lead or quicksilver. Coins were snipped, clipped, drilled, filled. "Sweated" coins were jangled for hours in a bag, and all the weight they lost collected in the seams. Parings could be taken from around the rim. "I am sorry to say it," the earl of Bellomont wrote from New York in 1699, "but 'tis an undoubted truth, the English here are soe profligate that I can not find a man fitt to be trusted, thats capable of businesse. . . . I was obliged to employ [as] Clerk of the Assembly this Session, one that was lately convicted of clipping and coining in this towne."

Even these coins had an air about them, like a party of dubious minor European royalty slumming it in America. Almost without exception they were royal coins—their fortunes hitched to the ups and downs of conquest and alliance, their titles reading like an Almanach de Gotha to a Ruritanian empire of world trade, and often incestuously related, their bloodlines having crossed and recrossed in the past. There were royals and crowns, ducats and ducatoons. There were tiny sultani, garnered from traffic in Arab North Africa, which colonists knew as Barbary ducats. Moidores came, and pistareens; minute little silver Ottoman sequins, or checkens, with a graceful crescent on the reverse; thumping German silver carolines with a fat king in a wig on the front. Pezzos sifted through from little Leghorn, scudi from the tiny Mediterranean island of Malta, florins from south Germany, and tales from China—the pagodas, oddly, came from Madras. There were English guineas, pistols French and Spanish, and Dutch guilders. More common still were Portuguese joes and half-joes, cousins to all the reals of Spain, those pieces of eight, which had prospered mightily since the count of Slik's day, and had now, like their Habsburg masters, adjusted themselves to the contingencies of empire: the Mexican pillar dollar, which showed the pillars of Hercules and bore the motto *Plus Ultra;* the central European thaler; the Seville dollar, the cob dollar, the globe dollar, and the Dutch dog dollar, which was actually meant to be a lion.

Even with this ragbag of dubious coinage, there was never enough to go around. Americans suffered from a persistent shortage of small change, and most of the coins were fairly large. In the last-chance saloon of America some noble old moidore or checken might suffer the final indignity of being cut into bits. This kind of small change, shaped like a wedge of cheese, was aptly known as "sharp money." A single silver piece of eight, for instance, was chiseled into two half-dollars, four quarters, or eight bits, like slices of a pie, a habit so ingrained that even now the United States' supposedly decimal currency has no twenty-cent coin, only a twenty-five-cent quarter, which many Americans persist in calling "two bits"—and some regional stock exchanges were still quoting prices in eighths of a dollar in 1998.

PHIPS WAS THE American who makes one comfortable fortune and goes on to make another. He had grown up hearing tales of the sea. In the yards, sailors spoke of galleons and treasure ships, of pirate gold and Peruvian silver, and Phips listened. On the water-front, in Caribbean islands, he kept his ears open. The story that caught his interest was the fate of the *Nuestra Senora*.

The curious dream of William Phips was of a miracle of sudden wealth. Long after Phips, in 1809, a traveler in New England found that "settlers indulge an unconquerable expectation of finding money buried in the earth. The money is supposed to have been buried by pirates; but the discovery of its burial place is hoped for only from dreams. Where dreams have conveyed some general infor-mation of the place, then mineral rods are resorted to, for ascertain-ing the precise spot at which to put the spade and pickax into the ground; and then charms and various observances, to defeat the watchfulness of the spirits that have the treasure in charge." The spirits are a good touch, a reminder that sudden wealth comes at a price. Treasure really was to be found now and then, in crumbling riverbanks, on lonely islands, under sands, and where X marked the spot. Herman Melville and Nathaniel Hawthorne, Mark Twain and Edgar Allan Poe all wrote stories that gave buried treasure the status of an American theme. A sense of solitude was soothed by a story that could attach a legend or two to the naked landscape: perhaps it reassured the lonely American that others had passed that way before, governors and kings, pirates and conquistadors, with their moidores, ducats, dollars, and doubloons.

Despite the information he had gleaned, Phips found that Boston could resist the prospect of a treasure hunt. So he sailed his own ship to London, seeking an audience with King Charles II. Social shoals and reefs needed careful and persistent sounding, and it took Phips a year to make the right contacts, but he flung himself into the task with utter self-confidence, going so far as to sell his ship to buy wigs and clothes, and to entertain in the required style. His determination was rewarded. Charles II, a chancer always short of money and keen on bold and sporting schemes, had a soft spot for Massachusetts. In 1652, during the interregnum that followed the execution of his father, Charles I, and his own restoration, Massachusetts had commissioned John Hull, a local goldsmith, to melt down bad coin and cast his own silver shillings, six- and three-penny bits, decorated with a pine, a willow, or an oak. Coining was technically a royal prerogative, but the situation was vague. Hull's contract gave him a shilling in every pound, and he headed off the Assembly's belated efforts to alter the terms to become one of the richest men in the colony, long remembered for dowering his daughter with her weight in silver shillings. She was rather small, but very fat. "Yes, you may take her," Hull told her suitor, "and you'll find her a heavy burden enough."

When Charles II finally gained his throne he was advised to stop the coining but, having once dodged his Cromwellian pursuers by hiding in the leaves of an old oak, he took Hull's Oak Tree shilling as a compliment, and called the people of Massachusetts "a parcel of honest dogs." (When he was eventually made to intervene, the colonists simply put an earlier date on the coins to make it look as if they had been struck before the ban.) Now Charles II agreed to become the humble Boston artisan's business partner, and Phips sailed back to Boston in command of a king's ship, just as he had promised his sweetheart: a frigate called the *Algier-Rose,* recently seized from Barbary pirates.

He immediately demanded that merchantmen and fishing boats in Boston should strike their colors, as they would to a regular navy ship. On being refused he fired across their bows, and then had them boarded and served with a bill for the cost of the powder and shot. Some days later he attempted to use his naval powers to impress a carpenter from another ship; a dockside brawl developed, Phips wading in to warn local constables that the governor had no authority in this matter—indeed, as one crewman put it, "the Governour and the Government here they did not value a fart."

The governor himself dismissed the case, sharply reminding Phips that "every body in Boston Knew very well what he was and from whence he came: therefore desired him not to carry it soe loftily amoung his country men." Phips, for his part, carried on shooting.

Boston was glad to see the ship and its troublesome captain and crew sail for the Bahamas on January 19, 1684. Phips had taken on three young Indian divers from his hometown, and where the sea foams murderously around coral reefs strung between the islands they worked in canoes, searching all over the reefs for the telltale shape of a sunken ship amid the coral thickets. It was ticklish work trying to locate the wrecks without sharing their fate, and as wreck after wreck turned up empty the crew began to grow mutinous, demanding that their captain turn pirate and lead them to living prey. Phips quelled the first mutiny by rushing on the ringleaders with his bare fists and knocking them down, but the months of idleness and failure were taking their toll, and Phips finally turned his crew loose in Jamaica, where they could all find work in the "bewiching Trade." A new crew came aboard, all pirates, too, but Phips knew he could rely on them not to mutiny for a few more months. He had also done some fishing of his own, for "by the Policy of his address, he fished out of a very old *Spaniard* (or *Portuguese*) a little Advice about the true Spot where lay the *Wreck* which he had been hitherto seeking, as unprosperously, as the *Chymists* have their *Aurifick Stone.*"

Almost two years after he had taken the *Algier-Rose* from the king, he sailed her back to England empty-handed. Charles II was dead and his brother, the unreliable James II, had no interest in foreign escapades. But Phips felt closer to the treasure, and within a year he had found new backers to give him two small ships. Once again he "set Sail for the *Fishing-Ground,* which had been so well *baited* half an Hundred Years before." If no treasure could be found, the ships would pay for their trip in English merchandise and sugar.

Back on the reefs, the divers worked their canoes for weeks before someone noticed what looked like a wooden spar sticking up from the coral. One of the divers "immediately dived, and found under a rock on which grew vast quantity of coral, first an enamelled pair of silver stirrups . . . which having done he found vast numbers of pieces of eight, which they brought up by thousands, sticking together, the sea water having dissolved some of the alloy of copper mixt with the silver, and made it into verdigrease, which has fastened them all together. There has likewise been a petrifaction on the top of them all, to about the thickness of half an inch," wrote Sir Hans Sloane, a naturalist who helped found the British Museum and who traveled with Phips on his third voyage a year later.

At the end of 1688 Phips was back in London. He brought with him 37,538 pounds of coined silver, all in pieces of eight; 25 pounds of gold, and 2,755 pounds of silver bullion, worth around $14 million in today's money. James II helped himself to 10 percent and knighted his new friend. Others were inspired. Daniel Defoe, the author of *Robinson Crusoe,* praised him for kick-starting the "projecting Humour" that animated London in his lifetime, which "had hardly any Hand to own it, till the Wreck-Voyage . . . performed so happily by Captain Phips . . . set a great many Heads on work to contrive something for themselves." The inrush of silver gave a fillip to the nascent stock exchange, more joint-stock companies were founded, more stocks were traded, and in 1694 the creation of the Bank of England changed the country's financial destiny forever.

Having scrupulously paid off his backers, who got a 7,000 percent return on their investment (the duke of Albemarle was so excited he could be found "melting his dividend of silver in his garden himself"), Sir William Phips—via another wreck or two—returned to Boston very rich. He built the brick house on Green Lane for his wife with his own hands. He had, it appeared, the Midas touch; and perhaps no one was very surprised when he received his appointment as the first royal governor of Massachusetts.

IT IS A VERY American story, a blueprint for many American fortune builders over the centuries to come. The insignificant origins, the lucky break, the ability to see an opportunity and to believe in it to the point of ruin are all familiar tropes in the stories of many of America's great inventors, salesmen, and visionaries. Yet Phips himself paid the price of sudden wealth. In 1690, goaded by the daring of French Canadian privateers and the complaints of the Boston merchants, he decided to teach the French a lesson. He laid siege to Port Royal, a hostile French outpost on Acadia, north of Boston. Surprised when Acadia surrendered without a fight, his militiamen looted the peninsula from top to bottom for twelve days while Phips himself stole from the French governor everything he could possibly carry away, established a puppet government, and returned to Boston in triumph with an altered sense of the French menace and a scheme to drive the French out of Canada forever.

His plan called for a land force to leave Albany, capture Montreal, and march down the St. Lawrence River to join in an amphibious assault on Quebec. Timing was everything. The soldiers moved off. Then the Boston fleet sailed, light on ordnance, heavy in men who had joined for the sake of Phips's style and luck, and the thought of Quebec's booty: twenty-five hundred exuberant militiamen crowded into thirty leaky and overloaded ships. Bad weather, adverse winds, and the failure to secure a pilot to guide the fleet up the St. Lawrence River brought them into the basin at Quebec very late in the season, the waters gelling greasily with the cold.

Phips could not know it, but the land assault on Montreal had already failed. He had lost any advantage of surprise, and the French had reinforced; but from Quebec's governor, the comte de Frontenac et de Palluau, he demanded instant surrender. Frontenac hit on a superb riposte: "I have no reply to make to your general but from the mouths of my cannon, and by gunshots." Phips's guns spoke first, and angrily, bombarding the city for two days, but when he improvised an attack by land the cannons he set up on shore were out of range. The French found theirs: ships were damaged and thirty men were killed. Finally, Phips ran out of ammunition.

Astonished and aggrieved by the failure of the French to give up, Phips reluctantly ordered the fleet home. But his luck was ebbing on the tide. As the Bostonians made their way down the St. Lawrence a dreadful storm blew up and four ships sank. The rest were scattered, to make their way back to Massachusetts through foul winds and hurling seas. Some ragged survivors crawled back to Dorchester, empty-handed; all they carried was an invisible dose of smallpox that went on to kill fifty-seven people in the town. Expectations in Boston were overthrown. "Some of the vessels are arrived, having lost some halfe their men, some more some even all. . . . Great Complaints there are that there was no suitable Care, nor provision for such an Army, men . . . having their Eyes and Cheeks Eaten by Ratts before found."[4]

To make matters worse, a rabble of angry survivors and keening widows was soon clamoring for pay and compensation. The plunder of Quebec had failed to materialize. The colonial treasury was empty.

---

4. Recently part of Sir William's sunken fleet has been investigated with a diligence he might find baffling, in a professional sense, since it contained nothing but rotten wood, muskets, and tableware.

❧

THIS KIND OF thing happened all the time, and no doubt Sir William Phips had friends who clapped him on the shoulder and wished him better hunting next time. History folded his failed assault on Quebec into the mostly forgotten saga of King William's War, one of the little proxy wars that all through the coming eighteenth century the English and the French prosecuted against each other half a world away from home. Other versions of that war with France were to be fought out on sea, on land, and through Indian allies, neither side able to strike a decisive blow until Wolfe died storming the Heights of Abraham in 1759, and the whole of French Canada was added to the British Empire.

Sir William Phips's own reputation—like his temper—suffered from the debacle. When he smashed his cane down over the head of a captain in the Royal Navy and assaulted a Boston port official, people affected outrage. Before long, his string of notable successes was picked apart and reembroidered as blazons of shame. People recalled his common origins. They accused his loyal wife of witchcraft, and sniped at his bloodless victory in Acadia. A hostile, priggish faction in the Assembly bound him to restore to Port Royal's former governor all the goods he had greedily plundered. Bad news travels fast. Distant friends at a faraway court began to desert him, and he was summoned to England to explain himself; but in London he died, quite suddenly, in 1695.

He was buried in the little church of St. Mary Woolnorth in the City, apparently hugging one last secret: the site of Bobadilla's fabulous treasure ship, complete with a table of pure gold, which had sunk on the reefs of Hispaniola in about 1500. The legend grew up that the details were in some way encoded in his tomb; but the tomb itself has disappeared.

MEMENTO MORI

REMEMBER — TO DIE

YOU are defired to Accompany the Corps of Sir *William Phipps,* Knight, from *Salters-Hall,* in *Swithins-Lane,* to the Parifh-Church of St. *Mary Woolnoth,* in *Lumbard-ftreet* ; On Thurfday the 21ft. of *February,* 169⁴⁄₅. At Five of the Clock in the After-noon precifely : And bring this Ticket with you.

William Phips, an illiterate colonial, made a fortune from the sea and almost single-handedly introduced Americans to the idea of vast and sudden wealth. Knighted for his treasure-hunting exploits, he died in London under a cloud. For America the cloud had a silver lining: the invention of paper money. (*Courtesy of the Massachusetts Historical Society*)

Nathaniel Hawthorne later attempted a sketch of Sir William Phips because, as he said, people are too apt to miss the humanity in names that crop up in the textbook; the sketch is a gem buried in the author's *Collected Works.* Treasure hunters consider Phips to be their patron saint, for they recognize his battles with rivals, bureaucrats, danger, and the sea, and the single-minded purpose that brought him fame and riches and disgrace. America in the long run owes more to Phips's failure than to his success.

Faced with popular outrage, the Massachusetts Assembly in Boston earnestly wondered how to pay the militiamen and the wid-ows. Their first instinct was to raise a loan from Boston merchants, but the merchants blandly declined, for they too needed the money just now. And then the Bostonians scented something new in the air, which seemed to hold the answer to their prayers.

It was nothing more than a scent, and it's hard to run it to earth. It may have been laid in French Canada, when a cash-starved garrison resorted to using playing cards as a sort of rudimentary currency, to be redeemed in hard cash when supplies arrived. In London in 1650 an anonymous pamphlet entitled "The Key to Wealth, or, a new Way for Improving of Trade: Lawfull, Easie, Safe and Effectual" appeared. The Key to Wealth was a new kind of money, made out of paper. Marco Polo had come across paper money in China three centuries before, but the pamphleteer was more likely to have been inspired by the experience of London silversmiths, who often stored other people's valuables in their strong rooms. The receipts they gave out in return were sometimes used as a kind of paper currency: instead of fetching the actual silver out of store, with all the risks that entailed, only the receipt from a respected silversmith needed to change hands between two merchants. Some silversmiths had gone on to realize the first principle of banking: that it is possible to issue receipts beyond the value of the silver in one's actual possession. Rather than lug silver or gold around, and risk having it stolen, people actually preferred a receipt from a reliable silversmith. On the rare occasions that someone came to take their silver away, the smith would cover the demand: in the course of trade it would likely come back to him in the end, for safety. If everyone came at once, he would naturally be ruined; but they seldom did.

In 1691, three years before the founding of the Bank of England and the earliest five-pound note, faraway Massachusetts became the first state since medieval China to issue its own paper currency. "We have found a way to stop the mouths and aswage the passion of the soldiers and seamen by a new mint raised here of paper money," one critic wrote, while the Massachusetts General Court more loftily referred to "the present poverty and calamities of this country, and through scarcity of money, the want of an adequate measure of commerce," before issuing "bills of credit" to the value of £7,000. They were printed on good paper from engraved copper plates. To a modern eye they look the wrong way up, five inches high by four inches wide: portrait rather than landscape. A fine scroll of twining lines across the top; no other decoration beyond the coat of arms of the colony. Each note was taken up with text, finished with a signature or two at the bottom. It looked like a small legal document, or a tiny proclamation.

Actually it could be thought of as a sort of writ, served by the present on the future. The people could take the money now, and pay up in the years ahead—when the corn was in, when the lumber was floated off, when those sloops came back from the West Indies with their silver and their sugar. The sooner they had the money, the quicker they could start making things happen—plant corn, chop timber, or outfit a sloop with the honey and the horses.

· 3 ·

THE GARDEN

Witchcraft—Coined Land—
An Open Invitation

"'Twas an honest and good method you took," said an open letter to the Massachusetts treasurer, "to pay by Bonds what you could not by Ready Cash. I therefore cannot a little wonder at the great indiscretion of our Countrymen who refuse to accept that, which they call Paper-money, as pay of equal value with the best Spanish silver."

The anonymous author was being disingenuous. People were coming face-to-face with paper money for the first time in Western history, and they weren't all ready to make the conceptual leap. You could bite on the best Spanish silver. Even wampum had had some weight, and a heap of money was a heap. Paper was worthless—"say what you like," an old Pennsylvanian grumbled, "but paper is paper and money is money." It was ten years before other colonies began to follow Massachusetts's lead, prodded on by the cost of fighting the French, or the Indians, or both together. King William's War, in which Phips played his hapless role, had dragged on into Queen Anne's War. King George's War of 1745 grew out of the War of

Jenkins's Ear; the French and Indian War of the 1750s culminated in Wolfe's capture of Quebec. In 1760 the French would formally surrender Canada at Montreal, and the British Empire in North America would be complete. There would be no more little wars, the British reflected, and no more paper money either.

Every time the colonists went to war, even if their contribution was only to fight skirmishes and launch border raids, they found themselves loaded with expenses. And they dealt with them by printing paper money. Sometimes the British sent out silver to help a colony "retire" its notes. Sometimes the notes were retired when the people paid their tax. But often they lingered on, more worn, more dubious from year to year, foxed by the touch of a forgotten promise, their value always slipping, sometimes gently and sometimes precipitously.

"What? is the word Paper a scandal to them? Is a Bond or Bill-of-Exchange for £1000, other than paper? And yet is it not as valuable as so much Silver or Gold, supposing the security of Payment is sufficient? Now what is the security of your Paper-money less than the Credit of the whole Country?"

The anonymous enthusiast was Cotton Mather, America's first homegrown philosopher; friend, neighbor, and biographer of Sir William Phips, America's first homegrown entrepreneur. It is tempting to see them as an American pairing, progenitors of a tension in American life that has trembled and flared up and down the years like an old family dispute: between action and consideration, between the necessary and the ideal, between rival conceptions of liberty, life, and the pursuit of happiness—and the money to pay for it.

Cotton Mather came from New England's aristocracy—the Cottons were his mother's family. He was born in 1663 and brought up in the shadow of the Old North Church, where both his father and his grandfather were ministers. Unlike Phips, who could barely read and whose faith was expressed in rare visits to the Mathers' church, he was literary and pious.

Almost his first words were prayers. By the age of eleven he could listen to a sermon delivered in English and jot it down in Latin for fun. At twelve he entered Harvard. Finally he joined the family firm at the Old North Church. He made a happy marriage, but his wife died young. He married again. Eventually he had fifteen children. When his second wife died he married a madwoman who brought him nothing but debt and domestic misery, mortifications relieved only by the attention of angels, who came to talk and wrestle with him in his study.

Phips was a vigorous, waterborne, treasure-seeking colonial of the seventeenth century, but Mather, who died in 1728, had his fundamental beliefs shaped by a century of puritan enthusiasm and approached them in an eighteenth-century frame of mind. He was a member of the Royal Society who backed the controversial new practice of inoculating for smallpox, and wrote treatises on political economy, but he also believed in witches, demons, angels, and the admission of spectral testimony in a court of law, as events would prove. With the help of his first wife he had once volunteered to take in a local girl bewitched by demons and together they saw to her cure; it was an experience that readied him for the outbreak of witchcraft and Satanism around the little town of Salem, Massachusetts, four years later. A court was convened to investigate.[1] Mather was the trial recorder, and his book *Wonders of the Invisible World* subsequently explained how a small community could be terrorized by a power beyond itself. He told how "the Devil, exhibiting himself ordinarily as a small black man, has decoyed a fearful knot of proud,

---

1. John Hull's son-in-law, whose wife had brought him the famous dowry of silver shillings, was the judge.

forward, ignorant, envious and malicious creatures, to lift themselves in his horrid service, by entering their names in a book by him tendered unto them."

The book itself was never produced (it belonged to the Devil), but twenty people were executed for witchcraft. Even Sir William Phips's wife was apparently accused, before the hysteria died away: simple settlers sensed that there was something diabolic about digging and diving for hidden treasure, piling up a fortune in secret. The model Puritan route called for patient toil under the eye of the community. Although sexual hysteria, collective delusion, jealousy, and an atmosphere in which it was acceptable to brand women as witches seem to have all contributed to the mania, it was invariably prompted by this lack of oversight. Four out of five of the accused women were "outlivers," the name given to those who had slipped their cables in the community and strayed out beyond the stricter boundaries of the parish.

Although the idea of recreating English villages, centered on the green and the church, had been long since abandoned, there still remained unspoken limits to how far out a settler ought to live. The woods had allowed early settlers in America to survive and even profit; but they were also the most alien feature of this New World. The Puritans took a gloomy satisfaction in picturing themselves cast into the wilderness, as they dutifully called it, with a frisson of horror as they surveyed the measureless immensity of the American forest. They sensed that it was another world, quite alien to them, and therefore dangerous. The lesson had been brought home to the Mayflower pilgrims within minutes of their landing, for a party of Indians had been seen watching from the beach as the first of the pilgrims rowed ashore. The Indians ran into the forest, and two men gave chase. They were Lincolnshire men who knew the treeless wold, and had spent years in the flat polders of Holland. Within moments they were tripped and snagged in the tangle of undergrowth and roots into which their quarry had so effortlessly disappeared.

Wild, vast, and turbulent as it was, the sea was by contrast a known quantity, well understood—a broad and navigable highway into the world, which men like Sir William Phips might sail to fame and fortune. There were monsters in it, to be sure, and mysteries; but people were used to them, and knew that competent sailors could read the face of the sea like a book. The woods were something else. The beaten paths which the colonists trod straggled out into nothingness at every village boundary, where the last of the cultivated fields ran out. There grew the trees, bigger than any the English had ever seen. They grew with such monstrous density that no one could begin to guess the forest's depth; and they flushed with fiery color in the fall. Up rivers, along Indian trails, the trees closed in, hiding everything. It was long since Europeans had experienced anything like it, for their forests were almost all chopped down; yet their fairy tales still rang with echoes of that lingering unease, and a bewildered man is literally a man lost in the wood, "bewildered" in the wild weald.

The Puritans reacted to the strange new world by peopling it with demons, and for years the Boston preachers drove home the dangers of the dark, unmeasured space in America, as in a man's soul.

WHAT MATHER WANTED was protection. America was the battleground in an almost physical struggle between good and evil, between the garden and the wilderness. In destroying the outlivers, he had hoped, the weakening bonds of a collective society would be reinforced. In the wake of the witch trials' sudden collapse, Mather altered his approach. He became a convert to the virtues of paper money, for like many conservatives he was prepared to be radical in defense of what he cherished. Newfangled paper money solved an older problem posed by his Boston Puritanism. Based on "the credit of the whole country" it would weave a web of action and industry around every community threatened by darkness and disintegration. Launched on the promise that it was as good as silver or gold, paper money seemed to be the logical fulfillment of American experience. However earnestly or plausibly the promise was made, it still remained a matter of faith, and such a faith in common purpose, in a wholesome future, in the bounty of God's providence, in the righteousness of one's fellow men, were just the beliefs on which this new country was being founded.[2]

If there was one form of literature beyond the Bible that early colonists understood, it was the written contract. Many of them had reached the New World with ink still drying on their fingers—indentured servants who promised to work for their passage, settlers who signed with the merchant companies responsible for various colonies, whole fraternities of incomers like the Mayflower Pilgrims who signed a famous contract on their mutual rights and duties while they were still at sea. The New World lacked precedents, and many aspects of life had to be agreed upon all over again. Europeans had little share in altering the system they were born into. The government and the law they obeyed, like the money they used, came to them from above; its sanction was historical. But as the first settlers had framed their contracts, their successors in every colony maintained the right of assembly for airing their grievances and articulating their desires. Almost every office in the country was elective, from the priest to the beadle, while the higher authorities were far away. Scattered along a thin strip of coastline, between the

---

2. Not that every minister knotted his brows over the problem quite so darkly. "Gentlemen! You must do by your Bills, as all wise men do by their Wives; Make the best of them," wrote the Rev. John Wise in 1721. "There is no doing without Wives. The great Skill is to cultivate the necessity and make it a Happiness." Wise was apparently reluctant to take his own medicine, later petitioning to have his salary paid in hard coin.

hungry sea and the unknown forests, settlers had made their own arrangements to stick together for aid and protection. Perhaps that explains why they so readily grasped the way paper money worked. Paper money was the social contract in motion, a signal of value that presumed upon the trust of a community.

The English at home never had to think twice about money: it was handed down to them by royal prerogative. In America money was always something defined by law—peas, wampum, or now paper. The whole community took on a debt, which would be discharged by taxes in the future. The value of silver and gold was in the cost of its production, already paid, and the perception of its present scarcity. Paper money cost nothing to produce; it was just a promise, like America.

So when Mather climbed into his pulpit at the Old North Church, and his Sunday morning congregation bent their steps piously through the trim Boston streets to hear him, they all knew that only a few miles from this steeple, these cobbles, even then, at the end of the first American century, began the wildwood. Every settlement was a garden hacked from the wilderness, and every bill drawn on its future—complete with its stylized borders of fronds and tendrils, flowers or patterns of knots—reflected the theme of cultivation and enclosure. Winthrop had asked God to "carry us into thy Garden, that we may eat and be filled with those pleasures, which the world knows not." To Robert Beverly in Virginia, "paradise itself seemed to be there, in its first native lustre." The word *paradise* means enclosure. The first settlers, particularly those driven by religious motives, had every intention of sticking together, and the conditions they faced encouraged them to do so. For it isn't just what goes into a garden that makes it good: it is what a garden keeps out.

The woods were dark, tangled, and mapless. Unknown savage feet beat silently down their invisible pathways. Tuft of feathers, clink of little shells; sometimes the animal calls weren't animal at all. Under the endless canopy of rustling leaves many things were shielded from God's sight—things of blood and bone, unholy sacraments, sticky feathers, painted skins, vanishing tricks.

Mather knew something that European theologians had never known, because it was a thousand years since anyone in the Old World had heard the murmur in the nearby woods. Such things had passed into the realm of superstitious memory. In America the outcome was still in jeopardy. The philosopher John Locke—who drew up a constitution for Carolina—once imagined a well-stocked farm of many thousands of acres, hacked miraculously out of the virgin forest of America. Without markets, he demonstrated, all but the acreage needed to support the farmer and his family revert to nature. It was a sinister image, this undoing of wealth, this reversal of God's promise. It implied that only movement, and markets, could unlock the dark continent: only money could hold the woods at bay. Money stitched communities together. It brought the backwoodsman out of the forest and the lawyer to the marketplace. It was indispensable, even to William Penn's (1644–1718) Holy Experiment—"I had in my view Society, Assistance, Busy Commerce, Instruction of Youth, Government of Peoples' Manners . . . distinct and beaten roads," he wrote: to which end he advised the would-be colonist to bring a third of all his wealth in money. "Where money has not been introduced," Mather wrote, "men are brutish and savage and nothing good has been cultivated."[3]

Money, Cotton Mather was saying, is civilization.

---

3. In *The Christian Philosopher* (1721). In his *Essays To Do Good* (1710), he argued that perhaps the greatest sin a person could fall into was stopping circulation of money by hoarding it.

IN 1729 A clever young man set out to allay the fears and reservations of colonial Americans with a pamphlet entitled "A Modest Enquiry into the Nature and Necessity of a Paper-Currency." Arguing not so much for paper money as for more of it, to follow the first Pennsylvania issue of £150,000, it was Benjamin Franklin's first foray into public life and, like everything else in Franklin's subtle and ingenious mind, it served a number of purposes all at once.

Franklin liked paper money just as much as Cotton Mather, but he was unaffected by the anxieties that plagued the old minister. The colonies were in a robust state: the forest was in retreat, the Indians were on the run, the population was growing fast. It's hard to picture Franklin struggling with angels: if he wanted a debate he had coffee-house friends, or he founded a debating club, or he simply wrote—a lot of his writing sounds like an argument. Mather's laager mentality seemed out-of-date. Even Boston seemed old-fashioned in a way. Franklin was brought up there: it had grown up like a European city, higgledy-piggledy in the crooked trampled spaces between house lots. He was also tired of working in his older brother's printing shop. Cotton Mather was still alive when young Franklin pointedly turned his back on Boston and took his skills to Philadelphia.

Philadelphia had sprung suddenly into existence when William Penn's surveyors platted 2,128 acres for houses, shops, and wharves in the form of a grid. The grid was inspired by unrealized plans that Sir Christopher Wren had drawn up for rebuilding London after the Great Fire of 1666. London was far too old to change. Philadelphia was brand-new. Its grid became the blueprint for America: eventually all its cities, all its land, were to be platted this way. Franklin was initially bamboozled by the new order. In his *Autobiography* he recalls walking up and down the streets munching a penny loaf, fresh off the boat. People stared at the newcomer, eating in the street: one of them was to become his wife. Franklin was made for Philadelphia.

For Franklin, platted land and paper money ran hand in hand. His "Modest Enquiry" explained how paper currency, secured against future tax revenues, turned future prosperity into cash right now. "A plentiful Currency," he explained, produced low interest rates:

> And this will be an Inducement to many to lay out their Money in Lands, rather than put it out to Use, by which Land will begin to rise in Value and bear a better Price: And at the same time it will tend to enliven Trade exceedingly, because People will find more Profit in employing their Money that way than in Usury.

He went on to argue the case for America as a land of opportunity—a land where money, or credit, being cheap, even the poor could advance by their wits:

> Many that understand that Business [i.e., trade] very well, but have not a Stock sufficient of their own, will be encouraged to borrow Money; to trade with, when they have it at a moderate interest.

This wasn't like Cotton Mather getting everyone to stick together. Franklin was talking expansively of the many, the people; he wrote about rising prices and a lively trade. He wanted people to borrow money and to grow: more people, more land. His "Modest Enquiry" was very well received; it got reprinted all through the colonies; and within a decade he had secured contracts to print paper money for New Jersey, Pennsylvania, and Delaware. Pennsylvania even paid him over again to destroy the notes when they wore out or were retired. Paper money came along with much government business. By the age of twenty-five, Franklin was a made man.

"Bills issued upon land," he had written, "are in effect coined land."

❧

BY THE MIDDLE of the eighteenth century, the matrix of land, debt and paper money which was to govern American destinies for more than a century was well established. A group of speculators would club together to purchase a huge tract of virgin land, paying in installments. It was up to them to have the land surveyed and to promote its sale to new settlers. The promoters were men of means and influence, and the influence invariably procured the means. Docile legislatures issued paper money. If the money depreciated, subsequent installments could be repaid at face value in a currency that was now worth less than before. Buying and selling land was the biggest business in America.

No stranger to such schemes himself, Franklin was a lifelong friend of paper money. Money, as he said, made men associate with one another; it enlivened and quickened, it turned over products and ideas, it encouraged the poor and ensured that the rich spread their wealth about them by buying things and employing people. Its presence acted as a magnet to new settlers and artisans.

Scientist, speculator, politican, promoter, Franklin was a boundary-breaker. He snapped his fingers at the wonders of the invisible world: everything, he sensed, had a rational explanation. Far from being a liability or a threat, the wilderness offered nothing but promise. The point with Franklin was to fill in the gaps—to banish ignorance, to settle the wilderness, to take blank sheets of paper and fill them with print

For Franklin was a printer. After the church, the colonial print shop was the focus of the colonial community. If the minister told you about the next life, the printer told you about this one. He used the mails incessantly, and was generally the town postmaster, familiar with all the latest news, orders, advertisements, and prices. Everyone dropped by the print shop for their news and mail, where they could buy pens, paper, ink, and envelopes. Some print shops offered "notions," whalebones, goose feathers, pickled sturgeon, chocolate, and Spanish snuff; flutes, patent medicines, and fiddle strings. Most printers bought rags for paper. Type, and even ink, would come from England; but ordinary paper was made at home mills. Printers advertised for rags in their newspapers:

> *Nice Delia's smock, which, neat and whole,*
> *No Man durst finger for his Soul;*
> *Turn'd to Gazette, now all the Town,*
> *May take it up, or smooth it down.*[4]

Franklin crammed his newspapers with arguments, sallies, and information culled from other newspapers. When he saw that every leaf on a tree had its own unique pattern of veins, as complex and idiosyncratic as anything in creation, he used what he called nature prints—the imprint of actual leaves—to make his paper money harder to forge. For his own almanac he invented aphorisms so pithy and well handled that they sounded like wisdom handed down from a departed generation, and afterward became so. He founded clubs, debating societies, and Masonic lodges up and down the country. Appointed postmaster general at the age of forty-seven, his fortune assured by a string of print shops through New England, Franklin put himself at the hub of a country which showed a marked urge to communicate.

He bought the job for £300, but it suited him and served him well. On the one hand he could send his own newspaper through

---

4. William Parks, advertising in his *Gazette*, July 26, 1744.

the mail for free; and on the other, he had a passion for correspondence, for closing the gaps. He wanted people writing letters and sharing their thoughts. He wanted to establish a correspondence between land and money. He was a great man for balance. He worked for several years to prevent the break-up of the British empire; afterward he worked on the Treaty of Paris to engineer an equable peace. He liked to hold many strings in his hand at once, just as he captured lightning with a silk ribbon. Electric Franklin! The French loved him, as much for his appreciation of good gossip as anything else.

His moneyless America could be a lonely, quiet place. Nineteenth century America, very moneyed, steam-driven, increasingly urban, would warmly respond to Thoreau's efforts to rediscover that primal isolation, ignoring the efforts of many eighteenth-century colonials to escape from it. Franklin's brand of self-seeking practicality had come to seem rather repellent. Mark Twain disliked Franklin's morals, and even affected to despise his marvelous stove, which Franklin gave to the world for nothing. Nathaniel Hawthorne pointed out that Poor Richard's proverbs, from the almanac Franklin printed every year, were "all about getting money or saving it." The man who had arrived in Philadelphia in 1723 with nothing but a Dutch dollar and a shilling in copper in his pockets would have agreed. "Never contradict anybody," he advised Jefferson. D. H. Lawrence wrote disgustedly: "The soul of man is a dark forest, with wild life in it. Think of Benjamin fencing it off!" Lawrence did not live on the edge of the dark forest.

Those who did saw little if any romance in it. Nobody much wrote about American landscape; nobody suggested that it could be painted or drawn. Description of a sort appeared in Thomas Jefferson's *Notes on Virginia,* but the title alone gives a fair indication of its style:

The Ohio is the most beautiful river on earth, its current
gentle, waters clear, and bosom smooth and unbroken by rocks
and rapids, a single instance only excepted.
It is ¼ mile wide at Fort Pitt:
500 yards at the mouth of the Great Kanhaway:
1 mile and 25 poles at Louisville.

Visitors without surveying rods often struggled to find anything
to say at all. Sarah Kemble Knight travelled overland between Boston and New York in 1704, and wrote of her experience of solitude
in the woods, travelling "without a thou't of anything but thoughts
themselves." Only people caught her eye, instead, speaking of money.

Every trader . . . rates their goods according to the time and
specie they pay in . . . a pay price, a money price, a pay as
money price, and trusting price. Pay is grain, pork, beef, etc., at
prices set by the General Court that year. Money is pieces of
eight, reals, or Boston or Bay shillings, (as they call them) or
good hard money, as sometimes silver coin is termed by them;
also wampum (viz: Indian beads,) which serve for change. Pay
as money . . . is provisions . . . one third cheaper than as the
Assembly in general Court sets it; and trust, as they and the
merchant agree for time. Now when the buyer comes to ask
for a commodity, sometimes before the merchant answers that
he has it, he says, "is your pay ready?" Perhaps the chap replies,
yes. "What do you pay in" says the merchant. The buyer having
answered, the price is set; as suppose he wants a six penny
knife; in pay, it is twelve pence; in pay as money, eight pence,
and in hard money, its own price (value), six pence. It seems a
very intricate way of trade . . .

But Americans seemed used to it, forced to think about money
from the root up. Money had become one of their tools, a wonderful

telescope that reduced the most baffling and impenetrable landscape to a familiar scale and brought colonists a sense of control over what was otherwise a tangled thicket, full of surprises. Beaver in the woods had prices on their heads; a deerskin went for around one dollar, still called a buck; forests were convertible into lumber by the cubic feet; land could be fenced, sold, and mortgaged; a whole emerging system ensured that the mysteries of America could be brought pretty rapidly to book, transferred, alienated, bought, and sold. The "hideous and desolate wilderness" of the first settlers could be turned into a recognizably civilized landscape. In time, every particle of the continent might be pried from its setting and value, like a diamond.

To outsiders, this trait was to seem very vulgar, like pricing love or beauty. But to the American, it was an inescapable response to the sheer size and mysteriousness of the continent beyond. No one had yet crossed it, let alone placed it upon the charts—its mountains, its lakes, its cannibal tribes, its rivers and golden kingdoms. America slipped and slithered in your gaze, a form vast and indefinable between the trees.

Franklin was still patiently explaining what he saw as the virtues of paper money when he want before a British parliamentary committee in 1764. This time he had more experience and more heft to his arguments. Paper money was the reason "whereby the province [Pennsylvania] has so greatly increased in inhabitants," he told them. It swept away "the invonvenient method of barter . . . gave new life to business, [and] promoted greatly the settlement of new lands (by lending small sums to beginners on easy interest) . . . New York and New Jersey," he added, "have also increased greatly during the same period, with the use of paper money; so that it does not appear to be of the ruinous nature ascribed to it."

Franklin tended to win his debates, but this was a tricky line to take. Americans had spent years telling the government how poor they were, being forced to print paper for want of real money; so it was perhaps too much to expect the government to listen to Franklin praising paper money as "the reason the province is so rich." The British suspected that paper money simply released unruly and uncontrollable ambitions; a stuffy attitude shared by plenty of Americans, and one which the Founding Fathers adopted for the United States twenty-five years later.

For most of the colonial period the colonies had nothing to do with each other—different traditions, different interests, different forms of worship. All they shared was a coastline and the ocean, governors appointed from across the sea, and a problem of cash flow that encouraged a few ideas like paper money. Yet the British felt that the formal pretext for paper-money issues had been removed. Canada was at last secure. It was unlikely that the colonists would have to go to war again, provided they kept within their bounds and didn't stir up the Indians. Using paper money to bolster colonial economies made no sense, when the point of having colonies was to provide raw materials at decent rates to the mother country. Franklin argued that rich colonies would buy more British goods; but the British saw through that. Busy and industrious colonies were as likely to smuggle in goods from elsewhere, or even learn to manufacture them themselves: a depreciating American currency would eventually price British goods out of the market. Five years after the fall of Quebec, Parliament blanketed their colonies with a ban on paper money in 1764.

The British government's disapproval set it against some of the most powerful people in the colonies. In Virginia, for instance, British merchants gave planters long credit on the security of their tobacco crop. The planters meanwhile were languorously heaving themselves up into a southern aristocracy, so they knew how to spend the money until a series of poor harvests in the 1750s left them struggling with debts. Squeezed to deliver more tobacco to pay them off, the planters hit on the idea of paying public dues in paper money, rathern than actual tobacco as before. At the same time, they rated a pound of tobacco at twopence, instead of the market rate of sixpence. Royal officials, including church parsons, were furious: they expected to be paid in tobacco at full value. So when the parsons objected and the planters insisted, the king intervened on the clergy's behalf, provoking the noted orator Patrick Henry to denounce him as a tyrant who had broken the compact he had with his people. The king, he thundered, had forfeited the people's obedience. Cries of "Treason!" greeted his tirade, but Henry held the floor and was finally carried out of the courtroom shoulder high, while the plaintiff was awarded damages of a penny. Paper money, as the British had suspected all along, was a standing invitation to rebellion.

Squelching paper money only made matters worse. The ban of 1764 confirmed Americans in their opinion that the House of Commons was dangerously out of touch. Britain saw fit to punish them together. They were encouraged to view their grievance as a shared inheritance.

There is a niggling list of grievances right at the beginning of the Declaration of Independence which seemed, at the time, crucially important, though few people nowadays read or remember them. The first two blame parliament for ignoring laws passed by colonial assemblies, and what they actually mean is: we agreed to have paper money, and you simply shut us down.

· 4 ·

THE ANTIQUARIANS

On Revolution—Motifs—Masons—
E Pluribus Unum

The American War of Independence was unique: never before had a nation gone to war without money to pay for it. Had the revolutionary Continental Congress managed to gather up all the gold and silver in the country, it wouldn't have covered the cost of a year's fighting. So when Congress started work in Philadelphia on May 10, 1775, a finance committee took four days to recommend that Congress issue bills of credit, or paper money, and on June 22, delegates voted the sum of 2 million Spanish milled dollars.

That vote was the first of many acts of faith that led to independence. Congress's authority, legal or moral, was vague. Congress was not a government; it was more like a charity. It had come together as a forum for airing colonial grievances. Because no one in England seemed disposed to listen, Congress found itself trying to conduct a war. But no one anywhere wanted to give or lend it money. Only the individual colonies had any right to tax their citizens, and members of Congress knew their limits. "Do you think, gentlemen," one of them asked, "that I will consent to load my constituents with taxes, when we can send to our printer, and get a wagonload of money, one quire of which will pay for the whole?"

Congress's trouble was that even nationalists couldn't tell where events were leading, whether to outright independence or a new compact with Parliament and the king. Tories, the loyalists, prayed for stalemate, or defeat. Radicals aspired to free the entire continent, from Newfoundland to the Bahamas, from European rule. Even firebrands could be suspicious of Congress—jealous of its power, in the language of the day—because they still hoped to establish the sovereignty of their own state. For a year or so, the famous thirteen colonies involved in the struggle might have been eighteen, or twelve: it depended on whether Georgia came in, or whether Barbados or Jamaica or even Canada would answer the rebel call.

The states never allowed Congress the right to tax their inhabitants, and most Americans—even in wartime—felt little urge to pay any tax at all, despite John Adams telling his Abigail to "pay every tax that is brought, if you sell my books or clothes or oxen, or your cows to pay it." Tom Paine wrote that "the man who pays his taxes does more for his country's good than the loudest talker in America." This was sophisticated stuff: the emphasis in No Taxation Without Representation lay generally on the first two words. Congress could only beg for supplies. Washington's army, shivering at Valley Forge through the winter of 1777/78, took the temperature of state enthusiasm in the raw and found the going very cold. But at least it was an army.

As a result of its first vote, Congress got paper money. It was denominated in Spanish "milled" dollars. Pounds and shillings would have been impractical—every colony had its own currency, depreciated at different rates, so that by the 1760s it took more than a thousand Maryland pounds to buy just one British pound, as if the colonists still cared. They had forgotten sterling. Only merchants involved in London trade certainly still had to bother with deadly handbooks like *The American Negotiator*, printed in London shortly before the revolution, which gave exchange rates between sterling and all the indigenous currencies of the American colonies. Thomas Jefferson, too, jotted down the local value of money whenever he crossed a colonial border, but when he sent a man to England to buy him books, he ditched *The American Negotiator* and his jottings, and sent him instead with thirty Dutch guilders and a silver coffeepot. The only coin worth much the same in all the rebellious colonies was the Spanish dollar.

Congress's paper dollars were to be redeemed in four installments of hard currency from November 1779, taken from state taxes. Congress thought that a paper currency backed by all the colonies together would act as "a new bond of union to the associated colonies," though Congress was not quite ready to tell each state what proportion of the whole it would be expected to pay. That was June 22. The following day Ben Franklin and John Adams joined a committee in charge of getting the bills printed.

FOR MOTIFS, THE committee turned to books in Franklin's library. They looked at the 1702 Mainz edition of Joachim Camerarius's *Symbolorum ac Emblematum Ethico-Politicorum*, as well as *Idea principis Christiano-Politici Symbolis* by Diego Saavedra; a copy of the 1660 edition is known to have been in America, and possibly belonged to Franklin. J. C. Weigels's *Emblematum Repositorum* provided the symbol and motto for the fifty-five-dollar bill, showing a sun coming out after a storm. A Philadelphia lawyer called Francis Hopkinson developed the symbols and mottoes for another seven denominations. The backs of the notes were decorated with Franklin's homely nature prints of various leaves—tansy, mulberry, filbert, raspberry, ragweed, buttercup, betony, sage, henbit, willow, grape, rose, and feverfew, along with a skeletonized elm leaf.

These prints contrasted fiercely with the images appearing on the front of the notes, because the committee's choice of symbols, mottoes, and devices seems to have been governed by the need to stress all that was elevated and philosophical about the revolution, far beyond the rumble of everyday politics. These were esoteric images which sprang from the alchemical tradition, seeking essences and patterns. Camerarius—a noted herbalist—provided rural images. A wild boar rushes a spear, grain is threshed with a flail, a heron and an eagle fight, a beaver gnaws a tree (with the motto *Perseverando*—By Perseverance), a storm whips at the sea. Saavedra supplied the motif of a harp with thirteen strings to represent the thirteen colonies, with the motto *Majora Minoribus Consonant*—Great and Small Agree, or "The large colonies are in harmony with the small colonies." Franklin himself devised the mottoes and motifs on the four smallest bills, for fractions of a dollar. They show the sun shining on a sundial—*Fugio. Mind Your Business.* On the back is an endless chain of thirteen links, and *American Congress We Are One.* The first set were engraved by Paul "The British Are Coming" Revere: the rebels had evacuated Boston and Revere couldn't reach his press, but he built a new one from scratch and cut one of his own engraved plates in half to work on the back, to deliver on time.

These paper dollars were called Continentals and were the earliest symbols of the United States. Nothing else had arisen as a rebel icon. The Stars and Stripes was two years off; the sentiments Old Glory was destined to arouse were primarily nineteenth century. The national anthem had yet to be composed, the Liberty Bell hadn't been rung, nobody had ever given a July Fourth oration, and the office of the president had yet to be invented, let alone a president elected. All the power of political advertising was vested in the Continental dollar bill.

The actual money value of Continentals was beside the point. It was never very high, and was to flicker and waver with the fortunes of war. Continentals finally sank like a stone as the British retreated and the rebellion looked like a success. For everyone wondered now what on earth Congress would do or find to redeem the money.

THE AMERICA THAT Franklin prefigured on his bills was so new, inclusive, and conspiratorial that a baffled public had to ask for an explanation of the devices and mottoes to be published in the newspapers.

Franklin was a Mason, and perhaps his colleague Francis Hopkinson (1737–91) was as well: Masonic records for the period are patchy. Hopkinson was the first lawyer to graduate from the College of Philadelphia. "He is one of your pretty, little, curious, ingenious men," John Adams observed: "His head is not bigger than a large apple." He performed on the harpsichord and claimed to be the first native-born American to produce "a Musical Composition," with his popular song "My Days Have Been So Wondrous Free." He conducted scientific experiments at home, wrote poems and gentle satires, visited England, signed the Declaration of Independence, and trained a house mouse to skip around the table and eat from his hand. Jefferson wrote him, "I Have but few Words, 3 of them are, I love you."

After working on the dollar, Hopkinson went on to design the American flag that Congress adopted in 1777, and the final design for the Great Seal of the United States also incorporated some of his suggestions. They carry echoes of his designs for the Continental currency, designs "much admired for their appropriate significancy."[1] The forty-dollar note showed a blazing altar, with thirteen stars shooting out in rays, below a representation of the all-seeing eye. The fifty-dollar bill showed the famous unfinished pyramid, of thirteen layers.

The Great Seal is reproduced on the back of the modern dollar bill. It has been there for almost seventy years. Some still find its design disturbing; it is certainly unique. Paper money around the world tends to portray famous people, landmarks, kings, queens, splendid new dams, characteristic animals, or funky graphics, rather as though it was produced by the local tourist board.[2] The dollar, on the contrary, glories in its weirdness. The Great Seal shows an eagle carrying a shield on one side, and an unfinished pyramid below a blazing eye on the other. The eye is generally taken to be the eye of God; but perhaps it is really the eye of the people—an unblinking, all-seeing eye that penetrates through conspiracies of power and warns the republic of threats to its liberty.

It first appeared on the back of the dollar bill in 1935, when Roosevelt's New Deal was being put together to drag America out of the Great Depression. Secretary of Agriculture Henry A. Wallace was idly contemplating a picture of the seal one day when the phrase *Novus Ordo Seclorum* struck him as meaning the New Deal of the Ages. He took the picture to President Roosevelt, who "was first struck by the representation of the 'All-Seeing Eye,' a Masonic representation of The Great Architect of the Universe," Wallace recalled. "Next he was impressed with the idea that the foundation for the

---

1. William Barton, *Memoirs of the Life of David Rittenhouse* (1813).
2. The Queen arrived on Bank of England currency only in 1965, just in time to capitalize on world tourism's postimperial affection for the monarchy.

new order of the ages had been laid in 1776 but that it would be completed only under the eye of the Great Architect." Both men were Masons. Both recognized that the eye in glory, the pyramid, and the repetition of the number thirteen had a Masonic resonance.

Wallace later recalled Roosevelt asking James Farley, his Roman Catholic postmaster general, "if he thought the Catholics would have any objection to the 'All-Seeing Eye' which he as a Mason looked on as a Masonic symbol of Deity. Farley said 'no, there would be no objection.'"

American Catholics, on the whole, don't go in for conspiracy theories, perhaps because they have occasionally been the butt of them. Plenty of other people have an objection to the Treasury Seal though. It usually suggests to them a Masonic, or even a satanic, plot to take over the republic. They imagine that Masons or whoever have created a state within the state, and are secretly running things their way. It's the sort of conviction that is hard to shake: if nobody argues with it, it proves that they have something to hide; but if they do, it proves the same thing. But the Eye in the Pyramid isn't a specifically Masonic symbol: it was simply an attractive, esoteric motif that the Masons picked up and started to use in the nineteenth century. Certainly its appearance on the Great Seal is the product of a conspiracy, but a conspiracy against British rule in which all Americans were expected to play a part.

THE GREAT SEAL'S motto, *E Pluribus Unum,* was supplied by Pierre Eugène Du Simitière, a learned and eccentric self-taught antiquarian who was celebrated as the founder, curator, and principal patron of the American Museum, situated in a house on Arch Street above Fourth Street in Philadelphia. Swiss by birth, Du Simitière had lived in the West Indies, where he cut silhouettes and painted portraits to support his passion for collecting. For nine years he roved the mainland from Rhode Island to South Carolina, assembling a most extraordinary collection of natural history specimens, native artifacts, books, cartoons, broadsides, coins, prints, manuscripts, and treaties. Like many victims of mania, he justified his magpie tendencies by referring to the book he intended to write, modestly entitled "Natural and Civil History of the West Indies and North America."

In 1774 he took two rooms in Philadelphia. One was rigged up as his studio, where he worked up drawings and miniatures of most of the notable inhabitants and visitors to the city, including George Washington, Pierre L'Enfant, and various British officers during the occupation. The other room became his American Museum, the first of its kind, a sort of wild—and small—ancestor of the Smithsonian and the Library of Congress, open to the public for a fee of a half dollar. He still meant to write a book, though it had now become a history of the revolution; in 1779 he applied unsuccessfully to Congress for a three-year grant as "Historiographer to the Congress of the United States." In 1781 thirteen of his portraits were engraved for him in Paris, giving Europeans their first glimpse of the leaders of the revolution, but pirate editions undermined his profits. Two years later he lost part of a finger; his health was ruined, and he died in poverty in 1785.

The motto he had proposed to members of a committee working to design the Great Seal could have been his own: "Out of Many, One." *E Pluribus, Unum* was also a suitable motto for the new country, and it was accepted without demur. Ever since then, though, people have wondered where it came from. There's a similar phrase in Virgil's *Georgics,* but it isn't a perfect match. Anyone scanning the classics for *e pluribus unum* has been looking too hard.

Du Simitière got the tag from the *Gentleman's Magazine,* a London monthly widely read on both sides of the Atlantic; in his time it was a more influential and solid institution than the government of the United States. Most people who could afford to subscribe had the *Gentleman's Magazine* in its bound annual edition in their libraries, and it was on the title page of this bound edition that the words *E Pluribus Unum* had appeared since 1731. So Du Simitière hadn't really had far to look.

The *Gentleman's Magazine* was published until 1922, when it bowed to commercial reality; perhaps too many gentlemen had died in the trenches of World War I; perhaps its articles were too long. Either way, it no longer ran as a monthly and the annual bound volume was no longer required: it shrank to become the *Gentleman's Quarterly,* which for years survived on library subscriptions and on conservative dentists who placed it in their waiting rooms as a sort of preliminary anaesthetic. In the 1980s, though, it transformed itself from a dull old gentlemanly thing into a snappy monthly with bare babes and fast cars, called simply *GQ.*

SYMBOLS SELECTED, layout decided, and printing accomplished, Treasurers of the United Colonies were appointed to issue the currency. A committee of gentlemen was formed to sign and number the notes. Someone must have remembered how John Hull used to take a shilling from every twenty he minted for Massachusetts, because these gentleman signers were paid a mean one and one third dollars for every thousand notes they completed.[3] Colonial

---

3. Henry Phillips Jr., *Historical Sketches of the Paper Currency of the American Colonies,* 2d. ser. (1866). With a dollar divided into eight reals, a third of a dollar was an awkward sum unless it was reckoned back into the local sterling equivalent at 4s. 6d. to the dollar, which produced one shilling and sevenpence.

paper money was invariably signed by men of local standing, who gave the money a certain credibility. But hardly anyone could command the same sort of recognition across the whole continental region; those few who could had better things to do than sign notes. The signatures of obscure elected gentlemen would celebrate the anonymity of a new, pan-American society.

By August Congress had upped its demands to $3 million. The gentlemen were still hard at work, and the money was not actually ready until November, by which time Congress had seen that even $3 million wasn't enough, and had ordered more money. The signers kept signing, two to a bill, one in brown and one in red, their numbers eventually swelling to more than 275 as Congress poured out more and more money in the hope of catching up with the depreciation of the bills. Signing bills was a purgatorial task, according to a nineteenth-century banker, whose "self-imposed limit was a thousand sheets (four thousand signatures) a day. For a single day . . . this would not be a hard task; but to follow it for weeks and months, as I did . . . would, if it were a punishment, be too inhuman to be inflicted upon the most guilty of criminals."

Six Morrises signed, and four Smiths. There were three Joneses, three Graffs, three Grays, three Sellers, and three Youngs; there were two Evanses, Shees, Eyres, Reeds, Reads, Budds, Nesbits, Hazlehursts, Gaithers, a couple of Stretches, a pair of Wilsons, two Salters, and a brace of Bonds, as well as Horatio and Rinaldo Johnson. There were men called Gamble and Conner and Cockey, and Sprogell, Kuhl, Levy, Garrison, Herandez, and Foulke. Cornelius Comegys, Zachariah Mackubin, Emmery Bedford, and Isaac All were signers. Some had plain names like Paul Cox and Daniel Hitt, chivalric surnames like Purviance, hobbity ones like Cranch and Ord, and unpronounceable names like Kaighn and Hillegas. There was a Darby Lux, a Hercules Courtenay, an Aquila Norris, and a

Belcher P. Smith. They were all private citizens who were sometimes paid by the hour and sometimes by piecework, and in the end they had signed not $3 million, but more than $241 million: $241,552,780 exactly. By 1780 one dollar in hard cash was worth forty dollars in Continentals.

DEPRECIATION RENDERS tangible what is normally invisible: the mood and confidence of the people. On November 7, 1775, the Philadelphia Committee of Safety learned that the Quakers of Philadelphia were refusing to accept the new notes, arguing that as pacifists they couldn't touch money created to fight a war. But since it could be shown that they had often used colonial paper money issued to help fight the French they were warned against any attempt to reject the Continentals, and in January 1776 Congress passed a stern resolution against anyone "lost to all virtue and regard for his country" who refused the bills or questioned their face value.[4] "Regard for his country," meaning America, was a brand-new concept.

It was not the last time Congress had to pass angry resolutions, though. Daniel Webster pointed out that you could no more "force value or credit into your money by penal laws" than "whip love into your mistress with a cowhide." Many, like Washington, saw in depreciation "melancholy proofs of the decay of public virtue." "A wagon load of money," wrote Washington, "will scarcely purchase a wagon load of provisions." "We have all been wrong in our notions of getting rich," wrote a wag in the *Pennsylvania Packet* (June 5,

---

4. Charles Bullock, *Essays on the Monetary History of the United States* (New York, 1900).

1779). "It is true, we have got money. I have more money than I ever had, but I am poorer than I ever was."

There were ugly sides to the situation. Wherever the British went—and at times they popped up almost everywhere—they naturally refused the Continentals, so that nervous citizens were reluctant to accept them at the best of times; and meanwhile, recognizing their value to the enemy, the British circulated fake Continentals in areas beyond their immediate military control. The depreciation struck at Washington's army as it tried to buy supplies to feed itself through several hard winters. By contrast, British troops quartered in New York were so well supplied with smart officers and George III's agreeably hard coin that the 1777/78 winter season, which Washington spent shivering at Valley Forge, was generally acclaimed as the most sparkling and brilliant the city had ever known.

Congress continued to insist that the notes would be redeemed in hard cash as soon as they fell due. "A bankrupt faithless republic would be a novelty in the political world," Congress assured the public, "and appear among respectable nations like a common prostitute among chaste and respectable matrons." No one believed a word of it, and five years after it was first issued, the popular prophecy was fulfilled when Congress in 1780 abruptly revalued the currency, at forty old dollars to one. New bills were issued, with the backing of the merchants. "We have now full confidence that this money will pass as gold and silver," Congress told its agents. "As we have no occasion to press the money, we would have you tender it without expressing any anxiety or earnestness thereupon." Within days the money began to sink.

The failings of the Continental currency were outweighed by its ultimate success in keeping armies in the field long enough to defeat the British and deliver independence. Foreign admirers found it hard to understand. French or English wars were generally and ultimately funded by the poor. They were dragooned into conscript armies, paid the bulk of wartime taxes, and lost life and property in the struggle. America fought and won a war with largely consensual aims, without any obvious resort to taxation at all; and the barest trickle of hard currency from France and Spain. It was a people's war—that much was revolutionary in itself.

It had been funded, as Franklin recognized, by a form of indirect taxation. He wrote dryly in a letter to a friend in 1780 that "Congress . . . is, as you suppose, not well skilled in finance. But their deficiency in knowledge has been amply supplied by good luck. They issued an immense quantity of paper bills to pay, clothe, arm, and feed their troops, and fit out ships; and with this paper, without taxes for the first three years, they fought and buffeted one of the most powerful nations of Europe. They hoped, notwithstanding its quantity, to have kept up the value of their paper. In this they were mistaken. But this depreciation, though in some circumstances inconvenient, has had the general good and great effect of operating as a tax, and perhaps the most equal of all taxes, since it depreciated in the hands of the holders of money, and thereby taxed them in proportion to the sums they held and the time they held it, which generally is in proportion to men's wealth."

Every time paper money changed hands, it had lost a little value: that little loss was the bearer's share of the expenses of the war. "Depreciation is an assessor," wrote Gouverneur Morris with enthusiasm, "that reaches every farthing and baffles every attempt to deceive." The longer someone held on to a bill, the larger the loss he would have accumulated when he came to exchange it for something—so business was brisk. More radical, perhaps, was the way this indirect tax struck at the rich in proportion to their riches. Once again, money had proved socially revolutionary in America, just as it had when Winthrop wrote his skit on the master and his servant,

150 years before; only this time it was money in excess, not scarcity, that caused it.

In the end, Continental currency, having run its course and done its job, "expired without a groan," as Thomas Jefferson put it. The phrase "not worth a Continental" entered the language. A barber wallpapered his shop with Continentals. An old soldier, wounded in the leg, supposedly used a bundle of his pay as a bandage, and coined the word "shinplaster," which was later used to describe any sort of money that could not be redeemed. A ship's crew discharged in Boston, and paid off in now worthless currency, found a way of making suits out of the paper bills and paraded through the streets. "For two or three years we constantly saw and were informed of creditors running away from their debtors, and the debtors pursuing them in triumph, and paying them without mercy," wrote Witherspoon. Creditors were caricatured trembling in attics, or lurking by the back window for a speedy getaway. A victory parade in Philadelphia turned into a riot of money, with the colors carried by people wearing paper-money cockades in their hats, and a dog tarred and feathered in Continentals let loose to run among them.

THE CONTINENTALS were supposed to be redeemed by state taxes. Unfortunately the states themselves were issuing their own paper currency—they were also fighting their own battles after all. Virginia's paper money showed a goddess grinding Albion under her boot—when Virginia currency sank to a thousand to one a pair of shoes cost five thousand dollars. North Carolina used a series of spooky rural mottoes—*A Righteous Cause The Protection Of Providence* or *Be Freedom And Independence Steadily Pursued*—followed a year later by mottoes in Latin. Many of the mottoes resembled threatening letters composed of newsprint: *Counterfeiters Beware* and *Do As You Would Be Done By*. In one state, the bills of a collapsed issue were buried in an elegant coffin with the honors of war, followed by a crowd. As it was lowered into the ground, several orations were given on the services it had rendered, as from former friends and benefactors, and at the end one speaker flourished a new state bill and cried: "Be thou also ready, for thou shalt surely die!" The prophecy was fulfilled shortly afterward.

THE SAGE

On Jefferson—Monticello— Measures—Southern Life

In 1777, a year after he had written the Declaration of Independence, Thomas Jefferson began work on a new house right on top of a hill in south Virginia, in the lee of the Blue Ridge Mountains. A red brick octagon surmounted by a shallow dome, Monticello became in its time the most widely admired building in America. The dome is circled by a white stone balustrade; beneath it, a pedimented porch and four deep sash windows. A pair of elegant verandas curve away from the house to reach two charming little pavilions—Mr. and Mrs. Jefferson lived in one of them while work was starting on the house. The whole conception was modest. Houses bigger and grander than this come right off the peg nowadays, but at Monticello no staircase sweeps down to the hall, the rooms are small, and even the lawn at the back of the house is only large enough for a game of croquet.

Jefferson was responsible for every inch of this curious house, which embodies his philosophy. He laid out the plans, performed the calculations, consulted the books, and—as much as he possibly could—oversaw the work. Monticello was—or so its architect believed—the right sort of house for a republic, expressing its builder's faith in life, liberty, and the pursuit of happiness. Its hallmarks were economy and precision. Jefferson thought them republican virtues, and tried to maintain them in his own conduct. The views from the house, like Jefferson's idealism, are immense. Each room downstairs has two aspects, over the lawn and the pavilions, or over the whole of southern Virginia. The room where Jefferson worked is pleasantly cluttered and his daybed, set into the party wall, communicates with the sitting room like a deep and comfy butler's hatch.

"Building up and pulling down are the delights of my life," Jefferson said. Monticello, in Virginia, was his republican dream home, rooted in the land. He died there on July 4, 1826. (*A View of the West Front and Garden,* watercolor by Jane Braddick Peticolas. *Monticello/Thomas Jefferson Foundation, Inc.*)

ONE OF TEN children, Thomas was born in 1743 on his father's plantation at Shadwell in Virginia. Peter Jefferson died when Tom was fourteen, but he had a doting big sister who helped bring him up and gave him a love of books and music. At sixteen he went to the College of William and Mary, already fluent in Greek and Latin, a Virginia swell with five thousand acres of his own who could ride and hunt and dance well. The college treated him to America's finest collection of scientific instruments, and there he studied under the expert jurist George Wythe. He married a rich widow and entered Virginia's House of Burgesses in 1769.

Jefferson was a big-boned, freckle-faced young man, too shy to be a speaker, with a gift for cool logic that brought him into the revolutionary movement. In 1775 he set out some of the best arguments for independence in his *Summary View of the Rights of British America,* which invoked the notion of popular sovereignty. God, he wrote, gave men liberty as he gave them life: "the hand of force may destroy, but cannot disjoin them," and so, "from the nature of things, every society must at all times possess within itself the sovereign powers of legislation." The withdrawal of the British gave Americans, at last, an opportunity to wield those powers themselves.

In the early 1780s, Jefferson was working as a farmer, a burgess in the Virginia House of Representatives, and as a delegate to the Confederate Congress. His work had only just begun.

In Jefferson's time there passed through Monticello a never-ending raft of foreign visitors and hopeful politicians, savants, gardeners, architects, inventors, financiers, and gawkers. Nowadays it is supported by a tide of paying visitors. Originally, from its stables to its fields, from the Negro shanties to the house itself, Monticello was rooted in the land. For Jefferson, as for most Virginians of his day, it was not simply that those who labor in the earth shall inherit the kingdom of heaven—that too—but that land was the only real form of property, bringing forth the only true return, its crops, by which God suffered mankind to exist. Property was the basis of civilized society. It gave men independence and allowed them to follow the dictates of their own consciences. It was in defense of their own property that they hesitated to interfere in the rights of others. Land, in the view of the Virginians, kept men honest and free.

When Jefferson had the virgin hilltop leveled and prepared, and raised a house on it, he was building what he hoped would be the Great Good Place for him and his family. It was largely his patronage and enthusiasm that made the young republic choose classical public buildings: "We wish to exhibit a grandeur of conception, a republican simplicity, and that true elegance of proportion, which correspond to a tempered freedom excluding Frivolity, the food of little minds." As secretary of state he advised the architect Pierre-Charles L'Enfant on the building of Washington—"I should prefer the adoption of some one of the models of antiquity"—and he designed the "academical village" at Charlottesville, the University of Virginia, with its rotunda a half-size image of the Pantheon in Rome. He turned out a number of commissions in that style himself, including seven houses, a church, two courthouses, and a state capitol.

At Monticello, Jefferson was marrying the classical, republican ideal with domesticity and, above all, land ownership. He took a nameless hill and hammered at it until it rang with classical associations and political echoes. This is what he wanted America to be: a great collection of special places. Monticello is very tightly packed, wrapped around the needs of the Jefferson family and the demands of the plantation. It's not a Georgian manor house at all. The Georgian house suggested class identity, one box much resembling the next, and Jefferson wanted to encourage variety. Conformity was a danger to freedom. The guarantee of freedom, as he saw it, was an independent mind, a connection with the soil, and the security of ownership. A family that honestly possessed some land and worked it diligently was well on the way to finding self-possession too: farming brought clarity to one's feelings and faculties. Jefferson's virtuous republic depended on these families, equal and free; and as they multiplied, so would the republic grow.

IN 1784 JEFFERSON headed a congressional committee to find out how to survey new land to the west as well and as quickly as possible with a view to feeding the citizens' righteous hunger for land and extending the boundaries of the United States. The result was the 1785 Land Ordinance, arguably the old Confederate Congress's greatest political achievement after the Declaration of Independence. Thomas Jefferson was the author of one and the architect of the other.

Every state except Maryland had vague historical claims on "empty" lands to the west, Virginia's claims overlapping all the others. Unresolved, the land question threatened to drive the Union apart. Maryland's condition for ratifying the Articles of Confederation was a "national domain," which meant settling colonial claims once and for all by giving over the disputed land to the United States. Jefferson supported the idea: he dreamed of lots of little states with names like Sylvania, Metropotamia, and Assonisipia joining the Union, carrying on the republican tradition.

IT COULD ALL BE swiftly achieved. With the tools now at the disposal of the United States, enormous tracts of fresh land could be divided up equitably and settled in an orderly manner. It had all been ridiculously haphazard under British rule, when a Massachusetts farmer's plot, for instance, might be described as "beginning at the Foot of the Gulley below his House and running three hundred and twenty Pole North Five Degrees West to Red Oak marked AB then running Eighty three Pole East to a Spruce Tree marked AB," and so on: dangerously vague when professional surveyors, who knew what they were doing, were so thin on the ground. Jefferson's father was one, and George Washington himself started out that way, with his tidy handwriting.

In Jefferson's time the widespread adoption of Gunter's chain, devised by an English surveyor in the early seventeenth century, let the unsung heroes of the American West, the chain-men, parcel up the wilderness. Gunter's chain contained a hundred links of eight inches, measuring sixty-six feet or twenty-two yards—a measure vital to the emphatically British game of cricket—but ten square chains made an acre, and 640 acres made a square mile, and this might be the perfect plot—a section—to offer to farmers.

Jefferson went slightly further. His thoughts on order and harmony had been slowly beginning to crystallize, for during his spell as governor of Virginia he had tried to make Virginia counties into squares; now he proposed dividing the lands into "hundreds," or townships ten geographical miles square, subdivided into a hundred lots of 850 acres each. The hundreds would mass to form ten new territories covering the whole Northwest Territory; once taken up and settled, they would become states in the Union.

Congress accepted the general idea. Without setting up any states for the time being, it suggested having fewer, bigger ones— "not less than three nor more than five." Congress didn't show the same zeal for hundreds either: it preferred to establish townships of six square miles, adjusted to lines of longitude and latitude every twenty-four miles. With the passage of the Land Ordinance, squared-off acreage became America's first successful foray into the techniques of mass production, "attended by the least possible expense, there being only two sides of the square to run in almost all cases." First used on an unmapped area twice as big as France, it would come to cover three quarters of the continental United States, from river valleys to rocky mountainsides, subtropical forest, subarctic tundra, and deserts, all neatly chopped up into 640-acre sections. Giovanni Grassi, the Jesuit president of Georgetown College from 1812 to 1817, explained how it worked:

> Before the land ceded by the Indians to the government is exposed to sale, it is surveyed by order of the public authorities, divided into townships and subdivided into sections. Each township is six miles square and divided into thirty-six sections. Each section contains 640 acres and each is distinguished by numbers from 1 to 36. Number 16, approximately in the center, is reserved for the support of a school and the three adjacent sections are set aside for the government, to be sold in the future if Congress should see fit.

The system's weakness only emerged gradually. A small farm of 640 or 320 acres suited a family in the temperate northeast. Much farther west the regular rains dry up, the little streams run out. The grass is thin, and 640 acres will not keep a cattle herd, even if water is discovered on the section. Western pioneers realized that they had to gather together to organize irrigation, put pressure on water monopolists, and break the rigid section rules. Out of that very experience, at the end of the nineteenth century, the biggest challenge to the dollar would emerge. In the meantime the West was as remote as the African interior.

The system's strength was apparent right away. Indians had of course named every inch of the continent, and the first white colonists like Governor Winthrop and his scouting party had gone around devising new ones. But the Land Ordinance encapsulated America in a code: a code that released a farmstead in Ohio or Tennessee. Anywhere in the survey—any place, really, in America—could be identified by a combination of numbers.

Jefferson was smitten by the number code. Nothing in old Europe could compare with it: millions of acres up for sale, to let the younger generation flourish like their fathers. And Jefferson was simultaneously thinking about money: how to put it, too, on a rational basis. Colonial paper money had been a closed system, like settlements hemmed about by woods. Jefferson was determined to create a new money for a new society, and his solution was linked from the start to the principles that ruled the wilderness with straight lines, as if it were a new city, like Philadelphia.

The American Revolution had taken the power of sovereignty from George III of England and was currently in the process of stowing it elsewhere, closer to home. Coinage, as Jefferson noted, was particularly an attribute of sovereignty—the right to strike coins and establish weights and measures was perhaps what kingship originally meant. Royal justice flowed from this right. In America the king had forfeited his rights by refusing to give colonists representation. Americans were entitled to begin all over again.

With increasing confidence Jefferson proposed a new, rational system of measures. It would allow ordinary people to picture costs or acreages, to calculate prices and figure their accounts. In the wake of Gunter's chain, Jefferson's rational, decimal currency would value the land in a way even a child could understand. The clearer the system, the less friction it would generate, leaving people to concentrate on the exercise of republican duty. Jefferson's first duty was to establish for good and all the value of the coins of the United States. He intended to set the measure, just as he had done with land in the Land Ordinance of 1785.

The money of a free republic should be gold and silver. Only land and gold could be considered "real" property. Paper money was only the beginning of a whole corrupt system of mysterious credit and deliberate depreciation, based on a legal fiction. Paper implied a promise that might be broken; created a kind of anxiety that promoted deceit and evasion; lured the unwary into all sorts of traps and pitfalls; created suckers and benefited swindlers. Paper money allowed values to be manipulated, and it always gravitated toward power. From speculation and promises it was a small step toward mild deceit. People in the slippery end of money and business always had hidden agendas; they were unable to act disinterestedly anymore—put on a front, talked things up, pulled in other people to sustain their schemes and fuel their hopes. Somebody would be cheated. They had stopped acting quietly and rationally for the good of their family, state, or country; they had become so desperate and selfish that they were prepared to dupe some people and corrupt others.

Plain men could scarcely understand it. Jefferson, all his life, was simply afraid of it.

THE MEASURE THAT Jefferson favored was based on tens: a decimal system. Jefferson already used decimal units to govern himself. An angry man, he advised a friend, should count to ten before speaking; if he was very angry, a hundred. The only state supposed to have based its units of measure on the decad, or rule of ten, was Plato's mythical Atlantis. Dollars, for instance, were divided into eights. Twelve pennies made a shilling, and twenty shillings made a pound: an absurd system. Jefferson argued that a schoolboy would struggle with adding up pennies and shillings, but "when he came to the pounds where he had only tens to carry forward, it was easy and free from error."

For all that, the duodecimal system was, and still is, embedded in the geometry of time and space. Twelve is the number of months in a year and of hours in a perfect day. Five twelves make sixty seconds or minutes; two twelves regulate the day; thirty twelves describe the 360 degrees of a circle. It is the number of Jesus' disciples, the days of Christmas, and inches to a foot. A visitor to Monticello noted "a colossal bust of Mr. Jefferson, perched on a column whose pedestal is ornamented with symbols of the twelve tribes of Israel and the twelve signs of the zodiac." The recurrence of the number wasn't arbitrary; but Jefferson disliked it because it was old. It smelled to him of priestly divination, obscurity for its own sake, and it went with the anointing of kings and their claims to supernatural status. It belonged in ancient Babylon, not in the new republic.

So he set about defining a decimal currency. Robert Morris, the Philadelphia financier and merchant who had organized American finances during the revolution, and Gouverneur Morris, his assistant, had been thinking about a decimal currency too. The two men were not related, but it was said that Robert Morris had taken advantage of the coincidence, relying on Gouverneur Morris's wooden leg: he installed Gouverneur Morris in a big downstairs office, where anyone who came to the lobby asking for Morris was shown in to see him. The visitor would address him confusedly as Gouverneur, and they would wind up talking about the wooden leg until they had run out of time. Meanwhile Robert Morris worked on undisturbed in a small room upstairs.

The Morris plan was to reconcile colonial money reckoned in pounds, shillings, and pence at various different rates. Some states had inflated wildly over the years; others had stuck more closely, though never very closely, to the sterling value. The lowest common denominator between the different state currencies was 1/1,400 of a silver Spanish dollar, or 1/1,600 of a British crown. Robert Morris suggested that the United States might use this sum, which he called a unit or a quarter, as the basis of a quasi-decimal currency, valuing a set of coins at five, eight, a hundred, five hundred, and a thousand units. To convert these denominations back into local currencies, you would divide fourteen hundred by the number of shillings locally equal to a dollar. Congress grappled unenthusiastically with this scheme for two years before Jefferson dismissed it as far too complex. The value of state money might change again. "As our object is to get rid of those currencies, the advantage derived from this coincidence will soon be past." He fastened instead on the Spanish dollar.

He called it the unit, probably only to make it clear that his whole system of coins derived from this one coin. A dollar was, by the 1780s, almost a generic term, and Congress declared in 1785 that the "money unit of the United States of America be one dollar." It accepted—in the main—the idea of making it decimal.

Jefferson proposed coining a half-dollar, a fifth or pistreen, a tenth or bit, and a twentieth or half-bit, all in silver; a copper hundredth; and a gold ten-dollar coin. In the end the pistreen, or fifth, was dropped in favor of a nondecimal quarter-dollar. Jefferson came up with some catchier names, too, filching "cent" from Robert Morris, who had imagined it as a coin worth a hundred of his peculiar little units; Jefferson inverted it, less logically making the cent a hundredth of his unit. Unashamedly Francophile, he came up with the disme, from the French dixième, and the eagle for the gold ten-dollar piece. Congress approved the details in October 1786.

Jefferson's decision to turn away from the rule of twelve was significant because the rule had not been devised by accident. Plato himself went to some lengths to point up the inadequacy of the rule of ten, or the decad, in his Atlantis allegory: it seems that Jefferson failed to appreciate that Atlantis—engulfed by a tidal wave—collapsed because its foundations were very subtly out of true: its defenses, which seemed so strong, were in reality too weak; a society based on decads became, literally, decadent.

The so-called Enlightenment, which shaped Jefferson's outlook, was in essence the discovery of man's sovereignty. The eighteenth-century rational mind was prone to underestimate the mind of God. Jefferson in later life worked long and hard at a new, expurgated version of the Gospels, rather as if he, not God, had a better sense of their drift. Like other Enlightenment prophets of the later eighteenth century, he thrilled at the prospect of shaking up the old arrangements.

Only man could improve a stagnant, changeless universe. This was most obvious in America, where "the swamp has to be drained,—cultivation has to creep up the sides of the hills,—roads have to be levelled,—railways . . . water . . . harbours . . . bogs . . . arterial drainage . . . sewerage . . . towns and cities . . . and the whole country to be made into a garden."[1] The garden was not the original Eden that early settlers had identified in the New World: it was to be made by men, in a burst of energetic purpose that left much less room for the two-way flow between king and subject, between nature and the farmer, between power and negotiation. The aggressive confidence of Enlightenment philosophy, perhaps the very phrase "arterial drainage" itself, spoke of the coming of nationalism, republicanism, and industrialism, founded on the exploitation of resources on an unexampled scale.

The creation of the dollar, all decimal, was tangled up in a very

---

1. James Harvey, *Paper Money: The Money of Civilisation* (Liverpool, 1877).

Jeffersonian paradox. Here was a man who proclaimed the right of every generation to establish its own ideal society, untrammeled by the claims of history: he calculated the length of a generation from actuarial tables and recommended a revolution every twenty years, as if the generations popped out neat as cough drops. He did away with primogeniture in Virginia law, and claimed that established weights and measures belonged to the past. But he laid down laws of his own that he saw as somehow exempt from the revolutionary command. The revolutions he envisaged would not overthrow any of his own cherished beliefs, which he supposed were timeless expressions of human rights, natural laws whittled clean of obscurity and monarchical favoritism; they might govern politics much as Newton's governed the physical universe. Revolution held no terrors for him. Revolution would simply return the country to the path of natural law set out in the Declaration of Independence and the Bill of Rights.

Thomas Jefferson was one of the founding fathers of the United States, and like other fathers his unofficial motto was "Don't do as I do, do as I say." He created the world's first decimal coinage, and his portrait also appears on the curious $2 bill. (Silhouette by Raphaelle Peale. *Monticello/Thomas Jefferson Foundation, Inc.*)

HIS LAST WORD on the subject was his Plan for Establishing Uniformity in the Coinage, Weights, and Measures of the United States, delivered on July 4, 1790. Perhaps Jefferson sensed that his plan came too late for the republic. He opened his speech with two paragraphs of schoolboy excuses: the order missed him on the road; he had been ill; he had been busy; new facts had very lately come to light. But the politician in him trusted that "these circumstances will apologize for the delay."

He planned for his fellow Americans "a thorough reformation of their whole system of measures, weights and coins, reducing every branch to the same decimal ratio already established in their coins, and thus bringing the calculation of the principal affairs of life within the arithmetic of every man who can multiply and divide plain numbers." Jefferson's system put ten inches in a foot, and ten ounces to a pound. A cubic inch of rainwater would weigh an ounce, the same weight as a silver dollar of 376 troy grains. Money and measure would run together.

Congress nodded sleepily as Jefferson droned happily through this field of figures, pecks, grains, avoirdupois. Few congressmen had the faintest idea what he was talking about anyway, and none of it, as it happened, would make a blind bit of difference. When Tom Jefferson was small the Appalachian Mountains were the limit, the end of the line for white settlers, but in 1750 a Virginia land agent had found a low valley that cut through the Appalachian ridge at 1,665 feet, from where Indian trails fanned out into what is now Tennessee and Kentucky. He called it the Cumberland Gap, after "Butcher" Cumberland, a famously vicious British general, and thirteen years later the British government, for imperial reasons, forbade settlement anywhere beyond the headwaters of rivers flowing into the Atlantic. They might as well have tried to dam the Ohio River. In March 1775, while patriotic assemblies were collecting their grievances, Daniel Boone and a party of thirty woodsmen began to blaze the trail beyond the gap, three hundred miles down to the Ohio River at Louisville.

Boone had spent years exploring the whole area. For two centuries white settlers had clung to the seaboard, watching the price of land go up as the fertility of the land declined. Boone saw the Kentucky bluegrass where the buffalo fed, with wild turkeys in abundance and glorious forests. Later he returned, leading a party of settlers who fell into an Indian ambush in which his own son was killed. Now a delicate peace had been arranged with the Cherokee over whiskey and trade goods—although a Cherokee chief, taking Boone by the hand, warned him he would find Kentucky a dark and bloody ground.

The legal barriers were overturned by the revolution, and the first settlers in the Northwest Territory arrived on the north bank of the Ohio in a boat called the *Mayflower*. A later party felt "almost inclined . . . in imitation of Columbus, in transport to kiss the soil of Kentucky." It was like the discovery of America all over again. In fifteen years more than a hundred thousand people followed Sweet Betsy from Pike across the Big Mountain. Within twenty years the trail, or Boone's Trace, was graded for wagons and became part of the Wilderness Road.

So by the time Jefferson set out his New American tool kit for Congress's inspection, the new man was showing a clean pair of heels. As farmers poured through the Cumberland Gap the mountain range was no longer on the edge of the frame; it was a hinge, the spine in the double-page spread of American colonization. It was too late for changing weights and measures: the first westerners had gone already with their Winchester bushels of the wrong old size and their Guildhall quarts and their clipped coins. They'd gone with the furlong chain and the six-mile square, the 640-acre section, and the 320-acre half-section and the quarter-section. They'd gone with their old tools, to measure it out all over again, the whiskey and the wheat, the virgin soil and the price of furs.

Jefferson didn't go after them. Two years later—seven years after America had defined the world's first decimal currency—Thomas Jefferson, as U.S. minister in Paris, had the satisfaction of seeing the French Assembly follow suit, instituting francs, centimes, and sous for the old livres. Jefferson loved the French. Even as the revolution careered beyond the control of the constitutionalists and into the days of the terror, he refused to be dismayed. "My own affections have been deeply wounded by some of the martyrs to this cause," he wrote to a friend in January 1793, "but rather than it should have failed, I would have seen half the earth desolated."

The French Assembly brought in kilos, meters, and millimeters. Affronted by the duodecimal arrangement of the hours, they legislated for twenty-hour days, ten-day weeks, and years of ten months. Seventeen hundred eighty-nine became Year I of the Revolution. They made minutes of one hundred seconds, though nobody could build the clocks. They made the entire spacing of the cosmos a matter of arbitrary arrangement, and watched as the whole ridiculous system they had built fell apart.

Napoleon formally dismantled most of the measurement system introduced by the philosophes. The meter, not incidentally, soon turned out to be inaccurate. That supposed absolute, lifted from the earth's own surface by theodolite and chain, had to be redefined three times in the nineteenth century.

IN 1786 Jefferson told the House that "in Virginia, where our towns are few, small and of course their demand for necessaries very limited, we have never been able to introduce a copper coin at all."

Silly as it sounds—how could anyone reject money?—it wasn't a trivial observation. Jefferson called southern Virginia an ocean, and certainly southern towns were much like ports in being full of idle men with a sailor's weakness for hard liquor. Where the so-called Tidewater lapped the jetties of successful plantations, hogsheads of tobacco or bales of cotton were loaded straight onto oceangoing ships; captains and planters did their deals on the veranda, mulling over whiskeys, exchanging the valuable products of the South for English finery: but the pianofortes and the lace were evidence, really, of the terrible ennui of southern white women, who had nothing to do. Slaves could do everything, from heavy work to housework. White women were decorative. Towns, with their ceaseless petty trades and exchanges, were few and far between: busy streets were as rare as bustling wives. Roads were terrible, and settlements seldom grew. Dominated by Tidewater plantations, which supplied America with its magnificent Virginia aristocracy—men like Madison, Monroe, Washington, and Jefferson himself—the existence of hardscrabble farms in the Piedmont, along with the presence of slaves, gave this society an acid edge.

Most of the land was idle too. Planters drove the economy of the South, and most could take care of themselves: whatever they thought, their estates were less like aristocratic estates in Europe than medieval monasteries. "My father had among his slaves carpenters, coopers, sawyers, blacksmiths, tanners, curriers, spinners, weavers and knitters, and even a distiller," a southerner recalled. Everything they required was produced on the estate—the plank, the cowhide, the meat and the wool, the flax, the cotton, and the fruit. There was no call here for money, except when "a professional shoemaker was hired for three or four months in the year to come and make up the shoes for the white part of the family."

The money of everyday life was inevitably of low account in the South. To Glasgow the tobacco went, to London and Lancashire the cotton. Accounts were settled with bills of lading, bills of exchange, and drafts drawn on distant bankers. Even the architecture of the South was oceanic: when great white plantation houses did appear, like beautiful cruise ships, they had to plow through a landscape littered with flotsam and jetsam—shanties for the slaves, no-account ramshackle fences for the beasts, barns and byres made of sticks. Southern crops ate up land in years; the planters then tended to move their operations on, and leave the land churned up and dying in their wake. It was easier to "up sticks" than to manure the land.

Money, and especially small money, was at a discount in a world where whites poor or rich were learning to look down on manual labor. No wonder no one tendered little cents. "Ain't worth a picayune," people said, for when the French held Louisiana, they used picaillons among their livres and sous. The picaillon was a small silver bit, and its name rubbed across onto the five-cent piece in the South. Idleness was a southern vice. Travelers were forever damning the expense of travel in the South, ameliorated, to be sure, by the ironbound traditions of southern hospitality. But even that hospitality was, in fact, no more than a monument to the loneliness of southern life.

SOME PEOPLE, storekeepers among them, battened on the South's carelessness. Most of the picayunes in circulation were not, in fact, five-cent pieces struck by the U.S. Mint, but little silver "medios," or half-reals, an overhang from the days of Spanish silver. The medio was worth six and a quarter cents. When you bought, say, a five-cent cigar with a half-bit, the shopkeeper would pocket the difference. On the other hand, if you offered a bit—twelve and a half cents—for a half-bit's worth of tobacco, you made do with a five-cent piece in change, the half-dime. When a shopkeeper had paid out ten half-dimes instead of ten half-reals, he made a twelve-and-a-half-cent profit. Congress was trying to stop this practice in 1875.

Perhaps the poor whites of the Piedmont would have done better not to follow the example of the Tidewater aristocracy, with their feigned indifference to money, their idle womenfolk, their touchy sense of honor. Thrift had no part in the emerging southern code that the poor whites adopted in fierce imitation of their richer neighbors. An obsession with blood and honor left little room for vulgar money. Visitors felt that it was an attitude that did nothing to help the poor "improve their station," while it aggravated the load borne by the middling sort. Jean Pierre Bissot in 1791 observed the consequences of the coin shortage; "it is calculated that in the towns the small expenses of a family are doubled on account of this difficulty. This circumstance reflects a striking want of order in the government and increases the misery of the poor."

A whole century before the revolution, an English economist lamented the scarcity of ordinary copper coins on Jamaica, which was awash with silver from the Spanish mines. Efforts should be made to bring in pennies, he thought, so that "the inhabitants would grow more thrifty than at present they are." The Jamaican poor found it hard to save money, "for they being accustomed to handle none other but a silver coin, the lowest denomination whereof is equal to five-pence sterling, learn to set no higher value upon five-pence, than an English beggar does on a farthing."

YET BENEATH THE laconic and chivalric gestures, money mattered terribly to upper-class Virginians. Their houses, horses, hounds, hands, and hospitality frequently sprang from a maze of debts. They ignored nickels and dimes because they were one harvest behind their creditors in England, not massively rich. Jefferson was no exception, dreaming of the day he would not "owe a shilling on earth."

Jefferson's problem with Monticello was that he couldn't afford it—not the wine, not the books, and above all not the cost of building and rebuilding the house. That bold architectural statement was more like an endless, rambling sentence from Jefferson's favorite book, *Tristram Shandy*, a shaggy-dog story, for it was never actually finished. Jefferson carried on building and altering Monticello all his life. Thirty years after he had started work half the rooms still wanted floors, and plastering; and much as it made a fine laboratory for a scientific man, as a family house it was frankly bizarre. The bedroom windows went down to the floor, but they were very short: visitors found it hard to dress in privacy, or to look out of the window. As for the rotunda, its symmetry was too exquisite to admit a humble stovepipe, so the vestibule beneath was perishingly cold in winter. Even access to the bedrooms was to be had only by "a little ladder of a staircase . . . very steep."

As an emblem of republican liberty, an expression of its architect's faith in the rural republic founded on classical values (with columns Doric, Corinthian, and Tuscan perfectly arranged), it was unfortunate that it rested on one classical institution that had nothing to do with the orders of architecture. Slavery was the classical inheritance to the fore at Monticello, however tastefully the slave quarters were screened from the house, or tucked beneath its verandas. One family enjoyed republican liberty at Monticello; dozens of others enjoyed republican slavery. Even when Jefferson praised those who labor in the earth, he was thinking of himself and his friends rather than the hundreds of Negroes whose actual labor freed up their master to express such elegant thoughts.

Jefferson knew as well as anyone that debt was the antithesis of liberty. A nation that owed money wasn't really free. Nor was a man. Franklin had said so: "The Borrower is a Slave to the Lender." When Jefferson later became president he was possessed by the moral need to slash government expenditures to the bone, doing all that was in his power to pay off the national debt. But Monticello kept him personally, permanently in debt. He kept the strictest accounts; he calibrated and calculated everything; but he could never keep proper track of his own finances. In his will he freed a number of his favorite slaves, but his executors sold them, instead, to pay his debts.

· 6 ·

THE MONARCHIST

On Ambition—The Constitution—
Shays's Rebellion—Yankee Wit—A National Debt—
A National Bank—Duels

One of the happy heirs to plantation society, Jefferson was born rich, lived rich, and was afraid of money. Alexander Hamilton was one of its victims, frightened of poverty and weakness. Mobility was in his blood.

He came from a line of fortune seekers and refugees, island-hoppers in the Caribbean: they escaped from one island prison to another paradise only to discover that it was a prison like the last. His mother, Rachel, "a woman of great beauty, brilliance and accomplishments," belonged to a respectable family of Huguenot planters on the British West Indian island of Nevis, before she was chivvied into marrying Johan Lavien, a Danish planter, on the island of St. Croix. Rachel wanted a new island, the family suspected he was very rich, and off she went. Lavien was not rich. They were not in love. They had a son, but in 1750 Lavien had his wife imprisoned to change "her ungodly mode of life." She fled St. Croix and returned to Nevis.

There she fell in with the amiable, drifting James Hamilton, a failed planter with blue blood and no money. Rachel lived with him for fifteen years. Her divorce from Lavien came through when Alexander Hamilton was two. Six years after that James Hamilton went off to St. Kitts; it was a business affair but he never came back, and his letters grew irregular, then stopped coming altogether. If Alexander Hamilton did grow up to become the father of the U.S. dollar, as people say, then the dollar has distinctly ramshackle grandparents.

Rachel was a capable woman. She opened a shop and sent Alexander and his older brother to work for local traders. When not at work, Alexander was schooled by a Jewish woman, and would regale his mother with the Decalogue in Hebrew, "standing by her side on a table." He learned how to manage accounts at work, and was good at French; his talents might have secured his future as a modest merchant in the West Indies. Then, when he was eleven years old, Rachel died.

Peter Lavien, her firstborn son, scooped up her money and property by law, and James Hamilton was not coming back, so a nephew of Rachel's became the boys' guardian. His own wife had recently died, and the boys had hardly settled before he committed suicide. Alexander was taken in by a family friend. At the age of twelve he confessed that he "would willingly risk my life tho' not my Character to exalt my Station."

Bitterly regretting "the grov'ling condition of a Clerk or the like to which my Fortune &c. condemns me," Hamilton was working over the ledgers in a trading house and learning how to manage figures and issue orders, when Fortune sent him a volcanic eruption. He wrote a dazzling essay about it that drew the attention of a newly arrived Presbyterian minister whose ambition was to be "a patron who draws genius out of obscurity." Few people have got what they wanted quite so easily. The Reverend Knox persuaded a group of merchants to send the boy to the mainland for an education.

Described as "the bastard brat of a Scotch pedlar," Alexander Hamilton rose on his merits to become Washington's treasury secretary, a brilliant radical who stopped the United States from becoming the first banana republic on the continent. He came to a tragically sticky end. (Portrait by John Trumbull. *Copyright National Portrait Gallery, Smithsonian Institution / Art Resource, NY*)

Hamilton never looked back. He was still only sixteen years old when he told Princeton to speed things up and get him to graduate in a year. The masters either balked at his presumption, or dreaded the challenge; so he went to King's College in New York. He wolfed down law, and as the break with England loomed he became, by turns, a pamphleteer, a volunteer, and an artillery captain. War broke out, and at twenty-one he was a lieutenant colonel serving as General Washington's aide-de-camp. One of Washington's rages gave him an excuse to get back to the war, just in time—Cornwallis had invaded Virginia, Governor Thomas Jefferson had run away, and the Yorktown siege by French and American troops was on. Hamilton led a night attack on a redoubt, under heavy fire. Washington missed his aide, and worried that he was "deliberately courting death." But soon after Cornwallis surrendered, ending the war. Hamilton married Betsey Schuyler, the daughter of a rich Hudson River Valley patroon. In 1783, he settled in New York, where he established a reputation as an able and successful lawyer.

The United States were still strung together by the old Articles of Confederation, but the loose connections that had enabled them to fight the British were producing, in the peace, clashes and arguments among them. The war hadn't made a nation out of the United States. The states had histories, but the United States were traveling light. The dates Americans had to remember were mostly recent. Their battles had yet to be glorified in legend. Some of their meager baggage seemed hardly to be theirs: a British tune, a French victory, Spanish money, English law, labor finagled from Africa, corn and turkeys pilfered from the Indians, and quantities of rum abstracted from the West Indies.

They were a quarrelsome lot, too, watching out for themselves, suspicious of their neighbors' motives, suspicious of their own rulers, jealous of their liberties. Madison compared New Jersey, paying port dues to Philadelphia or New York, to a cask tapped at both ends. Marylanders suspected Virginia of wanting boundaries to the Mississippi. People called themselves New Yorkers or Carolinians first; Columbians second; and seldom Americans.

All they really had in common was a starting point, 1776, and a credo, of the *Pike's Peak or Bust* kind—Jefferson's *Life, Liberty and the Pursuit of Happiness*. Some firmer association was needed to halt a slide toward anarchy, and Hamilton was barely twenty-eight when he called together a congress at Annapolis in 1786. It lacked authority but pointed the way forward, and inspired the states the next year to send delegates to work on drafting a proper federal Constitution.

In laying down the laws on money, the negotiators were extremely cautious. First of all they stripped individual states of their right to issue paper money: national unity required a single currency to stop states manipulating values just as they did in the bad old days, and had been doing ever since the revolution. The states could make only "silver and gold a legal tender in the payment of debts." The power to regulate the currency, to fix the currency units and the value of gold and silver relative to one another, was vested in Congress. Permission for the federal government "to emit bills of credit" was struck down, leaving it only the right "to coin money, regulate the value thereof, and of foreign coin, and fix the standard of weights and measures." One Delaware delegate thought that including a right to issue paper money would be "as alarming as the mark of the beast in Revelation."

Thomas Jefferson was away in Paris as U.S. minister, but Hamilton made a speech. He proposed a president for life, life senators, and the abolition of the states—a monarchy in republican dress. It lasted five hours, "praised by every body . . . supported by none." Later speakers felt that the intellectual atmosphere of the debates had been enlarged. Hamilton retired to New York City while the delegates thrashed out their Constitution, and when it was settled he campaigned for it brilliantly. He wrote most of the so-called Federalist Papers, which urged the adoption of the Constitution from every possible angle. Privately he had "no objections to a trial being made of this thing of a republic." The papers seethed with arguments, and North Carolina worried about what would happen if the pope was elected president.

A rebellion broke out in Massachusetts. In 1786 Daniel Shays, a former continental officer and veteran of Lexington, Bunker Hill, and Saratoga, led an armed revolt against the state. Hundreds of farmers joined him. Some of them brought pitchforks and others took their guns off the wall. The casus belli, inevitably, was money.

Farmers like Shays had gone into debt in the days of free and easy paper money, and their troubles had begun when Massachusetts decided to return to hard coin. There was a money squeeze, a sudden deflation, and creditors calling for their debts to be repaid. But farmers didn't have any coin. Some were being forced to sell their farms at fire-sale prices to raise cash to repay minor debts. Resistance began with the courts, which ordered the payments to be enforced; there was massive civil disobedience and in summer 1786 Shays put himself at the head of an angry rabble and marched on the state armory.

The rebellion, in the event, was defused. The state militia dispersed the pitchfork army at Springfield. Shays and the other ringleaders were arrested, lectured, and sent home, but they had raised the specter of real anarchy and bloodshed overtaking the nation, and the anxious public rallied for the Constitution, for order and stability, when the time came for casting their votes.

The Constitution was adopted in 1789. Washington was elected president, and he invited Jefferson, aged forty-six, to be secretary of state. Hamilton was appointed secretary of the treasury at the age of thirty-four.

The first federal Congress came together in 1789 in a mood of anticlimax. Few of the new delegates bothered to make it to the official opening in New York, and it took another three weeks to reach a quorum. Nobody was sure how a federal government ought to behave, or even what to do next, and while Adams fussed over protocol, suggesting that the sergeant-at-arms be known as Usher of the Black Rod as if this were the British Parliament, George Washington presided over dinners where no one was allowed to talk, and "played on the table with a knife and fork like a drum stick." Delegates didn't know what to call him—Adams again, to radical cheers and hoots, had offered the title His Excellency the President. Washington, naturally, was no wiser as how to address them, and had no clear idea of their powers. On his first appearance in the Senate to lay out the details of an Indian treaty he was negotiating, the senators started him into "a violent fret" by referring the matter to a committee.

The greatest unknown was the prodigious amount of money that the country had borrowed from foreign powers and its own citizens to fight the British, which everyone expected to take years, if not decades, to sort out. The U.S.A. was only a pastoral country. Three and a half million people lived in its villages and farmsteads, a mere two hundred thousand in its towns. If the U.S. was small, it also looked weak. British Canada frowned down from the forty-ninth parallel, bristling with redcoats and loyalists. The Spanish Empire—moribund already at its core, but still capable of flashes of energy and intention—had Florida and the whole of the Southwest up to California, where its Catholic missions straggled out toward vast unexplored territory. French Louisiana was a huge amorphous stretch of central North America, most of the Mississippi basin from New Orleans up to the same unexplored territory to the north. The thirteen United States flanked a small section of the coast, the smallest unit on the map.

Americans stayed farmers for several generations, and most of their deals were made by bartering goods. Few of them handled money regularly while some two hundred thousand slaves, of course, had no dealings with money at all.

But there were the debts. Congress was responsible for much American debt, and the rest had been incurred by individual states. France, Spain, and Holland were owed extravagant sums, but much more was owed to ordinary Americans in the shape of chits, receipts, IOUs, and even verbal assurances that the revolutionaries had issued in return for goods and services—including military service. Nobody quite knew how much was owed, or to whom: it was like the northwest, unexplored territory, and more frightening.

Hamilton had done the sums when he delivered his "Report on the Public Credit" on January 14, 1790. Foreigners were owed $12 million. The states' debts could be estimated at $25 million. The federal debt amounted to $42,414,085.56.

And there lay Hamilton's opportunity: "It is a well-known fact that, in countries where the national debt is properly funded, and an object of established confidence, it answers most of the purposes of money," Hamilton explained to Congress. The debt would make money. The government would pay regular interest on the national debt, dollar for dollar, in hard coin that would come from import duties, and selling off public land. Anything left over could go to pay the principal. Investors who knew that the interest would be regularly paid in gold or silver would confidently buy debt certificates from one another, and their value, currently bumping along at a shilling to the pound, would promptly rise. As soon as debt became a desirable commodity, like land or tobacco, it could form the basis of a circulating currency.

The glacial logic of Hamilton's scheme sliced through the fuzzy afterglow of the revolution, because it rewarded the speculators who had bought up the IOUs issued to soldiers who had risked life and limb in the sacred cause, and even merchants who had patriotically supplied the army, and who had long since sold—been forced to sell—them for ready cash. Hamilton regretted this, but he could see no other way forward. He pointed out that even the speculators had, after all, demonstrated a faith in the United States.

Not everyone suffered tweaks of conscience. "Poor soldiers! I am tired of hearing about the poor soldiers," sneered Jeremiah Wadsworth, who was a businessman and a representative. The moment Hamilton's scheme was made public, unscrupulous "jobbers" like Wadsworth started hunting down all the government paper they could lay their hands on. They scoured the back country in the spring of 1791, and it was said that wagon-loads of gold went rolling down to the Carolinas, while vessels "freighted for speculation" carried agents south with instructions to go knocking on doors like Aladdin's uncle, offering to purchase old paper that almost everyone had given up on, for a little hard cash, anything from five to two shillings on the pound. It could take weeks or months for the common knowledge of New York to reach farmers and merchants in the Carolina woods or on the banks of the Savannah. Moneymen stood to make a killing. No matter: at least the terrible logjam of old debt was beginning to shift.

Now Hamilton proposed that the federal government should take responsibility for all of America's public debt, including the debt of individual states: a policy that became known, with biblical simplicity, as Assumption. It got right to the heart of Hamilton's thinking on government and justice, because Assumption really would lift central government into new realms of power and responsibility. As one of Hamilton's supporters explained in the House, "if the general government has the payment of all the debts, it must of course have all the revenue, and if it possesses the whole revenue, it is equal, in other words, to the whole power." States' rights advocates understood this. If the federal government took over their debts, it assumed a power to settle their affairs in the national interest.

Hamilton had long ago decided that the nation eclipsed the states. Americans should spread the risks and share the opportunities. A common debt was a common responsibility. The benefits of life in America were open to all. It was not for Virginia to repudiate its debts to British merchants, and thereby drag down the states together. It was not for Rhode Island to push its credit at the expense of its neighbors. Nor might tinpot local tyrants continue to exploit their social position and their interlocking local interests to play fast and loose with the reputation of their own, and the united, states.

Mainland America, as Hamilton had long since discovered, was still a collection of small islands. A political and social elite, empowered by birth and the control of land, controlled the destiny of each state, and Hamilton knew all too well the provincial superiorities, the listlessness and stupidity of island life. For all the revolutionary talk, Americans behaved with "the passiveness of sheep." They let powerful local families sew up legislatures and fix the rules in their own interests. The hullabaloo about states' rights was raised by well-born demagogues eager to maintain their provincial stranglehold and pursue their selfish interests.

This was where Jefferson and Hamilton were bound to clash. Jefferson thought it was enough to write a Constitution, and declare neutrality in foreign affairs and noninterference with legitimate activities at home. Jefferson seemed to see America's future in the same nation of small tradesmen and farmers it was on the eve of the revolution—a young republic like Athena, born of Zeus, springing from his skull fully formed, fully armed, completely prepared.

Hamilton was too cynical not to find this idea completely mindboggling, and ambitious enough to find it depressing. Hamilton was pushing for a social revolution. He envisioned a power capable of defending itself abroad and at home, one powerful, indivisible government capable of offering opportunities freely and equally to every citizen. To be free she had to command respect. Beating the British army had won the new country some credibility, but a nation couldn't be perpetually farrowing itself in wars. The costs of peace and freedom required that the supreme government have credit—literally, the credit to borrow money, at favorable rates, whenever necessary.

Money, not status, would be the source and measure of American values. Access to money would free the people from their habits of deference, and let them step past the old, ingrained inequities of birth and class to bust open the bonds of precedent and provincialism. States' independence meant division. Division created weakness. Union made for growth and enterprise, security and peace.

SOUTHERNERS DETECTED a hidden agenda. Most of the debt was owed by northern states, and most of the creditors were northern businessmen. Hamilton might invoke a national interest, but the South stood to gain very little by Assumption.

Hamilton's masterstroke was finding a way to bring the South around at no cost to himself or to his program. It was all on the level of symbolism, and symbols were free. Everyone agreed that a national government required a national capital, and several states fancied the honor. Hamilton, alone among old revolutionaries, had no feelings about it. He was born on an obscure little island. He had no particular state. As happy with New York as Philadelphia, he would have gone easily to the Susquehanna or the Potomac. Without Assumption, the question was anyway academic: a toothless federal government hardly needed a capital. He was not the only one who recognized as much. Unless the issue of Assumption was settled, and the question of a national capital fixed, "there will be no funding bill agreed to, our credit will burst and vanish, and the States separate, to take care, every one of itself." So Thomas Jefferson wrote to his friend Monroe.

By an irony that Jefferson never enjoyed, it was he who finally gave Hamilton the key to unlock his program in the legislature. Robert Morris had been approached with the prospect of a capital at Germantown in Pennsylvania in return for the necessary votes, but the Pennsylvanians were still slowly chewing it over when Hamilton and Jefferson met for the first time, at Washington's house on Broadway. They left together, sauntering down Broadway arm in arm while Hamilton sketched again the dangers to the Union if Assumption failed. Broadly speaking, he observed, the South wanted the capital. The North, in general, wanted Assumption. A dinner was arranged for the next evening.

Years later, after Hamilton's death, Jefferson would say that Hamilton had tricked him. It was an unequal bargain. For although the nation's capital did rise on the Potomac, for years to come "This famed metropolis, where fancy sees / Squares in morasses, obelisks in trees" remained a benighted village, enveloped in woods and a purgatorial climate. Even before the British burned them down in 1815, its public buildings were a gimcrack disgrace: Abigail Adams, the first first lady to move there, miserably hung out her washing to dry in the main salon of the White House. Nobody liked it.

In return, Hamilton got the assumption of the state debts, and the whole money program that was to stand on it, which attracted wealth and talent in a way L'Enfant's Washington signally failed to do for almost a century afterward. Hamilton's scheme for American money went up very much faster, and spread its tentacles very much deeper into American public—and private—life than anything that happened in Washington, D.C. It pleased the Philadelphians, who got America's first federal building in the shape of the neoclassical Mint on Chestnut Street and it delighted the cream of society, from the Binghams and the Morrises to the merchant princes of New York, Baltimore, and New Orleans.

THERE WAS ANOTHER dinner. Jefferson, Hamilton, and Adams met in April 1791. As talk turned philosophical, Adams declared that the British Constitution, purged of its corruption, would be the most perfect "ever devised by the wit of man." Hamilton responded lightly that it would be an impracticable government. "As it stands at present, with all its supposed defects, it is the most perfect government which ever existed," he suggested. It is unlikely that he was advocating corruption or a monarchy for America, but he was certainly approving the way that royal patronage kept power balanced between the Crown, the hereditary chamber, and the elective Commons.

Jefferson reacted as though stung. The Sage of Monticello had always suspected Hamilton of monarchical sympathies, but his airy dismissal of the c-word was the last straw. Hamilton, he suddenly saw, was himself incorrigibly corrupt, and all his schemes were founded on corruption. From then on the rift between the two men widened into an ideological gulf between town and country, states' rights and federalism, hard money and paper money. Hamilton's Federalists, said the Jefferson Republicans, were British stooges; the Republicans, said the Federalists, "spoke all French." The heat grew tremendous. The invective was lacerating. Each side kept a newspaper primed with licentious details on the other. Jefferson told Washington he thought Hamilton was a dangerous traitor. Duels were fought. Politics grew very bitter, and rather dangerous.

CERTAINLY THIS SMALL, dapper, handsome man, who was so clever and so diligent, had considerable powers of fascination. Women found him sexy and charming, and he was a terrific speaker, unlike Jefferson. It is said that Congress never let Hamilton present his arguments in person, because they doubted their ability to resist his oratory. It made no difference apparently. Hamilton presented money as the most reasonable thing in the world, and made his cash-starved listeners glow with a sense of coming order and prosperity. The way he conjured money out of the thin air was hypnotic.

Once he had secured an agreement on paying off the national debt, the value of government securities rose from $15 million to $45 million. Hamilton's magic added $30 million to the national economy. Money, as we know, works because it works: Hamilton inspired people to believe.

The larger the debt, the more paper money he could make available. He described paper money as a "lively sort" of money, in opposition to "dead" gold and silver. Paper money could skim about, in packets and pockets, paid in at one address and withdrawn at another, easily split and quickly spent. Gold and silver followed trade like a broken trooper in the rear guard of a victorious army: a heavy sort of money, lugged about in chests, always slow and always in open danger. As confidence in his paper dollars grew, so business would grow more lively. With the population growing too, imports and exports would rise, federal revenue would rise, and the debt would be retired in an orderly manner. Perhaps the debt, in fact, need never be retired: Hamilton the Federalist liked a public debt. Its existence anchored everyone, regardless of their home state, to the federal system.

But Americans of his generation had been deceived by paper money before. Hamilton was alive to the danger that a government would be tempted to multiply its debts in order to produce more money—which means a resort to the printing press, just as had happened in the days of the Continentals. What he proposed was a new, privately owned national bank, modeled—though he was careful not to rub it in—on the Bank of England, to carry on the whole debt and money operation. A private bank would be immune to political pressures. Misbehavior at the bank would frighten off investors, its credit would sink, and its stockholders would suffer. From purely selfish motives, the stockholders would strive to maintain its credit.

Founding any sort of company or corporation meant getting permission in the form of a government charter, because the right of corporations to exist in the early days of capitalism wasn't guaranteed, and the idea of creating a semifictional legal entity that could act like a man yet live forever still seemed odd. Nowadays we can buy companies off the shelf and we are inured to the idea of corporations actually paying less tax than anyone else, so it is the old caution that perhaps seems odd; but Americans knew that their revolution had been sparked off by the British government's decision to allow the biggest government-chartered corporation of all time, the East India Company, to sell its tea in Boston.

Hamilton began with a plan to turn $500,000 in hard money into $10 million, almost overnight. Like a conjurer, Hamilton takes an empty box that he calls the Bank of the United States. The box has an Ionic portico and stands at the corner of Chestnut Street and Third in Philadelphia. It is given a value—$10 million, say—and since $10 million is a lot of money, rather more than all the gold and silver circulating in the country, people are invited to share in buying it. The government is offered a fifth, at $2 million.

The government does not have $2 million. No problem: the bank's job, after all, is to lend money, and the government can be its first customer. The government borrows the money from the bank and promises to repay it in eight annual installments. Now the game is in play. The government can't run off with the money. It might default, but it has those import duties as collateral, not to mention western lands. The terms are slightly less generous for the next investors. They are the general public, and they must buy the bank's remaining $8 million worth of stock using some hard cash, and the rest in government securities, which bear the 6 percent interest rate paid by import duties.

The public fought to pay in, as it happened: all shares in the bank were sold in an hour, after which the bank was directly earning the 6 percent interest on the government securities. The securities do actually pay their 6 percent regularly, and the bank can use them to back a currency issue. The money is printed on paper, it's paper money, and when the bank lends it out it charges the going rate, 6 percent. It looks now like a going concern and everyone wants to invest, for which they need the 6 percent bonds issued by the government. As soon as the government has everyone clamoring for its bonds, the bank is perfectly justified in using those bonds as its capital.

The government money in, the public subscriptions, the issuing of banknotes, the setting of dates for interest payments and installments—all depend on the whole affair happening in one grand moment, like a gala festival. But Hamilton doesn't want the machine to be hermetic. He's building a nation, and besides the drip of gold from people who import goods, his system calls for a tax that will fall on people who think themselves absolved from all contact with the government or money. Whiskey fits the bill, and so the coils of government snake up to the borderlands, where whiskey making is a profitable way of turning huge loads of corn that nobody could possibly carry away into something every red-blooded southern male drinks with his breakfast tea.

Jefferson's supporters were furious about the whiskey tax—it sounded just like a measure devised by a British government to bring the people to heel. They were apoplectic about the whole idea of a national bank, which seemed too cozy with a federal government they also instinctively distrusted, and the whole plan might have collapsed if George Washington had not finagled a settlement for the capital slightly farther downriver than originally licensed—quite close, in fact, to Mount Vernon. He and the South needed Congress to approve the site, the sooner the better, for if the Bank of the United States went to Philadelphia, the move to Washington might never actually occur. Hamilton adroitly got Congress to pass his bill for a bank in return for turning a blind eye to the new siting of Washington.

THERE WAS ONE last hitch. At the end of February 1791 Hamilton's bill for a bank had passed the House and Senate and lay with the president for assent. Washington was bothered by the opposition of his fellow Virginians to the bill, and he asked the attorney general and Jefferson for their views in writing. His greatest fear was that the bill was unconstitutional, and the Virginians did their best to persuade them that it was.

Nothing in the Constitution specifically authorized the government to establish a bank. "To take a single step beyond the boundaries thus specifically drawn around the powers of Congress," Jefferson warned, "is to take possession of a boundless field of power no longer susceptible of any definition." The powers delegated to the federal Congress were explicit, and all other powers were reserved to the states. Any step beyond those enumerated powers would encroach on the rights of the states, and topple the whole system of checks and balances that so carefully spread power between the national government, the states, and the people. The public would have to use the bank; but the bank would not have to serve the public.

Asking Madison to draw him up a veto message, Washington sent both opinions on to Hamilton for a reply. Hamilton kept the president guessing for several days, and it was at the eleventh hour that Washington read his defense of the bank, a classic exposition of the doctrine of implied powers. Hamilton argued that if the U.S. government was a sovereign power, it was entitled to use the best means at its disposal to achieve its constitutional ends. The word in the Constitution was "necessary." Jefferson's narrow interpretation might imply that the federal government had no necessary duty to provide lighthouses, buoys, or beacons at sea, because its duty "to regulate commerce" did not specifically demand them. Yet the government paid for them as a matter of course, because they were useful; and the bank was useful, too. If the government was to collect taxes, regulate trade, borrow money, or provide for the common defense, it was fully entitled to create a corporation that would help it do all these things.

For Washington's sake, Hamilton went over the old ground. The Constitution certainly forbade the government from issuing money itself, and Hamilton thought this wise, for it was "a moral certainty" that any government that had the power to print money would resort to it in the end, rather than levy taxes that would make it unpopular. This government, he reckoned, had shown its wisdom "in never trusting itself with the use of so seducing and dangerous an expedient." A bank owned and operated by the government would fool nobody. But a privately run bank could be trusted. Its paper money would have to be redeemed in gold or silver on demand. Private interest would ensure that to preserve the bank's existence, it would not overextend itself and lend more paper money than it could redeem, whereas the slightest suspicion that money was subject to "public necessity . . . would continually corrode the vitals of the credit of the bank." Of course any government would also want to keep its bank solvent, "but what government ever uniformly consulted its true interests in opposition to the temptations of momentary exigencies? What nation was ever blessed with a constant succession of upright and wise administrators?"

George Washington had been here before, one month earlier, when the House of Representatives decided that the image of the president should not appear on the nation's coinage. "However well pleased they might be with the head of the great man now their President," the Virginia statesman John Page pointed out, "they may have no great reason to be pleased with some of his successors."

On February 25, 1791, Washington signed the bill into law.

HAMILTON HAD succeeded in keeping money and government apart; but Jefferson saw it differently. In his view, Hamilton had raised the Bank of the United States into a new governing institution by sleight of hand. It had a twenty-year charter, issued paper dollars, took deposits, and made loans. It took the government's revenue, and lent the government money. Eventually it opened branches in Boston, New York, Washington, Charleston, Norfolk, Baltimore, Savannah, and New Orleans.

Ever since that dinner with Hamilton and Adams, Jefferson knew that Hamilton was trying to fasten Old Corruption onto the republic. Corruption was, very simply, paper money: by shuffling and manipulating artificial paper wealth—banknotes, debt certificates, stock—the Anglomen, as Jefferson called them, could exert an influence over the country out of all proportion to their real worth. They would buy up legislatures and demoralize the people. Privately owned, privately run, unrepresentative, unaccountable, the bank was more than an unattractive alliance of old Tories, foreign merchants, and speculators: it was a network of tunnels and covered ways that threatened to undermine and overwhelm the classical simplicity of the original Republican edifice.

Jefferson was undoubtedly right. Hamilton's approach to money did suggest some sort of a trick; it was a con game, however pure its motives. But Jefferson's own dream of a rural republic where people used money like matchsticks in a friendly game of poker was never really very plausible. Money won't be confined. It runs into the street. Money likes making friends. Money can't bear to be idle, can't keep to itself, can't help but chase after the latest fad or the hottest show. Fickle as love, it will gladly promise itself to anyone. Money's curious, prying, venturesome, and unforgiving: you can't lock money up when the sound of the band wafts through the grille.

But that is what he wanted to do all the same. Money frightened him. He preferred not to acknowledge its charms, perhaps because they worked on him so powerfully. Jefferson's money would have been like a pale duenna, glancing down the street, slipping billets-doux through the casement for fevered romantic assignations; instead he dreamed of money that behaved with decorum and self-possession, infallibly retiring when the talk got hot. It never shirked a duty but it never listened to blandishments. Small wonder that Jefferson was afraid. Money was a strumpet; Jefferson remained nervously aloof. He loved his wife to the day she died; in Paris he dallied, in a respectable French way, with the English actress Maria Cosway; but he found himself, in the end, comfortably and privately attached to a girl called Sally Hemings. She was young enough to be his daughter. She was also literally his slave.

Hamilton understood money better than Jefferson, and he took its character into consideration when he devised the rules for it. Oddly enough, he was a perfect dupe when he propelled himself into an affair. The woman he was involved with was no Sally Hemings, no pretty country girl with homely ideas: she was an insinuating woman with a husband, both of them up for a spot of blackmail. No one ever rightly understood why Hamilton took such a risk with his reputation: in the end, to seize the ground from his political opponents, he made a full, published confession. It was a bold move, and it partly worked. Jefferson, facing the same sort of scurrilous rumormongering for his relationship with Hemings, simply shut his mouth and faced it out.

THE BANK OF the United States favored its political friends, and gave reluctant accommodation to its enemies. Soon they began to demand that state legislatures should grant them banking charters too—generally fobbed off with the bland assurance that, since anyone could buy bank stock, new banks were unnecessary.

Aaron Burr, the very successful New York lawyer, representative, later vice president, imperialist, and traitor, found a way through. An outbreak of yellow fever in 1798 was blamed on polluted water drawn from city wells or carted in from the countryside for sale. Six prominent citizens, including Alexander Hamilton and Aaron Burr, suggested that "a plentiful supply of fresh water" should be arranged as a matter of urgency. Hamilton's contribution was to propose that the council should incorporate a company to do the works, rather than carry them out itself.

Hamilton had nothing much more to do with the plan, which was taken on by Burr, supported by a number of respectable city businessmen, mostly but not exclusively Republicans like himself. The Manhattan Company was chartered to raise dams and divert streams all over the city, and it might "employ all such surplus capital as may belong or accrue to the said company in the purchase of public or other stock or in any other monied transactions or operations not inconsistent with the constitution and laws . . . for the sole benefit of the said company." Burr pointed out that without the clause, the waterworks would never get off the ground; and most people, if they thought about it at all, believed that the Manhattan Company would engage in trade.

A year after the Manhattan Company got its charter, when a young woman was found drowned in one of its new wells, the man accused of dropping her in was successfully defended in court by Hamilton and Burr. Hamilton was already aware he had been tricked. Burr's Manhattan Company was a bank, and a huge bank too, which just happened to have a waterworks attached,[1] and very accommodating to Republican grandees in the city. Hamilton wrote to a friend, "I have been present when he [Burr] had contended against banking systems with earnestness and with the same arguments that Jefferson would use. . . . Yet he has lately, by a trick, established a bank—a perfect monster in its principles but a very convenient instrument of *profit* and *influence*."

Dueling hovered hotly over politics in the early days, influenced its atmosphere, and occasionally eliminated its practitioners. Duels were fought up and down the country, and politics, of course, furnished plenty of slights and insults to provoke them. The shift toward party affiliation was not formal or complete—party was still a pejorative, implying that a man had abdicated his sovereign intelligence. Personal honor still counted for everything. In 1801 Hamilton's eldest son fought a duel and followed his father's advice to fire into the air. His opponent shot him and he was brought to The Grange and laid on a bed. His parents lay on either side of him for a day and a night until he died.

By 1801 Burr was the vice president of America, under Jefferson. Three years later on July 11, 1804, at seven o'clock Alexander Hamilton left The Grange. He had drawn up his will, and written two farewell letters to his wife. He rode to the Haarlem pier, took a

---

1. Honorably run, by all accounts, and pumping out water late into the nineteenth century, even though it could no longer be sold, because the directors feared that if it stopped, the charter would lapse and the bank collapse. The Manhattan Company merged with Chase National in the 1950s, to make Chase Manhattan.

wherry to Weehawken, New Jersey, and walked for twenty minutes to his rendezvous. Nobody quite knows what Hamilton was supposed to have said that drove Burr to challenge him. Burr shot Hamilton through the liver. He died the following day, around 2 P.M., on July 12, 1804. He was forty-nine.

Thomas Jefferson lived until 1826. Magisterial to the last, he was waited on by death in the house he had designed and built, in a bed of his own construction, on a date he might have chosen, July 4. The Thomas Jefferson Memorial Foundation has gone to great lengths to re-create the house Jefferson knew since it bought it in 1923. It has bought books for his library, planted his trees, restored his bed, found his writing desk, and laid his china for dinner. More than half a million people make the pilgrimage every year.

Few people know it, but Hamilton's house, The Grange, also still exists. Through the agency of the New York Parks Authority it belongs, as surely as Monticello, to the nation. It is a modest clapboard mansion in a plain Federalist style, painted white, that originally stood among fields in Upper Manhattan. It has been moved twice since then, and anyone with a taste for the ironies of decline may inspect it today, jammed up gracelessly against a row of speculative terraces and a nineteenth-century Baptist church on Convent Avenue in New York City. Monticello is immovable and unrepeatable. The Grange, though, is effectively homeless: as it wanders through Upper Manhattan at the whim of the Parks Authority it offers something of Hamilton's own rootlessness, and its fate seems emblematic of Hamilton's bittersweet reputation in America.

Jefferson was doctrinaire in his way, with a devious streak, a hypocritical tendency, and a habit of tilting at windmills and straining at gnats. In some curious way, his most characteristic acts were failures: his most successful were positively Hamiltonian, right down to the Louisiana Purchase. Hamilton could have defended the Purchase on his own terms; Jefferson was forced to sidestep the question of implied powers by entering into the burlesque role of an old Virginia uncle: "The Executive, in seizing the fugitive occurrence which so much advances the good of their country, have done an act beyond the Constitution. . . . It is the case of the guardian investing the money of his ward in purchasing an important adjacent territory, and saying to him when of age, I did this for your own good!"

Hamilton does not command the affections of the people. He probably did more than anyone to ensure that the United States did not become the first banana republic on the continent, but modern Republicans would like to replace him on the ten-dollar bill with Ronald Reagan.

· 7 ·

THE DOLLAR SIGN

On the Dollar Sign—
Pounds, Shillings, and Pence—The U.S. Mint

Two-bit means cheap. A red cent is worth the same as a plug nickel. You can *look like a million dollars,* a faintly weird ambition; pose *the $64,000 question, pass the buck,* and *up the ante.* You can spend your *penny, two bits,* or one of the *toadskins—buckaroo, fin, Vee,* or *nickel note, sawbuck, double sawbuck,* and *C-note,* even fifty *G,* and hope to get *a bang for your buck.* A *five and dime* is a store that sells cheap goods. A *nickelodeon* played a record for five cents. You can be *busted* or *loaded, flat broke, shiny broke, beat for the yolk, melted out,* or *made.* Perhaps you have *to squeeze every dollar till the eagle shits,* but if you're *on the money* you can be *in the money,* maybe *rolling in it,* once other people *lay it on you.*

A GI might be a *doughboy: dough* means money, because everyone "kneads" it—*spondulicks, dinero, moola,* or *tin. Rhino* has been used since 1670, long before anyone had seen a rhinoceros. *Berries, bones, dead presidents,* and *scratch* must be taken on trust: I've never heard anyone use them, even in the movies, so they may be literary inventions; I also suspect *oscar, pap, plaster,* and *rivets. Greenback, folding green, long green* don't count as real slang, only idiom; if *cabbage, kale,* and *lettuce* are for real, they're just a bit limp.

Slang comes and goes. *Shove the queer* now, and you'll be accused of violent homophobia; a century ago you'd be guilty of passing counterfeits. A *Bungtown copper* was once a phony cent: by the time small towns all over New England started claiming the distinction of being the original Bungtown, people had presumably forgotten what *bung* meant fifty years before (Bungtown=Shitsville). *"Not worth a Continental"* is the sort of thing foreigners say when they've learned the language out of a book.

Etymologists have a hard time keeping up. Did rap artists lately take *ducat* from a book, or has it been hiding from philologists since the eighteenth century? *Buck* itself has been traced to Sacramento in the Gold Rush ("mulcted for the sum of twenty bucks"), which probably only goes to show the limitations of slang dictionaries (that "mulcted" has a phony ring, too), because buck and dollar have been interchangeable ever since a buckskin brought a dollar-load of goods at the store; only nobody quite wrote it down right ("He has been robbed of the value of 300 Bucks," 1748, Ohio River, isn't all there). To this very day, etymologists can't explain *spondulicks* or *rutabaga,* which doesn't matter very much.

But it's the dollar sign itself that nobody can account for. When the fourth edition of *Webster's Dictionary* came out in 1859, an explanation was tantalizingly close: the Webster's people could categorically affirm that $ had made its first appearance within living memory. Somebody, somewhere, knew what it meant. But the years passed, and nobody stepped forward with a claim. Nobody sought patent rights or royalties on what has since become perhaps the most widely recognized symbol in the world, and nobody anywhere knows exactly what it is, or where it comes from, or how it got to be that way.

It is perfectly unmistakable. The $ means money and nothing else at all. The euro symbol is a Greek E. R is for rouble, Y is for yen, F is for francs, and they can all be tapped out on a standard keyboard. £ for British pounds looks more obscure at first glance, but it's only a stylized L, standing for libro, the Latin for a pound (like libre in French and the Italian libro).

But the S in the $ isn't S for dollar, or thaler, or peso. Theories abound. Is it S for Spanish? Or could the two uprights and the S represent the Pillars of Hercules with curling pennant that appeared on old pieces of eight? Could it be an 8 itself, oddly cropped? Is it U plus S? Colonial Americans *used* dollars, it was true, but they didn't often write them down as such—they kept accounts in sterling. If necessary they used the letter D: Jefferson, for instance, gave it a horizontal bar like the line on the British pound sign. *Webster's Dictionary* found no evidence of prerevolutionary Americans using the dollar sign at all.

In 1912 a math professor at Berkeley, Florian Cajori, undertook a study of the origins of the dollar sign. When Spaniards had shortened the word *pesos* to PS, they put the S higher, tethered to the P by a line like the string of a balloon. He imagined that someone once cut the string, allowing the P to sink into invisibility while the S—trailing its string like this, $—floated into history. He tracked its first appearance to a letter written in New Orleans in 1778, its first printing to Chauncey Lee's *The American Accomptant* of 1797. *The American Accomptant* is a very interesting book, and obviously maintains its influence in the trade, closely studied even now by the multinational accountancy firms who provide Wall Street with so much valuable advice. Lee was a true patriot, a decimal enthusiast, and a complete idiot. His professional heirs can probably even spell the word *accountant* better than he did. The only sensible claim in his entire book is that the federal government's newfangled decimal currency was actually quite simple to use. Had he stopped there the world might not have thanked him much, and his book would have been oddly short, but it would have had at least that one merit. Instead, Lee set out to explain how federal money worked. He gave illustrations. He performed calculations. He wrote at considerable length. *The American Accomptant* graphically demonstrated that however much Lee admired federal money he completely failed to get the point of it.

The point, as Jefferson had said, was to bring "the calculation of the principal affairs of life within the arithmetic of every man who can multiply and divide plain numbers." The Sage of Monticello supposed that any schoolboy could add and carry the ones, the tens, and so on, and write down the answer to two decimal places. Chauncey Lee proved him wrong. Lee seemed to think that people would want to go around writing things like 2,400 cents, or 48 dimes, and he came up with helpful little squiggles and symbols to represent them, utterly missing the whole point of the exercise, which was to have any sum of money neatly expressed in terms of a dollar—$24 or $4.80. We say: a dollar fifty. Lee says: fifteen dimes. We say: that will be four dollars thirty-six. Lee says: that will be six cents, three dimes, and four dollars. As the great numismatist Eric P. Newman puts it so felicitously, "Lee's system was thus conceptually obsolete, impractical and very difficult to transcribe." It would be nice to think that Lee wrote the whole book very drunk one night in a bar, at the dictation of a total stranger even drunker than he was; but the truth is sadder still. For all Jefferson's splendid claims for the decimal dollar, in 1797—as we will shortly discover—almost nobody knew what he was talking about. Chauncey Lee was one of the nobodies.

Meanwhile Cajori himself was anyway wrong about Chauncey Lee: the only symbol that looks like a dollar sign is one he uses (superfluously) for a dime. The first true printed dollar sign appeared in a pamphlet published in the summer of 1799.

Cajori's article elicited a flurry of correspondence, and his attention was drawn to a memo from New York in 1776 that distinctly used the dollar sign: "Treasurer to advance Captain Wismer $580 for bounty." So the dollar sign, like the dollar itself, was born in the year of the revolution. It seemed a happily patriotic solution.

Wrong all the same. In 1770 an Irish-born trader called John Fitzpatrick opened a store at Manchac in the Gulf of Mexico. The territory was first under British rule, then Spanish, then French; it was still French when Jefferson bought it parceled up into the Louisiana Purchase, but Fitzpatrick was long dead by then: all through the War of Independence and Spanish occupation he had run his store as a remote and highly technical subject of King George III, until his death in 1791.

This man used a squiggle a bit like $ to stand for dollar in his books for 1768. He used it incoherently. "Some at 8½$ and Others at 9 Dollars," he might write; and that, as far as anyone yet knows, is the best we have: the earliest use of the symbol in the history of the world.

But like the little picture of the cornflake packet on the packet of cornflakes, showing a tiny picture of a cornflake packet with a smaller picture of the cornflake packet on it, and so on ad infinitum, we may never get to the bottom of the mystery, because John Fitzpatrick put the dollar sign in his correspondence, too. When Bell invented the telephone, whom did he ring? If Fitzpatrick invented the $ sign, how could his correspondents have known what he meant?

Either way, Fitzpatrick's squiggle would become the most eagerly recognized symbol in the world. It came to define the currency of thirty countries. But John Fitzpatrick, who died in obscurity, never visited one of them.[1]

---

1. He never visited the U.S. because, of course, it did not exist when he arrived; West Florida, after the revolution, was handed over to the Spanish. The other countries

Far from ousting shillings and pence overnight, dollars and cents actually made sluggish headway against the system Jefferson had condemned for its obscurity. Neither the revolutionary generation, nor the one after, found it at all easy to think in terms of "federal money." In spite of Jefferson's argument that the decimal system was clearer and simpler, people were perfectly used to dealing in Spanish coins and giving them British valuations. Even the dollar, capstone of the Jeffersonian system, struggled for recognition. Into the 1850s the people of New England called a dollar six shillings. Nine shillings was $1.50; ten and six meant $1.75. A Spanish real was a New York shilling; eight reals made a dollar, and one real was worth twelve and a half cents. Ten reals made $1.25, or ten shillings, though in Virginia a dollar and a quarter meant seven shillings and sixpence.

Americans had to price things in curious fractions, according to the coins available to them. Goods went for 6¼, 12½, 18¾, 25, 37½, 50, 62½, and 75 cents. Things cost $1¼ or $5⅞. A decade before the Civil War, in 1852, the *New York Herald* was still running ads valuing goods at six shillings, 37½ cents, 62½ cents, and $9¾.

The Bank of the United States kept the general government's accounts in dollars, but many of the states carried on using pounds in making up their books. Maryland waited until 1812 before it deigned to pass an "Act recognising the coin of the United States," and New Hampshire did not actually drop its legal right to use the shilling as a unit until it was confirmed two to one by a plebiscite in 1947.[2]

---

using the $ symbol are Australia, Bahamas, Barbados, Belize, Brazil, Canada, Cayman Islands, Chile, China, Colombia, Cuba, Dominica, Ethiopia, Guyana, Honduras, Hong Kong, Jamaica, Liberia, Malaysia, Mexico, New Zealand, Nicaragua, Peru, Philippines, Singapore, Taiwan, Trinidad, Uruguay, and Vietnam.

2. We will never know if the people of New Hampshire really did want to drop the shilling, because the crucial question was entangled in another one about ballot reform.

Part of the trouble was the state of the U.S. Mint, for which both Hamilton and Jefferson share some blame. The Mint was erected on the site of an old brewery in Philadelphia in 1791, and Jefferson, who liked coins, saw it as his pet. He got his old friend David Rittenhouse, America's top scientist, installed as director, and Benjamin Rush, its greatest physician and chemist, as treasurer. Later he and Hamilton fought for control of the Mint, and Hamilton, as secretary of the treasury, eventually won.

Despite its resounding title, its illustrious employees, and the fact that the Mint was the first federal building erected in America, it was a cheap outfit that never worked very well. What little machinery it owned was mostly homemade, and until 1836 it was powered by a horse. In theory anyone could bring in their silver—teapots, ingots, foreign coins—to be turned into splendid dollars for a small charge, but nobody did. The Mint, being too poor to buy its own supplies of silver, never had minted dollars on hand to exchange for the incoming coin and silver bullion, which left busy capitalists to wait weeks, even months, before they got the coin. It was finally demonstrated that the first $3 million worth of coin had cost $300,000 to manufacture. Calls grew for the closure of the Mint, much to the satisfaction of the reliable English manufacturer Thomas Boulton, who offered to make America's coinage for her, humiliatingly cheap. Jefferson declined, for reasons of honor and security.

Operating more subtly against the Mint was the so-called mint ratio, which Hamilton had set to define the value of gold and silver relative to each other. He pronounced an ounce of gold to be worth fifteen ounces of silver. For a fixed amount of silver the U.S. would always stake you another fixed amount of gold.

But Hamilton's ratio was out of kilter and was bound to be. The real market ratio was forever moving up and down as one metal or the other looked more scarce. Discover a big gold mine, and the price of gold went down. Should some needy European prince disgorge the family silver, the price of silver might wilt. European markets were big enough to set the prices of gold and silver worldwide: the United States' paltry stock had no influence on the market price at all.

Europeans valued gold more highly than did the American Mint, and for years very little gold coin was made in the United States. But silver ran into trouble too. The Mint's shiny new silver dollars didn't stay at home. The world was full of horrible old Spanish dollars, rubbed and chopped and hard to tell apart, and Hamilton's old friends the West Indian merchants gradually discovered that they could exchange smart new U.S. coins on the islands at face value for grubby old Spanish pieces of a slightly higher weight, which they shipped back to the Mint for recoining. The Mint did the work, and the merchant took the profit. The situation got so out of hand that in 1806 Jefferson stepped in to stop the Mint turning out any more of his beloved silver dollars, which were not coined again for thirty years.

Copper coins had their own ways of disappearing from circulation. To begin with, nobody took them very seriously—Congress actually wouldn't declare the copper cent to be legal tender, allowing anyone, including the banks, to refuse them. The first design was modeled on a portrait of Martha Washington and gave her wild staring eyes and starting hair. It was dubbed "Liberty in fright." A replacement effigy turned out to be modeled on the artist's mistress, though the artist's friends insisted she was only a "blowsy barmaid." Shopkeepers collected all the cents, which they couldn't bank, in small barrels, and sold them to craftsmen who melted them down again for their own copper work. Other people had uses for them too. Women took to using cents to keep cooking apples green, or to stop apple butter burning. Sometimes people died using cents to fix the color of pickled cucumbers (copper and vinegar is a poisonous mix). Undertakers used them to seal the eyes of the dead. A slaver took almost the whole output of 1799 cents, drilled them with a hole for stringing, and shipped them out from Salem to buy slaves in Africa; his ship sank and the coins were lost, which served him right. Years later, sympathizers would give runaway slaves from the South a cent, which had been carefully notched, the position of the notch acting as a bona fide to people who sheltered them on the Underground Railroad.

In the South itself, cents were used on spindles, and as low-friction bases for gambling wheels; hotel managers shaved off one side, stamped a room number on the blank, and attached them to keys. The fact that the North appreciated small coins more than the South didn't always keep them in circulation either: they were made into screwdrivers, levers, keys, and even gearwheels. In New England they were nailed onto the ridgepoles of new buildings, for luck, and with the coming of the railways—a very Northern venture—they were turned into commemorative souvenirs, or charms. When Lincoln's funeral train steamed slowly home to Illinois, thousands of cents were laid on the track to be flattened by its wheels; just as they were forty years later when the body of the assassinated President McKinley was taken back to Ohio.

Idle pranksters altered the E in CENT to give anyone looking too closely at their change a shock—the start of a curious subcultural activity that was to produce Columbia seated on a chamber pot and better, wilder reinterpretations of the Indian-head nickel. Out on the frontier, the cents were shaved and notched to serve as rifle sights. In 1857 the so-called large cent was finally abandoned, and a whole generation of small boys was inspired to start coin collections.

What with the lack of gold, the ban on silver dollars, and the difficulties of the large cent, the Mint's total output by 1830 was one coin per head of population. Had Congress followed the British practice, and set the silver dollar and the gold eagle as standard coins, they could have issued all the others as tokens, or "fiduciary" coins, containing less silver or gold than their face value, because small coins didn't have to be valuable in themselves: they were bound to be valuable because they were useful. Congress balked at doing this because it feared that the public would see it as a devaluation, of the sort that used to be practiced by unscrupulous monarchs, and the country had to wait until 1853 before it happened.

It was not until the revolution was eighty years old and Americans had the amenities of railway travel, steamboats, chain hotels, most of the states of the Midwest, and the telegraph that they were finally united with a currency they could call their own. Acts to allow foreign coins to pass as legal tender for a limited period were renewed in 1806, 1816, 1819, 1823, 1827, and 1834, but right up to 1853—piping their eyes to the "Star-Spangled Banner," unfurling the flag at every hustings and convention, wildly if erroneously celebrating the Fourth of July all the while—the change in America's pocket was almost anything but American. Some was French, most of it Spanish, and a modicum, at least, was British.

Whatever Jefferson said, it looked as though only paper money could fill the yawning gap between what Americans could afford in silver and gold, and what God and nature were inviting them to achieve.

THE AMERICAN SYSTEM
OF JACOB PERKINS

A Monomaniacal Inventor—Counterfeiting—
Iron Writing—Money and Land—
Portraits and Landscapes

Either Hamilton or Jefferson could have claimed paternity of the dollar. Each man saw it upholding the framework of the republic they wanted built. Jefferson's dollar was on the farm; Hamilton's was more lawyerly, alive to the moral laxity of men but not corrupted by it.

It was noticeable, though, that the dollar never grew to resemble either of them very closely. Its features belonged—and still do—to a pleasant Massachusetts inventor called Jacob Perkins, who took up the dollar as a problem that required a solution. The problem was counterfeiting, and the way he solved it changed America.

COUNTERFEITING WAS an old American tradition, as old as paper money itself. There wasn't much anyone could do to prevent it. Anything one engraver could put on a copper printing plate, another engraver could copy. But copper was the necessary compromise: soft enough for an engraver to work on with his burin, hard enough to last. Copperplates could make around five thousand impressions before showing signs of wear, a stupendous number in the early days of printing—especially in the colonies, where paper and type were scarce and the market for printed matter was rather small. In the rare event that an illustration needed to be printed more than five thousand times, the printer would call in the engraver to go over his original work and freshen the plate up. A reengraved plate was never identical to the original, but this didn't matter terribly until the arrival of paper money. Then the print runs grew longer, and the variations were disastrous: before long, popular issues of paper currency were only an approximation of the original. This was the very weakness that counterfeiters tended to exploit.

Printers made deliberate spelling mistakes, hoping to catch the forgers out, grew extravagant with their swirls and borders, and wrote their copperplate in different styles and sizes, without much hope of successfully warding off the counterfeiters. And in the end they resorted to metaphysics. The Eden of colonial America was open to the danger of betrayal. Every colonial bank bill carried the hopeful legend *To Counterfeit Is Death.* Dozens of counterfeit artists blithely copied out the phrase. In Georgia in 1769 a fuller version of the motto appeared in abracadabra, like a spell:

TIEFRET.NUOCEDIVSIYGRELCFOTIFENEBTUOHTIWHTAEDTCAOT.

Reassembled, it sounded more prosaic: To counterfeit is death without benefit of clergy vide act.[1] A Captain Schuyler once pro-

---

1. Without benefit of clergy didn't mean a malefactor was deprived of his Last Rites; it referred to an ancient privilege of the clergy to escape capital punishment. Being a priest or minister was no excuse.

posed that New York's money show "an eye in a cloud, a cart and coffins, three felons on a gallows, a weeping father and mother, with several small children, a burning pit, human figures being forced into it by fiends, [and] a label with the words 'Let the name of a Money Maker rot.' " As a suggestion for X-rated money it fell flat; it too was only a more lurid version of *To Counterfeit Is Death.*

And even that turned out to be an empty threat, largely because Money Makers were not as universally detested as Captain Schuyler liked to think. Sometimes they were hanged, but juries often hesitated to send forgers to the gallows. Typically a convicted Rhode Island goldsmith in 1742 stood an hour in the pillory, had his ears cropped, and was sold into service to pay his fine and costs. The crime was common because forging paper money was a mammoth temptation.

The simplest way was to add a nought to a genuine bill, or scratch out the original sum and write in a bigger one, rather in the spirit of the old lady at Bloomingdales, on page 4, but this was amateur stuff; the copperplate was big time. Many professional counterfeiters from the old country were transported free of charge to this paradise of paper money by British courts; but forgers might well be people of social standing—goldsmiths, silversmiths, or merchants, like the prominent Rhode Island Quaker John Potter, a member of the legislature whose own signature appeared on Rhode Island's legal notes. He easily arranged to take a printer friend on a tour of the Newport pressrooms where the money was produced, which told them all they needed to know about the ink, the paper, and the technique.

His own printer set to work to counterfeit the notes, and Potter had the gall to take his counterfeits back to the legitimate printer and point out some telltale variations. As Potter hoped, the printer assumed they were genuine examples of his own work, and explained how worn plates had to be reengraved from time to time; he offered to sign a statement swearing that the bills were genuine. When he was eventually discovered, Potter paid a ten-thousand-pound fine to avoid having his ears cropped. People used to point him out as the man with the most valuable ears in the colony.

There were forgers with brand marks, forgers with missing ears, counterfeit gangs ("it is a sort of Disgrace for one reputed honest to be seen among them"), black counterfeiters, women like Mary Peck Butterworth who had seven children and did all her counterfeiting in the kitchen with a damp cheesecloth and a hot iron.[2] But Owen Sullivan was the best. Having trained as a goldsmith, he turned out to be a gifted plate engraver who fell for counterfeiting with irrepressible relish. In jail in 1749 he started engraving a plate for a forty-shilling New Hampshire note in his cell. He was no sooner out than his racket was busted once again—two hours in the pillory, twenty lashes. Then he moved to Rhode Island to reproduce the colony's latest design for a sixteen-pound note, working with a gang of "shovers" whose job was to pass them. When the whole gang was caught in 1752, Sullivan told them what to say, and all went free except Sullivan and an associate who had, it turned out, betrayed them.

Public opinion in Rhode Island was all for Sullivan; people felt he had been served a dirty trick, and even the executioner did the branding as discreetly as he dared and gave his ears no more than a little nick. So determined was Sullivan to see his former accomplice get his punishment that they actually brought him out of prison to watch; whereupon he seized a cutlass from a guard, leapt into the ring, and encouraged the executioner to do his duty with rigor. Then Sullivan jumped into the crowd and disappeared.

---

2. Because she used the cheesecloth to take off an impression from a genuine note, then burned the cloth, the eventual prosecution failed for lack of evidence: the authorities were unable to produce the printing plates.

He resurfaced in Dutchess County, New York, as the master-mind of the Dover Money Club, which went into operation with twenty-nine accomplices and new plates for colonial bills from all over America. The Money Club shovers were arrested now and then, but they were hard to convict and the trail to Sullivan was always cold until a bounty hunter, Cornet Eliphalet Beacher, was given a warrant by the Supreme Court of New York and a corps of mounted assistants. Beacher forced a suspect to lead him to the master's den, the clubhouse. They arrived at a swamp in a large wood. The guide removed some bushes from a cliff face and then a tree stump hiding the mouth of a cave. A tunnel brought the bounty hunters to a large, comfortable room, which even had a window set into another part of the hill. Sullivan had escaped to the mountains and stayed up there nearly a week, hungry and cold, before he went into hiding in the house of a friend. Beacher and his men eventually found him there, after spotting a piece of fresh dirt on the floor. They had to shift a bed aside, despite the protests of its occupant, and prize up a loose plank. Underneath they found a passage cut in the earth. Sullivan was persuaded to come out. He was still boasting. He could imitate every note he had ever seen, he said, and he slyly offered to show Beacher how an inimitable plate could be designed. But the secret remained his: Beacher marched him off to the New York Supreme Court, which sentenced him to be hanged.

Sullivan seemed incapable of regret, let alone remorse. He was not unusual. Counterfeiters seemed not only to enjoy their work, but to relish the notoriety: the noose around their necks struck many as the crowning moment of their criminal careers. As one silversmith, Gilbert Belcher, cheerfully confessed in his own gallows speech, "No gain afforded me so much pleasure as that which I acquired by illicit means."

Meanwhile public sympathy for Sullivan was running high. A hangman could not be found, the gallows were cut down overnight, and Sullivan's last speech was rapidly set and printed for the public. He boasted of making twelve thousand pounds in Rhode Island paper, of which he had passed sixteen hundred pounds in one day, ten thousand pounds or more in New Hampshire bills, and at least three thousand pounds in New York money. He had contempt for the money dealers who asked him to identify which notes he had actually forged. "You must find that out by your learning," he replied.

He took a large plug of tobacco. He turned to face the crowd. Just before they let the trap drop he made a funny remark. "I cannot help smiling," he said, "as 'tis the nature of the beast."

THE BRITISH GOVERNMENT'S counterfeiting operation is said to be the first example of economic warfare, certainly the first of its kind. Tom Paine wrote in one of his *Crisis* letters to General Howe, March 21, 1778: "You, sir, have the honor of adding a new vice to the military catalogue; and the reason, perhaps, why the invention was reserved for you, is, because no general before was mean enough even to think of it."

It was mean, but it seemed moral: the Continental currency they forged was illegal anyway. The more public their operations, the more successfully they cast doubt on the currency. In April 1777 New York papers carried the following announcement:

> Persons going into other Colonies may be supplied with any Number of counterfeit Congress-Notes, for the Price of the Paper per Ream. They are so neatly and exactly executed that there is no Risque in getting them off, it being almost impossible to discover, that they are not genuine. This has been proved by Bills to a very large Amount, which have already been successfully circulated. Enquire for Q.E.D. at the Coffee-House, from 11 P.M. to 4 A.M. during the present month.

The unfinished pyramid of thirteen courses appears on the back of the modern dollar bill, but it first appeared on the Continental currency issued to pay for the American Revolution, along with other bold and esoteric motifs. Benjamin Franklin—printer, postmaster, ambassador, philosopher, polymath, and revolutionary—devised these so-called Nature Prints to foil counterfeiters.

❧

BORN IN MASSACHUSETTS in 1766, Jacob Perkins was one of those early American tinkerers who stalked the frontiers of technology. He grew up with an uncanny ability to see abstract problems in practical terms. He was apprenticed to a goldsmith. When he was only fifteen the old goldsmith died, leaving him the shop, and in spite of his youth Perkins grabbed hold of his business and made it pay. A swift grasp of the properties of metals was the springboard of his career. He devised a machine to make carpenters' nails, at a time when every nail in the world was still handmade and most of the nails in America were imported from England (in Virginia they had been used as money). Even Thomas Jefferson ran a nail foundry at Monticello to generate income for the estate.

Perkins became a legend in the small world of early American engineers—mostly Philadelphia engineers really, because most inventive men seemed to wind up there in the first decades of the nineteenth century. Stocky and short, with receding hair and a mobile and amusing face, he loved an audience and delighted in spectacular demonstrations. His head whirled with ideas. A doctor friend recalled getting some practical advice from him that struck him as simple and ingenious, but he was scarcely out of the door before Perkins called, "Come back, Doctor, and I will show you a better plan." The doctor took the new sketch, but before he had crossed the yard Perkins called him back. Finally he reached the street, with Perkins at the gate calling after him: "Doctor, if you don't find that to work right, come back, and I will show you a d——d sight better plan than either, which I have this moment thought of."

Perkins's inventions never made him rich. In the course of a long and busy life he was either picking up new ideas and dropping them again just when they were set to blossom into an elusive fortune, or else doggedly pursuing them down a blind alley. He had a happy marriage, industrious children, and the knack of keeping friends, despite his tendency to get so excited by new ideas that he was quite capable of mulling over somebody else's in such detail that he would come to see it as his own, to the point of happily explaining the whole apparatus to the very man who had first thought of it.

He was a showman and couldn't help it. Once for a bet he devised a practical ship's pump out of an old leather boot, some

Jacob Perkins invented steel engraving: his American System of currency printing stamped the dollar with the mark of the machine age and allowed nineteenth-century America to surf home on a tide of colorful paper dollars. (Portrait by Charles Willson Peale, ca. 1816. *The Historical and Interpretive Collections of the Franklin Institute, Philadelphia, PA. Photograph courtesy of Charles Penniman, Philadelphia, PA*)

board, and two broom handles in twenty-seven minutes. He devoted years to a steam gun that could mow down an infantry regiment in ten minutes.[3] He fired out patents like bullets too. He had plans to make morocco leather, improve fire engines, perfect water mills. He patented new locks for banks, a watermarked paper, boilers, valves, tubes, and a screw propeller. Following a remark from his wife, he left "bedsteads and sofas" much improved. He patented a spoon. He lived at a time when every avenue of science was wide and open, steam power was still a marvel, and almost everything in the

---

3. A fellow American witnessed a demonstration in London before the duke of Wellington. The duke of Sussex was there too, "and when the bullets flew pretty thick and the discharge came to a climax, I heard him say to the duke of Wellington, in an undertone—'Wonderful, wonderful, d——d wonderful'; then again 'Wonderful, wonderful, d——d wonderful'; then again 'Wonderful, d——d wonderful.' And so he went on, without variation. It was in fact, save the profanity, a very good commentary upon the performance."

world from washing up to traveling to the next state still depended on sheer physical effort.

Perkins invented the first true refrigerator in 1834; two years later he came up with air-conditioning, which made life possible in otherwise uninhabitable parts of the world like Washington, D.C. Late in life he was also responsible for creating the world's first postage stamp, the lustrous Penny Black. Before that, though, he had come up with the first substantial advance in printing methods in two centuries.

The germ of the whole scheme came to Perkins in 1788, when the Massachusetts Assembly asked him to engrave a steel die for striking copper coins. He was still by trade a goldsmith and engraving was in his line. His first insight was that small steel dies like the one he was engraving—sixty-four small dies to be exact—could be clamped together to form a plate for printing paper money far superior to copperplate. Each tiny die would be a miniature marvel of the engraver's art, and the whole plate would be the work of many hands. No counterfeiter would be able to faithfully reproduce one of the features on the note without fluffing another, for if he was good at faces he would be stumped by crosshatching; the meticulous crosshatcher would despair of duplicating an artistically engraved picture, called a vignette. If necessary, the legitimate printer could switch the dies to vary the design, or add new ones: counterfeiters would be hard-pressed to keep up.

None of this would count if the dies had to be reengraved. The trick was to come up with a tougher plate, and for this Perkins did away with copper altogether. Not without difficulty—he had to pick over tons of steel to find the uniform quality he needed—Perkins invented a way to "anneal" or soften steel so that an engraver could work on it, and to "case harden" it again without damaging the engraving. This then became the master plate. By 1804 he had a method of duplicating hard steel plates he called siderography, "iron writing," or transfer. The result was a printing plate that could be used thirty thousand times. A fresh plate, identical to the last, would then replace it. Not only was the steel more durable than copper, but it also took—and held—the most detailed work an engraver could aspire to produce.

Developing labor-saving devices because labor was expensive and money was scarce was one of the hallmarks of American industry, from the days when it was carried out in little machine shops on city streets to the age of factory towns and expensive laboratories. In Perkins's day, the classic of this kind was Eli Whitney's simple cotton gin, which he had invented in 1793 while on a vacation in the South. The gin automatically raked cotton seeds from the cotton lint, so that one man could produce fifty pounds of clean cotton a day instead of one. Whitney, who disapproved of slavery, naively thought that he had solved the South's manpower problem, and that slavery would dwindle away. Instead, Whitney's cotton gin gave the American South a piece of cheap technology that turned cotton into America's biggest single money-earner. The market for cheap, comfortable cotton was insatiable. It made cotton-plantation owners so rich, and slavery so profitable, that America lost any chance she might have had for solving the slave question peacefully and cheaply. From then on, cotton and slavery went west with the frontier, driven ever deeper into the culture and economy of the South (the Old South, where cotton didn't grow so well, simply took to slave-breeding).

Perkins's slot-in-and-snap-together printing system for paper money turned every would-be counterfeiter into the equivalent of the man who cleaned by hand a pound of cotton in a day: by his own reckoning it would take a counterfeiter many months of unremitting labor to forge a copperplate replica of one of his own notes. In that sense it was turning the American tradition of simplifying a process on its head. But Perkins had hit on the essential principle of mass production at the same moment as Eli Whitney: perfect uniformity, standardization, and interchangeable parts. Swiftly it became known around the world as the American System.

Perkins was assured that he had finally carried paper money beyond the clutches of the most dextrous counterfeiter. His dollar bills bore the imprint of the machine age. Instead of trying to compare two dollars,[4] searching for variations, anyone who held a Perkins dollar was able to compare several identical vignettes repeated over and over on the same bill, like rows of identical buttons. "The Transfer Press," it was later reported, "is the triumph of Mr. Perkins' invention; it is the foundation upon which the whole superstructure of the art of bank note engraving rests. It may be likened to the lever of Archimedes, in its power to move the world."[5] Quite apart from the time and trouble spent engraving the original dies, it was unlikely anyone else could follow his procedures, which involved dark and costly work with mufflers, smoldering leather, forges, and dashes of cold water. It was years before anyone improved on his methods.

In order that the public knew what to expect from a genuine note, he suggested that all banknotes be made exactly alike, except for the bank's name and the town. In 1804, convinced that at last he had created the inimitable note, the Holy Grail of paper money, he published *The Permanent Stereotype Steel Plate, with Observations on its Importance, and an Explanation of its Construction and Uses*, which

---

4. Not always practical. "In my time," wrote an Indiana pioneer of the 1820s, "rarely indeed, could two cash dollars be seen circulating together."

5. "Remarks on the Manufacture of Bank Notes and Other Promises to Pay." Addressed to the Bankers of the Southern Confederacy. Columbia, South Carolina: 1864.

challenged any bank who used his method to present him with a forgery of his note and get its money back. Twenty-six banks had been using his process for three years without suffering a single forgery, and the results were so astonishing that every bank in Massachusetts was shortly required by law to use Perkins's protective methods.

They got better and better. When he reached Philadelphia he joined forces with Cyril Durand, another prolific inventor who had produced a machine that could rule straight or wavy lines on a printing plate, and he took on a new ornamental lathe that turned out the dwindling loops a spirograph produces on paper. None of these was easy to copy by hand. But Perkins decided that the eye tended to glaze over these whorls and loops and hatches. They looked too geometric. Pictures were much more easily read by the public, and variations in a picture were easier to spot. So Perkins took on several high-class American engravers to produce "vignettes." Cyril Durand's brother Asher Durand introduced Greek goddesses onto paper money because they were tasteful and pretty and hard to copy; he later turned his back on engraving and became a distinguished landscape painter in the so-called Hudson River School. Gideon Fairman was a blacksmith who developed an aptitude for engraving and eventually chose to work on a reproduction of probably the best-known portrait in world history, Gilbert Stuart's 1795 portrait of President Washington.

Fairman's rendering of Stuart's Washington has been reproduced at least 14 billion times since it first appeared on the U.S. dollar bill in 1929. It finds its way onto T-shirts, chocolates, and government web sites. By all accounts it is taken from one of the worst likenesses of Washington ever produced: infinitely more human portraits of the president were done by the Philadelphia artist Rembrandt Peale. It was not really Gilbert Stuart's fault that his picture worked out so pumpkinlike and expressionless. Stuart was first rate: he had worked in London with the great progenitor of American painting, Benjamin West, and competed for sitters successfully against some of the giant names of British art. Unfortunately for Stuart, Washington sat for him while he was trying to get used to a new set of false teeth, "clumsily formed of Sea-horse Ivory, to imitate both teeth and gums, [which] filled his mouth very uncomfortably." The president clapped them in every time he sat, hoping that they would grow more comfortable if he used them; in the end he abandoned them.

"Mr. Stuart himself told me that he never had painted a Man so difficult to engage in conversation, as was his custom, in order to elicit the natural expression, which can only be selected and caught in varied discourse. The teeth were at fault," explained Rembrandt Peale. He might have enjoyed his innocent schadenfreude rather less had he known how the American public would always like this stiff, stubborn portrait, mutton jaw and all. Stuart produced a total of three portraits of Washington and then, seeing how his bread was buttered, III replicas. In fact he lived off Washington's face. Long before his portraits of the president appeared on the currency, he lightly referred to them as his "one-hundred-dollar bills." The original, so-called Athenaeum head was never finished; like its companion piece, a portrait of Martha Washington, it remains a sketch on oils and may be seen at the Boston Museum of Fine Arts.

NO SOONER HAD Perkins launched his stereotype method of printing than Jefferson's platted land went into mass production. The Louisiana Purchase and the leadership of men like Daniel Boone had opened the West to white settlement, and surveyors working their chains across a seemingly inexhaustible supply of new, good farming land united young and eager Americans with millions of virgin acres at the reasonable price of two dollars an acre.

The Mississippi basin was the size of western Europe, and it was settled in a matter of years. Kentucky and Tennessee were already states of the Union when Ohio joined in 1803. Louisiana came in 1812, then Indiana in 1816, Mississippi in 1817, Illinois in 1818, Alabama in 1819, Missouri in 1821: all products of boom years, as were Arkansas in 1836 and Michigan in 1837. The new settlers rapidly went on to construct around themselves all the institutions of a civilized society—law codes and courthouse, jail and church, tier upon tier of representation in various types of government. County authorities, state legislatures, even federal government and all their various departments were thrown together with stupendous speed, just like balloon-frame housing on the treeless Plains a generation later, culminating in the arrival at Washington of a parcel of new senators and representatives, speaking for states the size of European countries, which thirty years before had neither names nor white inhabitants.

No one had been quite sure how America would grow—Jefferson, for one, thought it quite likely that several distinct countries united by bonds of friendship would be hacked out of the wilderness—but in the event the sheer speed of growth dropped every new mile of settled territory into the lap of the United States. "The American republic invites nobody to come," explained the State Department in 1819. "We will keep out nobody. Arrivals will suffer no disadvantages as aliens. But they can expect no advantages either. Native-born and foreign-born face equal opportunities. What happens to them depends entirely on their individual ability and exertions, and on good fortune."

Good fortune seemed guaranteed by the absence or lowness of taxes and the sheer availability of good farmland at a price that dropped as low as $1.25 an acre in the 1820s. Payments could be spread over a number of years—until the crops and the money came in. America's population almost doubled in twenty years after 1800; by 1820 it was close to 10 million, and 80 percent was down to native fertility. All the same, a hundred thousand people arrived in the five years before 1820, free to come as they pleased. Half of them stayed in New York and Philadelphia. The other half headed straight for the Ohio River.

Capital came too. But capital was always scarce, and the scarcity of money sharpened the distinction between the Old World and the New. Banks in the Old World gathered together the accumulated capital of ages of enterprise and made it available to trusted people, and Old World money always had this musty atmosphere of accretion. Year after year, out at interest, quietly growing, Old World money was patted and fed by a patient army of lawyers and bankers. Old World money slid from hand to hand by the complex and respected laws of entail and primogeniture; it furnished dowries, allowances, and remittances, and it ruled the horizons of all the most respectable people in Europe, people with what was delicately called a private income.

In the New World, banks did the exact opposite: they took on projects and used them to create money the way Hamilton had instructed. The banks' job was to collect capital from every possible source—especially the fictitious capital of government bonds—and use it as a reserve on which to issue a magnificent supply of paper money. The money would pay for a scheme and then, once the scheme had reached fruition, repay the original investors many times over. So American money had a sell-by date, like Cinderella's golden coach and horses; the point was to spend it, crank up the scheme, get it in gear, and go spinning off into the future in a shower of sparks and a jet of steam. Anyone unwise enough to take money to hoard was left with the pumpkin and a few white mice. Canada, which eventually combined something of the U.S.'s opportunities with a more fixedly Old World manner, is still seen by Americans as a *Cinderella* in the first act.

Except for foreign coins and the pitiful output of the U.S. Mint, it was private banks, of all shapes and sizes, that supplied the new republic with all its money. Every bank that issued paper dollars, from Hamilton's great Bank of the United States chartered by the federal government, down to banks operating within particular states on charters from the local legislature, was privately owned and privately run. Whether the states had the constitutional right to set up banks or not, nobody seriously challenged their legality.

Banks feasted on government-backed schemes, or failed with them, and bank dollar bills were like steam to the machine. The essential generator, the typical scheme itself up to the Civil War, was buying and selling land. Banks were falling over themselves to lend, springing up everywhere to service the demand. Everyone borrowed, with everyone around going into debt too. Raising a mortgage on a new farm sounded just the thing. Prices for farm produce were climbing. Money was easy. Booms developed. Mortgage debt rose from $3 million in 1815 to $16.8 million in 1818, a fivefold increase in just three years.

Jacob Perkins really had devised the lever of Archimedes, and it often seemed to have the power to move the American world. Copperplate paper currency would have been as easily counterfeited as the revolutionary Continentals, but Perkins's American System underpinned the paper dollars that paid for the expansion of early-nineteenth-century America. Whenever you took a dollar, you were accepting from a stranger a straightforward promise to pay: you were basically buying into someone else's scheme. Right up to the moment when you spent it again, and passed the buck, you were lending a dollar's worth of your time and energy to the entrepreneurs who had issued the dollar in the first place.

Within living memory, the newly created U.S.A. had boasted just three banks. By the time Jefferson became president there were thirty-one banks in the country, thirty of them chartered by states. On Jefferson's watch the number of banks trebled—by 1805 there were seventy-five banks and ninety by 1811. It was always Jefferson's fate to wind up transfixed on the pin of historical irony. It wasn't that he approved of banks: he hated them. He also championed human liberty and kept slaves; treasured independence and lived in debt; sang the virtues of open republicanism and bought Louisiana on the sly. Now that he was president of the United States he protected the rights of states to do as they saw fit, and was consistent in supposing that any number of little evils was preferable to a centralized Bank of the United States.

In every color, and from every hand, paper dollars poured in on the young republic. More and more people went into debt to buy America, and more and more banks were created to satisfy them. There were 90 banks in 1811; two years later there were 208.

AMERICAN BANKERS adopted Perkins's system to make things difficult for counterfeiters, but across the Atlantic banknotes issued by the Bank of England were still no more than pieces of elegant copperplate handwriting on handsome paper. The Bank of England proceeded on the assumption that no one would ever dare try to forge them: it relied on the fear of God, the panoply of the law, and the vengeance of the Crown, for detection meant death, even hanging, drawing, and quartering, a gruesome medieval punishment reserved for treason and counterfeiting. For a while, at least, the bank's lordly stance seemed justified. It was fifty years before someone had the effrontery to forge a note, and the directors of the Bank of England were stunned—as well as irritated. "There is no calculating how much longer Bank notes might have been free from imitation," wrote a bank historian, "had this man not shewn with what ease they might be counterfeited." Americans would have been stunned it took someone so long.

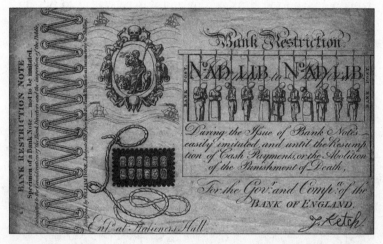

Cruikshank's savage cartoon banknote skewered the Bank of England's lofty disdain for antiforgery devices—including the American System presented by Jacob Perkins.

When the English took on Napoleon and France between 1797 and 1815, the Bank of England suspended gold payments and issued only paper currency. One result was an explosion of counterfeiting, as the Bank of England pushed its easily forged paper money into the national economy in place of gold. Deterrents had failed: eight thousand forged notes were detected in 1801, eighteen thousand ten years later, and by 1817 the number had reached thirty-one thousand. The public felt that its notes were a sort of cruelty inflicted on the poor, like putting a cake in the hands of a starving man and telling him not to eat it. The popular cartoonist George Cruikshank drew a spoof pound note with the loops of the copperplate lettering replaced by a hangman's noose, the center adorned by a busy gibbet, and Britannia herself devouring babies. So many people were being hanged that in 1818 a Royal Commission was finally appointed in London to look into the question of an inimitable note, and the Bank of England was persuaded to put up a prize to be given to anyone who could find a way to eradicate the forgeries.

The sum on offer was rumored to be colossal. One hundred thousand pounds in 1818 represented almost half a million dollars, and it was gilt-edged Bank of England money, the annual income of the richest family in Britain, and probably more than the richest men in America could see in a decade.

Perkins heard about the prize from the British minister in Washington, who was a profound admirer of the beautiful work done on the dollar with his steel plates, and he at once decided to lead an expedition to London. Throwing over all his other projects he assembled his engravers and his workmen, including the engraver of Washington's portrait, Gideon Fairman, and set off for England with twenty-six cases of equipment on the fast-sailing packet *Telegraph,* under Captain Hector Coffin, on May 31, 1819. He sat as a guest at the captain's table, and by the time they arrived four weeks later, young Captain Coffin was a backer.

FOR TWO YEARS Perkins and his champions, who included the Royal Society of Arts, labored to convince Sir William Congreve's bank committee that the American System was superior to any other they could devise. He was kept in funds by English private banks, who leaped at his printing system as Massachusetts banks had done a decade earlier. Only the Bank of England proceeded cautiously. Writing to Captain Coffin at the end of the year, Perkins confided that "such is the demand for our plates for private banks, that we only wish for *the honor of the thing* that the bank of England should *at present* adopt our plan—That they will be finally compelled to do it, I have no doubt in fact, all the people declare it must be so—We were told yesterday from the best authority that one of Sir Willm. Congreaves' workmen had said, that Sir Willm. had been as cross as a bear, ever since our specimens were exhibited to the commissioners, that he had said that he expected the American plan would be adopted."

Perkins and his team engraved and printed sample notes for the bank. The committee thought highly of them, and a separate committee set up by the Royal Society of Arts liked the idea of commissioning the greatest artists in the country to produce vignettes. Only Sir William Congreve—an ambitious engineer who had invented the science of rocket artillery—refused his support. He understood the qualification "inimitable" to mean a banknote that could not under any circumstances be reproduced well enough to fool the public, even if that involved putting the entire machinery of the Bank of England to work on the problem. By using all their skill and the bank's resources, including time, engravers and printers at the bank made passable imitations of the Perkins pound notes.

Perkins naturally objected. The counterfeiters so regularly being marched to the gallows were rarely equipped with the broad resources of the Bank of England: they simply saw an easy target and took their chance. In every practical sense, Perkins had made the target unattainable; private banks in England and the Bank of Ireland too had adopted his methods, and he bombarded the committee with testimonials from American banks that had been using his plates for years without loss. He pointed out that unlike rival schemes, his system was up and running and ready right away. Nothing would move Sir William Congreve. He had a violent aversion to the American System, and seems to have done everything he could to turn the committee against it. The magnificent prize of one hundred thousand pounds was never awarded, for in the end the Bank of England decided not to make any changes to its notes after all. With the end of the French wars, the bank went back onto gold payments in 1819. The amount of paper it issued declined, and so did the number of counterfeits. A public relations crisis was averted, then forgotten. So far as the records show, Perkins never received a penny for his efforts.

WHILE PERKINS STAYED on in England, enjoying the atmosphere of the world's workshop, calling his family together to dispense American hospitality in his new home, and dying there twenty-seven years later at the age of eighty-three, his system flourished in America. Banknote-engraving burgeoned in the space of a few years into what one visitor called the only true American contribution to the arts—faint praise for sure, but still a recognition of the exceptional level of skill and taste American artists had brought to their banknotes. The U.S. was still young and derivative, but its money was unique, much altered from the old revolutionary currencies with their spooky Masonic or alchemical devices cut in copperplate. The Bank of England might not recognize it, but the tool that Perkins gave banknote engravers had swept the eighteenth century away.

WHEN THE NEW farm sections in the West were stamped from the surveyors' grids, they were eerily well matched to the new dollars that paid for them—a whole section was made up of 640 acres, a whole dollar was composed of sixty-four dies. The dollars, run together, made up a formidable expanse of easy credit, just as the sections, run together, had begun to assemble themselves into a broad new landscape. Americans saw what they had found as wilderness, horribly unvaried and featureless. Measuring it out was the only way to comprehend it; buying it, selling it, erecting farms and felling trees, peopling the land turned it gradually into something tamer. It was then that it became a landscape, when it was worked and inhabited.

The country that greeted any traveler going west of Pittsburgh in the 1820s was worked and given shape by men and women whose life histories had come to converge on a particular piece of God's own country, teeming with their children, patterned by their houses, fields, crops, animals, churches, stores. It was many years before railroad companies sent out delightful illustrated brochures to draw the world's attention to these happy landscapes in a serious effort to populate their lines. Long before railroads, the best picture of what was happening behind the Alleghenies and over the Ohio River was peddled by the dollar.

Nineteenth-century American painters who tackled native landscapes with such fire and light were inevitably struck by what the English-born artist Thomas Cole called tongue in cheek "the grand defect in American scenery—the want of associations, such as arise amid the scenes of the old world." In the western wilderness there was "no ruined tower to tell of outrage, no gorgeous temple to speak of ostentation," in fact no moral painterly code to follow at all. Time, in America, was only just about to begin.

The wild grandeur of the unclaimed wilderness, stretching mile upon mile across a huge uncharted continent whose enormous size had only begun to be appreciated, hit American artists of the period like a thunderstroke. The land, as they saw it, was still fresh from the

Dollar bills peddled the American dream. Images like these on a state bank bill of 1819 helped change public perceptions of the West, while the money paid for the actual transformation.

hand of God. Cole's knowledge of English factory towns and a deeply man-worked countryside helped set the tone for the Hudson River School of artists who followed him into the American wilderness. "Those scenes of solitude from which the hand of nature has never been lifted, affect the mind with a more deep toned emotion that aught which the hand of man has touched," Cole continued. "Amid them the consequent associations are of God the creator—they are his undefiled works, and mind is cast into the contemplation of eternal things."

From Niagara to the Catskills, from Pike's Peak to the Great Plains, Thomas Cole and his successors—Frederic Church, Alfred Bierstadt, Asher Durand, and others—returned with the message that this was, indeed, a promised land, newly minted by the Creator for the delectation of a chosen people. "American associations are not so much of the past as of the present and the future," Cole concluded. "Where the wolf roams, the plough shall glisten, on the gray crag shall rise temple and tower—mighty deeds shall be done in the now pathless wilderness: and poets yet unborn shall sanctify the soil."

The painters had to hack their way laboriously into the wilderness to find what they were after, knowing that in a matter of years their wild camping grounds would become farms, towns, holiday resorts. Sometimes they projected farmsteads into their canvases, where no farmstead yet existed; sometimes they picked out a lonely house and an acre or two of tree stumps in a field, set against the lonely grandeur of a distant peak and the poignant magnificence of ancient trees. Here was an empire on the march, and the sublime would fall before it! It would be priced and peopled, bought and sold: time and change had broken in upon the New World. Church's painting of the Niagara Falls leaves the dullest viewer slightly damp: so much spray, so much volume of water, so many tiny moments of ebullition and sliding away are represented there! And this bewildering force of nature has been pouring its energy out for all eternity unseen—until this moment, by a tiny figure in a buff coat, standing on the viewing platform.

PERKINS'S AMERICAN System channeled this landscape art into the service of the humble banknote. Of course the dollar was a cramped little canvas, and in black and white it could hardly aspire to Durand's light effects to suggest that a new dawn was breaking upon God's handiwork. But it maneuvered in the same artistic space and tried to summarize in line what the painted canvas could suggest in light and shape and size. Where the painters dreamed, the engravers bustled: sometimes they were the same men. Their painterly vision of God's own discordant order leaned perceptibly toward scenes of reaping and binding, of plump sheaves dotting the fields, of distant cabins and smiling acres.

Liberated by the steel plate to produce images so fine they were almost photographic in their depiction of detail, almost every decent

State banknotes were unashamed boosters. This early-nineteenth-century vision of western ease and plenty reassured investors that the wilderness held no terrors.

engraver in America did work for the banknote companies, chronicling the rise of this new civilization. No longer upright and poster-shaped, like little proclamations from the wary edges of the wilderness, dollars spread to embrace the new horizons offered by the unfolding frontier. They became landscape in shape, longer and larger than modern dollar bills. They read left to right as well, like storybooks, telling stories that the people who handled the money could readily understand. Imagine the new immigrant, westward bound, receiving in his change the very picture of his hopes! Imagine how an eastern farm boy reacted to seeing all his dreams crystallized and made official on a dollar bill! What a story all those engravings told, of a rugged continent being turned into landscape: a wilderness converted, section by section, into private property as thousands of new settlers crowded into the Ohio valley and beyond.

For artists and engravers the excitement was obvious, and the power of the message was unmistakable. When the squatters in Texas lost their appeal to join the Union in 1836, they put old Daniel Boone on their dollar bills simply to show that they were pioneers of the same old stock—and certainly on a par with the Missouri settlers, who had got themselves a state. For banks in New England and the middle states, artists presented soot and smokestacks, steam and cogs and dark satanic mills, as innocent blazons of progress.

They showed the farms and ferryboats of the West, and farming scenes and fixtures in exact detail—a hog-slaughtering, a tree-felling, an ox at the plow. Here's an authentic grain cradle; there an early mechanical reaper (you can tell it's a Hussey by its hand rake); a harrow, a hay thrower, a mechanical weeder. Here's cotton picking, turpentine. A surveyor with three assistants squints through his theodolite beside a fallen tree. Even one alchemist creeps onto the vignettes. Whaling and sailors, tobacco barrels drumming on the docks, teamsters driving their wagons through a turnpike, shanty boats for trappers, horse-drawn barges, cog railways—all these and more appeared on the dollar bills.

The railroad turned out to be the most popular subject of all: dollar bills chart the breakneck development of American rail-roads from etchings of early British-built trains to the steaming behemoths of continental locomotion, smokestack, cowcatcher, and tender. There was, of course, a rose-tinted, booster angle to the vignettes but there was never a medium like it for putting an ency-clopedia of stirring images into the public mind. Dollar bills of the early nineteenth century helped to create the American dream.

In artistic terms only vignettes with the immediacy and economy of a political cartoon could ever hope to handle the breakneck speed of America's development. Charged with an image of a continent tamed, the little canvas was cheap, common, and traveled unblush-ingly from hand to hand, peddling a landscape that ordinary people were making, a landscape that belonged to them.

For in America the great land-grab was a popular, democratic movement. No towers, temples, or memento mori: nothing in the landscape reflected the feudal inheritance of great landowners. Landscape paintings might be sold to wealthy connoisseurs, but they were also shown—for a quarter—to the general public, who took their seats in front of a picture behind a curtain and gasped as they plunged into the frozen world of the Labrador coast or a ruminative western sunrise.

Americans were always ingenious in supplying themselves with money. With the sudden and total disappearance of small change during the Civil War, towns, railroads, churches, and stores issued their own "shinplaster" or "scrip."

The Delaware City Bank boasted four separate vignettes on the face of its one-dollar bill—a girl in a nightdress and laurel crown lounging against a shield; a passenger train thundering across the prairie; a haymaker resting with his sickle; and a very small picture of what might be a rat, but must be a dog. The City Trust dressed up the Delaware girl in curtains, while a gentleman in a top hat gestured to a distant ship for the benefit of a Mohawk brave dangling his hand dangerously close to the American eagle's beak. Native Americans were often pictured on the dollar, where they served the image of progress. Their attitudes suggested a noble sort of resignation. The feathered brave, half-naked and erect, watches the coming of the ships, behind which rolls the whole irrepressible caravan of technology and progress. Perhaps the brave is alone: poignant sentinel of a vanishing order, he philosophizes glumly from his thorny crag above a burgeoning city, climbing upward from the river. Perhaps he brings his family around him; then the Indian matron often points the way, gesturing toward the plow and the wheatsheaf. As time went on, the Indian was to fade from the picture, with the Indian princess, pagan and free, who had represented America for centuries, replaced by a classical goddess.

Cupids, cherubs, and putti swag their bills. Aurora rises from the sea in her chariot to dew the morning, and Apollo, god of the sun, races his chariot through the sky. Hebe, goddess of youth, appears as cupbearer to the gods. The Phoenix rises from its ashes, a symbol of rebirth. Spring nestles in her pretty bower, an allegorical figure with her child. If the bank lay near the sea, then it might draw on images of Thetis the sea goddess, or Neptune, his chariot pulled by the hippocampus, half horse and half dolphin, his son Triton, dolphins, and mermaids. Sometimes it was pretty girls for their own sake—the three Graces, elegant nymphs—or something bound to strike a spark and perhaps be kept as a souvenir. The dollar bill issued by the Bank of Saint Nicholas in New York showed Santa Claus with a bag of goodies about to disappear down a chimney.

Peace, prosperity, and Santa Claus. Western tastes were more robust: "Get a real furioso plate, one that will take with all creation—flaming with cupids, locomotives, rural scenery, and Hercules kicking the world over."

The pretty milkmaids, planted acres, reaping machines, and vanishing Indians all denoted healthful country. Not wild. Not wilderness at all: only the new country learning to make sense of itself, applying "civilized" notions of order and purpose to a near-frontier situation that would unroll from one state to the next for the entire century. The painters had greater license to plumb the ambiguities of the West: one famously enigmatic painting seems to show an Indian and his half-breed son slipping downriver in their punt with what may be a baby bear or a cat or a prick-eared dog in their prow, all idle but intent, all easiness and danger too. Dollar bills more brusquely projected hope and plenty. No half-breeds here, only a whole new breed of men and women fitted to the task of breaking open a new country.

Nothing like these paper dollars, or the settling of the land, had ever been seen before—they certainly defied the common European experience. Mass-produced on the American System, Perkins's dollars spurred on the buying and selling of land at a rate unequaled in human history. Leapfrogging from one frontier to the next, a migration unknown to recent European history started to unfold as year by year the people who figured on dollar bills tore into the wilderness delineated for the last time in American high art. A martian beamed down into a shaver's shop in early-nineteenth-century America would have been able to get a fair idea of the level and direction of American civilization by looking at the money. You didn't have to be a martian: only one of the thousands and tens of thousands of new Americans who, perhaps scarcely better prepared, now swarmed westward across the continent.

· 9 ·

A PHILADELPHIA STORY

On Philadelphia—A Banker's Heaven—A Monster—
Perfect Money—Andrew Jackson

When Jacob Perkins left for England in 1819 he sailed from the nation's busiest port, the only real city in all North America. It was the place where European visitors—who always liked it—could put up at the United States Hotel, arranging to draw their money from the Bank of the United States. It was not incidentally the home of the U.S. Mint. Many of the country's leading merchants, brokers, and bankers lived and worked there too; it was the financial capital of America, and its Chestnut Street was the Wall Street of its time. The city was Philadelphia.

Never again would one city so utterly dominate America, or stand so sharply at its cutting edge. It was a city brimming with intelligence and energy—oxygen itself was first discovered there by the scientist Joseph Priestly who, newly arrived from England, relished the company: all the most forward scientific thinking in the country was thought out under the aegis of the city's American Philosophical Society. It boasted the finest doctors and the subtlest lawyers. In 1791 the Virginians had fought Hamilton's schemes to give Philadelphia a powerful bank for fear that it would kill their hopes for a capital on the Potomac. For more than a decade Philadelphia was the capital in name, as well as fact, until Washington, D.C., was rigged into life, obedient to the compromise struck between Jefferson and Hamilton. Even then the federal government could afford to take only the bureaucrats away; Philadelphia kept anyone who was rich or interesting or learned or ambitious. This was a city that knew exactly where it stood. Not until the late 1810s did the government in Washington possess astronomical instruments to allow them to work out their longitude. Nobody at bottom much cared when the British burned down the Capitol in 1814.

The Liberty Bell, Freedom Hall, the first Supreme Court, the hallowed ground where the Declaration of Independence was signed, all reminded Philadelphia of its historic role and duties to the nation, and while Washington, D.C., struggled to figure out its position in the country, Philadelphians were stooping over America like scientists peering into a petri dish. Philadelphia was the only place to study electricity, scientific agriculture, economics, or Indian linguistics. American entomology kicked off with *Melsheimer's Catalogue of Insects of Pennsylvania* in 1806. The exposition of America—all the exploring, tracking, and mapping, all the recording in watercolor of birds and beasts, all the flora- and fauna-collecting of the continent—was conducted from Philadelphia, where the pioneers who demolished Buffon always returned footsore and astonishing to give their lectures to Philadelphians or to stuff the first American natural history museum (founded and run by the local portraitist Charles Willson Peale) with treasures from the interior. Even Lewis and Clark, the trailblazers of America's Manifest Destiny, left for the Pacific only after they had been briefed, and kitted out, in Philadelphia; and the first authoritative edition of their journals was published there in 1815.

By 1820 there were ten industries in America that could claim to be worth a hundred thousand dollars a year, and Philadelphia publishing was one of them. The first American edition of *Encyclopaedia Britannica* was printed in Philadelphia, A–Ant emerging in 1790 and Z–Zym twenty-two quarto volumes later in 1802. Marshall's fantastically pompous and dreary five-volume *Life of Washington*[1] was a classic Philadelphia project—it took a city printer to find enough type—and so, in its way, was the much sprightlier semifictional *The Life and Memorable Actions of George Washington* in a hundred best-selling pages by "Parson" Weems, full of cherry tree stories. Barlow's unreadable patriotic epic, *The Columbiad,* and Wilson's superb *Ornithology in America* all came out in the early years of the new century, then Benjamin Smith Barton's *Elements of Botany* and Nuttall's *Genera of North American Plants,* with John Torrey's *Flora of the Northern and Middle Sections of the United States* following in 1824.

Painters gathered at the Academy of Fine Arts, founded in 1805 by the elderly banker George Clymer, who had signed the Declaration of Independence, to display a collection of Italian paintings. The first American artist to paint the wilderness, Thomas Doughty, a Philadelphian, had his maiden exhibition in the city in 1816. The first American lithograph was made here in 1818. America's best engravers took advantage of Philadelphia's publishing tradition, and two skilled Englishmen moved here to produce a portfolio of aquatints, *Picturesque Views of American Scenery,* issued in 1820/21. The *Port Folio,* founded here in 1801, was the country's top literary journal, when the port itself could only be Philadelphia. Physiognomy was treated by the pantograph, which produced mechanical

---

1. John Adams described it as "a Mausoleum, 100 feet square at the base and 200 feet high."

reproductions of a profile. There were plays,[2] there were the first terraced houses ("Philadelphia rows"), the first *Builder's Assistant* (1818–21), which laid out the Greek orders for the first time, and the young William Strickland's Greek Bank of the U.S. (1819–24), which "excels in elegance and equals in utility, the edifice, not only of the bank of England, but of any banking house in the world," according to an English critic in the 1830s. It was a building of imposing weight, and where shadow and sunlight played across its deeply carved white marble facade Philadelphia kept the money that paid for the oxygen, the lawyers, the expertise, the books, plays, and Philadelphia rows.

The city attracted fallen monarchs. Iturbide had been the Empress of Mexico. Joseph Bonaparte, Napoleon's brother, was the ex-king of Italy, now at Point Breeze, near Bordentown (he landed in New York, but was greeted by a porter shouting, "Hey, Boney, lend us a hand with the valise!"). A king of Spain wintered here and kept a pew at the Catholic church, while the prince of Canino and Musignano was a resident member of the American Philosophical Society and a keen bird-watcher, who first described Bonaparte's gull, the smallest of the gulls, still to be seen in season along the reedy banks of the Delaware.[3]

As for emperors, Philadelphia had its own. Nicholas Biddle was known as Czar Nicholas to his friends. He was a Philadelphia blueblood with a patrician sense of republican duty. Born in 1786, named after an uncle who died heroically at sea in the revolution, he

---

2. English actor overhears chimney sweep: "I say, Bill, look! There goes Cooper the player man." "Hold your tongue, John," says his companion. "Who knows what you may come to yourself."

3. Not every royalist liked Philadelphia. "As in the other American cities, most of the women wore black, no doubt so as not to vary the endless monotony of the country," wrote the bitter Bourbon supporter De Montlezun in 1818. The girls were pretty, but they had bad teeth, big feet, and "something disagreeable about the length of their legs."

graduated with the highest honors from Princeton at the age of fifteen: the same age that Jacob Perkins became master of his forge. Biddle had a hand in almost everything that made Philadelphia excel. In 1804, after a few weary years practicing law, he visited Paris as secretary to the American minister, James Monroe, where he bought pictures for the Philadelphia Academy of Fine Arts. He attended Napoleon's coronation—an event that ultimately gave Philadelphia some of its royal tenants—and traveled in Italy when one of them, Joseph, was still its king. From Italy he passed on to the Aegean and became, in fact, the first American tourist to visit Greece. Seized with the realization that the world contained two truths, the Bible and Greek architecture, in 1807 he rounded off his tour with a spell as secretary to James Monroe in London before he returned to Philadelphia, the Athens of America.

There Biddle revealed himself as a Jeffersonian paragon. He married an heiress, settled at Andalusia, a country seat on the Delaware, and became an authority on farming and horticulture. (Biddles, needless to say, still live at Andalusia.) He forced grapes in his hothouses and brought the first Alderney cattle to the country. He took over the editorship of the *Port Folio* and was chosen—by Jefferson himself—to bring out the first public edition of Lewis and Clark's journals, which opened up to its readers the rich possibilities of the American West. He was a legislator in the Pennsylvania House of Representatives and president of the Philadelphia Society for the Promotion of Agriculture. He was popular, witty, clever. When James Monroe became president he made him a director of the second Bank of the United States. Biddle protested his ignorance of banking, but he did his duty. And it was in 1817 that he added his voice to those of the other six members of the bank committee to sum up everything about the new country that Philadelphia could see best.

"Your committee," they wrote, "could not refrain from casting their eyes over the map of the United States and indulging themselves in the most pleasing anticipations." You can actually hear them rubbing their hands! "They see before them a country including within its bounds an extent of surface and fertility of soil affording ample space and presenting a certain reward for the labor of almost innumerable inhabitants; cities increasing in magnitude, in number, in wealth, and magnificence; the ample surplus of the varied productions of almost every climate on the globe flowing into those cities to be consumed or transported to countries abroad, producing an internal and external commerce which will keep millions of money on the wing between contiguous and distant cities, sections, and divisions of this great country."

The contiguities! The fertility and extent! And millions of money on the wing—angel dollars, in a banker's heaven!

THE DIRECTORS OF the bank who gave themselves over to this most unbankerly panegyric to America's future prosperity betrayed their inexperience, for it does not do for central bankers to sound like stock boosters. But the temptation was irresistible, for the War of 1812 had ended and young America was on a spree. But when Liverpool's cotton importers turned to cheaper Indian supplies the great land boom collapsed. The price of cotton at New Orleans halved at the beginning of 1819. The price of land then dropped 50 to 75 percent. State banks set up in the flush times found themselves overextended, with inadequate collateral in low-priced lands. They started going bust, and the Bank of the United States—feeling the pinch itself—called in its paper and busted yet more of them. Chains of paper currency tottered and fell; debtors found themselves forced to repay their loans in hard money. America's debts started piling up toward Philadelphia, where the Bank of the United States grimly took over thousands of mortgages to western lands. "The people were ruined, but the Bank was saved," wrote William Gouge, bitterly, and Senator Benton howled in Washington in 1818: "All the flourishing cities of the west are mortgaged to this money power. They may be devoured by it at any minute. They are in the jaws of the monster! A lump of butter in the mouth of a dog! One gulp, one swallow, and all is gone!" It was America's first financial crisis.

And what was this monster, exactly, this slavering dog poised to devour the butter? Nothing more than the successor to that sinister bugaboo of the Jefferson Republicans, the Bank of the United States, whose premises still stand in Philadelphia, shuttered and rather crumbling now, facing the city library across Third Street. Founded in 1791 on a charter set to run for twenty years, it had been in its time the grandest circulator of credit, the biggest money-printing operation in the country. It handled federal funds, moving money around the country on the government's behalf, taking taxes, and furnishing federal salaries. It took care to ensure that the dollars printed by smaller state banks could be redeemed in gold and silver, as promised. Its own, quietly distinguished banknotes were as good as gold. It kept a very adequate reserve and lent cautiously to respectable businessmen and the government.

Its days were numbered, even so. Its twenty-year charter would no doubt have been renewed had Hamilton lived, for the bank had done a creditable job. In 1804 it had helped Jefferson double the size of the country for four cents an acre, buying the whole of Louisiana from the French. Without the bank the money might not have materialized, and the United States would be a different country altogether. Even Albert Gallatin, Jefferson's secretary of the treasury, came to think the bank was useful, but Gallatin was a Swiss immigrant and the Swiss famously have no natural resistance to banks. The rest of Jefferson's supporters feared the bank and loathed its influence. They were not naive. They looked at the concentration of money in the hands of the bank and shuddered to think of the power the bank's wealthy stockholders might come to wield over government, a power to subvert the popular will.

They never failed to point out that most of the bank's stockholders were not even American: more than half its twenty-five thousand shares had been bought by British investors. Gallatin observed that foreigners had no vote, and argued that America should take British capital, cheap at the price of an annual dividend, rather than go hunting for loans in Europe. He warned that if the Republicans made good their determination to let the bank's charter lapse in 1811, more than $7 million in hard cash would be whipped out of the country to refund the stockholders. Nobody listened, and Congress in 1811 killed the bank. The consequences were just as Gallatin had predicted: a shortage of gold and silver, which led all the banks in America to stop redeeming their notes at all. For five giddy years, the country was on a paper standard.

The Second Bank of the United States arose in 1816, if not quite on the still-warm ashes of its predecessor then only five years later and a hundred yards away, on Chestnut Street and Fourth, where it was widely admired as the finest bank building in the world. Although the consequences of having no bank at all had become all too evident, it naturally provoked the same suspicions that had killed its forerunner. Maryland slapped a tax on its Baltimore branch, arguing that since it was not chartered by the state, its presence infringed Maryland's sovereign rights. The Supreme Court Chief Justice John Marshall, one of Jefferson's cousins, ruled against the tax: in a famous judgment he said that the power to tax was the power to destroy. He upheld Hamilton's argument that Congress had the power to establish a federal bank, since it had a right to make "all laws which shall be necessary and proper, for carrying into execution the foregoing powers," which included the power to tax, to borrow money, to regulate commerce, to declare and conduct a war. Marshall was profoundly profederal, and Jefferson always hated him. But the balance of forces between federalists and the states was about to swing the other way.

BIDDLE TOOK UP the bank's presidency in January 1823, with the avowed intention of giving the country better money. There was, as the economists have discovered, something impossibly unbankerly about Nicholas Biddle: he was, as one of them put it, "incorrigibly jaunty and pagan." Asked to contribute to a girl's autograph album, he improvised a whole poem to describe how he had forsaken literature for finance:

> *I prefer my last letter from Barings or Hope*
> *To the finest epistles of Pliny or Pope;*
> *My "much-esteemed favors" from Paris, to those*
> *Which brought on poor Helen an Iliad of woes;*
> *One lot of good bills from Prime, Bell, or the Biddles,*
> *To whole volumes of epics or satires or Idyls;*
> *Nay, two lines of plain prose with a good name upon it*
> *To the tenderest fourteen ever squeezed in a sonnet.*
> *Why, I would not accept—not for Hebe's account—*
> *The very best draft from Helicon's fount,*
> *Nor give—this it grieves me to say to their faces—*
> *More than three days of grace to all the three Graces.*
> *Then their music of spheres! Can it thrill through the soul*

Like kegs of new dollars as inward they roll?
And Cecelia herself, though her lyre was divine,
Never gave to the world notes equal to mine.

Which was perfectly true—Biddle turned out to have a flair for finance, and he knew what his country needed: a single currency that would be valid anywhere in America. Bank of the U.S. dollar bills were watertight, and could be turned into silver or gold on demand at any of the bank's twenty-nine branches. The government, of course, banked with the bank, which handled its earnings from land sales and import duties, and since these were often paid in state banknotes Biddle had an opportunity to supervise the state banks too by promptly presenting them with their dollar bills for redemption. If they were insolvent or overextended they were soon found out, and the survivors learned to be cautious and sensible, keeping up safe reserves of silver and gold, watching the progress of their loans more carefully, issuing less money and to better clients. In trying to bring the finances of the country into one transparent system it never seems to have occurred to him that anyone could want anything else. He paid no attention to people who thought Philadelphia was already too much in control, people who suspected that he controlled Philadelphia.

By the late 1820s Biddle had achieved his ambition for the dollar, which was as sound and healthy as any currency in the world, backed by silver and gold ultimately drawn from the accumulations of the Old World—Britain especially. The undeveloped nature of the country provided plenty of scope for enterprise. State banks could grasp opportunities on the spot that Philadelphia could not see; but Philadelphia kept them from enthusiasm. You might have thought the money question was solved.

It was in this mood of confident assurance that Biddle told a committee that he could have destroyed any bank in the country had he wanted to. This was grand finance. For supporters of General Andrew Jackson, the new president, it was also rather too much. It was, in fact, what they had suspected all along.

IT WOULD HAVE been hard to find anyone in America less like Nicholas Biddle than Andrew Jackson. They differed in temperament, taste, age, style, upbringing, and experience, but for all that, Biddle still voted for Jackson in 1828. Four years later they were at daggers drawn.

Banknote engravers chronicled the rise of American civilization. Ten-dollar bills were popularly known as sawbucks, after the shape of the familiar Roman numeral.

Born in 1767, Jackson came from a family of Ulstermen, poor tenant farmers in the Carolinas. He had no expectations, nothing to keep him from trekking west through the Cumberland Gap into Tennessee when he was seventeen. He was able to gain a smattering of law, and so hung out his shingle as a prosecuting attorney. There was nothing average about Jackson: he was tall and, with his clear blue eyes and high cheekbones, even handsome, but it was his manner that men and women found irresistible. Before long he had been appointed a judge of the Superior Court of Tennessee, in a state where toughness counted for more than precise legal knowledge. He was shrewd and honest. In 1802, without any military experience beyond his ability to shoot straight, he was elected major general of the state militia.

He had a shoot-from-the-hip, drinking, dueling, d—n you style that naturally endeared him to the settlers in Tennessee. While frontiersmen in the new West tended to be democratic in their views, they liked this natural-born frontier aristocrat, his mix of physical toughness, hard drinking, and freedom from fear. It was a rudimentary sort of aristocracy, held together by an equestrian class code that was distinctly rougher in Tennessee than in, say, Virginia. Jackson was rougher than his idol, Thomas Jefferson.

Jackson's attitude to the Indian question was a case in point. Jefferson had recognized that Indian nations could never stand alone, like islands. They would have to civilize themselves and join the republic; the alternative was annihilation. Jackson agreed, but with the emphasis on annihilation. Frontiersmen were not prepared to wait for civilization to trickle through to the Indians. In the Creek War of 1813 Jackson showed his eagerness to wipe out Indian opposition. In 1830, as president, he would sweep yet more Indians off their ancestral lands with a stroke of a pen and a column of irregulars. As a result of his successes in the Creek War, he was asked to shift his commission to the regular army, which needed someone to bring them a victory after a series of military failures in the 1812 war against the British. Washington had been burned, Hull had surrendered; the only American victories were at sea.

Jackson took command of the department of the South, and on January 8, 1815, he destroyed the British in the Battle of New

Orleans. They lost their commander and two thousand men were killed or wounded; Jackson lost seven men, and six were wounded. The battle was a kind of personal revenge: Jackson still bore the scar from the revolutionary war, when a British officer had clubbed the daring twelve-year-old with a rifle butt. It was also a cause for national jubilation. The fact that it had been fought three weeks after the diplomats signed a peace in Paris made the whole thing, if anything, slightly more satisfactory. New Orleans was a murderous joke at the enemy's expense.

After that it was inevitable that he should gravitate toward politics, making his first tilt at the presidency nine years later, in 1824, with a result so tight that it was decided by a casting vote in the electoral college. Heading home from Washington to Tennessee, it dawned on Jackson that he had been the victim of a "corrupt bargain" between Henry Clay, the great Whig fixer, and the new president, John Quincy Adams.[4]

The realization thrilled him. Jackson was a capital hater. Every year he seemed to discover new things to hate—the British, Henry Clay, Indians, the city of Washington. After his first duel—fought when he was twenty-one—he gave up mercy as a bad job and aimed to kill, and thanks to an unhappy irregularity in his marriage he fought as many as twenty duels. He had a knack for coming up against the hard things in life and was condemned to live with excruciating physical pain. In 1806 he was hit by a ball of lead, which stuck close to his heart, wrapped in little bits of cloth and dirt; it was impossible to remove, and eventually Jackson developed a pulmonary abscess. In 1813, Jesse Hart Benton shot him twice in the left arm. One of the bullets stuck fast against the bone (bits of which

---

4. On his deathbed, he regretted, "I did not hang Calhoun and shoot Clay." Calhoun stood for slavery and the South. John Quincy Adams had the same hate list too, but longer; he added Jackson himself and Daniel Webster who "used up their faculties in base and dirty tricks to thwart my progress in life."

came out through his skin over the next six months). In the Creek War, Jackson caught dysentery and malaria, which encouraged him for the rest of his life to dose himself with calomel, a mercury compound, and stupendous quantities of a remedy called sugar of lead, which he drank, bathed in, and squirted into his eyes when his sight was failing. His teeth fell out, he coughed slime, he was subject to fevers, faints, stomachaches, and migraine.

Riddled with bullets, suffused with lead, nicknamed Old Hickory for a wood like iron, Andrew Jackson was a hard-money man by instinct and experience. He admired gold and silver and damned paper money of every sort. He was afraid of nothing and nobody, with one significant exception. Four years after his political defeat he was convincingly elected president in 1828, and it was then that he confessed to an abiding fear derived from an early reading of English history. "I think it right to be perfectly frank with you," he wrote Nicholas Biddle at the Bank of the United States. "I do not dislike your bank any more than all banks. But ever since I read the history of the South Sea Bubble I have been afraid of Banks."

MARX SAID THAT when history repeats itself the original tragedy returns as farce, and the so-called bank war set to break out in 1832 may demonstrate the point. It was to be the clash between Hamilton and Jefferson all over again, the urbane financier slugging it out with the rural sage. It had an unmistakably stagy quality, cardboard swords, leering villainy, and presidential "By the Eternals!" included, when the roles were reenacted forty years later.

Biddle had the easy charm that can strike people as a form of insincerity. Jackson could feign the most terrible rages, which left his victims to wonder, miserably, whether they had killed the old man;

and there is a persistent suggestion that Jackson's attack on Biddle and the bank was something of a stunt. Jackson was almost too roaringly iconoclastic. The presence of the paying public was never forgotten. On his final return from Washington, in 1837, Jackson handed out 150 half-dollars to children, telling their parents: "This is our country's eagle. It will do for the little one to cut his teeth on now, but teach him to love and defend it." The sentiments were utterly sincere; that is what makes the struggle so interesting.

MONEY WAS MISBEHAVING in America. Philadelphia should have known as much, because knowing about America was Philadelphia's self-appointed duty. But even the foreigners who gravitated to Philadelphia as the nicest place to be recognized that Philadelphia was not, in fact, much like America at all.

The country was not confident, cultivated, or prosperous. It was largely infected by a mixture of anxiety and hope. It wasn't only on the developing frontier that life felt rough and unsettled, dominated by wild excitement and a never-ending fear of failure. It was a country—many countries—where Old World clarities, however suffocating and narrow, had been replaced by the painful dazzle of opportunity and the murky possibilities of defeat.

10

UNEASY MONEY

Sources of Unease—Counterfeit Detectors— Carpetbaggers—Confidence Men—Wildcats

When Jackson told Biddle he was afraid of banks, the general was taking up a strategic position. He'd been voted in without a coherent program, simply as the man who licked the British at New Orleans. His opponents tried to turn that around: they liked to paint him as a military chief who would drag down the country as Napoleon had dragged down France. He would trample blindly on the carefully constructed system of checks and balances that reined in the power of the chief executive. But to others he seemed like the last of the revolutionary generation in politics, and no better man could be found to reassert the founding principles of the republic. He was wildly popular. A huge throng followed him to the Capitol for his inauguration as president and cheered when he broke with tradition and politely bowed to them. The crowd considered itself invited back to the White House, where they trampled on the silk upholstery for a better view and ate up all the ice cream, smashed the glasses, gobbled jellies with golden spoons, and eventually had to be lured onto the lawn with steaming bowls of hot punch; the windows were thrown open to help people get out. Jackson men thought the day had gone rather well. Jackson's White House was always afterward open to all comers, as one visitor observed, "from the Vice-President to an intoxicated canal laborer in a dirty red plaid cloak. It is a striking picture of democracy, & truth to tell, it strikes me with disgust."

The new president faced a political minefield. The nation was arguably less united now than at any time since the revolution. The slaveholding South wanted free trade to boost its cotton exports. The North wanted a protectionist tariff for its industries. The West wanted the federal government to pay for internal improvements, like canals and turnpike roads, pushed on by the nimblest politician in the country, Henry Clay. A spiritual descendant of Alexander Hamilton, Clay had started to look to the government in the 1820s to promote America's development and to match the efforts of individuals. Government should put in canals, roads, and harbors, do all it could to boost settlement in the West, and tax imported goods to shelter America's baby industries. Like Perkins's printing methods, Clay's policy was also called the American System: it resembled early mass production in that it pushed the idea of standardized benefits for all. Like Hamilton thirty years before, Clay was sure that America's pursuit of happiness depended on being strong enough to keep meddling European powers out of the Western Hemisphere. Jefferson's well-meaning hopes for a loose-limbed rural republic—or even several—were just old hat now. The world was to be dominated by rapacious industrial powers, eager in their pursuit of new resources and fresh markets.

Whichever way Jackson swung, he risked alienating some crucial section of his support—workers in Pennsylvania, perhaps, farmers in the Southwest. His political opponents rubbed their hands together and predicted his imminent downfall.

Jackson trumped them all, following a gut instinct that chimed perfectly with public feeling. By seizing on the money question he sidestepped the trickiest issues of the day and put himself at the head of a large section of the population who felt alienated and alarmed by the growth of banks, and the dancing tribes of paper money. He united everyone against the "money power."

THE MONEY POWER itself—the bankers and the Biddles—were slow to get the point. It was, after all, their job to deal in money, and perhaps it was because they dealt with money so easily every day that they failed to notice something that outsiders who visited the country chorused one after another: they all said that America's most distinct national characteristic was an obsession with money. Even a thoughtful enthusiast like Alexis de Tocqueville found it "at the bottom of everything"; he decided that money was inevitably the measure of existence in a democracy. Hamilton had apparently been pushing at an open door when he tried to make money the yardstick of Americans' ambition and the principle of social order: the dollar seemed to do the work that class or creed did in Europe. It was America's bishop, its king, its squire. What Michael Chevalier in 1839 called a "passion for money" was not a greedy passion, in the main: it simply reflected the importance of dollars and cents in a society that had no other standard to work to.

Rich, literary, and disinterested, Biddle was ill placed to understand that. The money standard was not as well established as Biddle could have hoped but more important to ordinary Americans than he might have guessed. The result was a rumble of public discontent. The revolutionary impulse in Europe went into guillotining nobles, curbing the power of the clergy, or writing and rewriting liberal constitutions. In America it often hurled itself against money instead, because this was the country's guiding institution. The way money worked defined, for many people, the direction the republic was traveling. Whether people thought that the greatest threat to American liberty and well-being was the money power, or that credit was a shining gift that would allow them to unlock the riches of the country, it was always money that was the locus of American hopes and American fears; and when Americans were disturbed or made uneasy or felt the opportunities slipping from their grasp, they looked suspiciously at the money to provide a remedy or an explanation.

THE YEARS BETWEEN 1804, when Perkins invented the inimitable note, and the Civil War of 1861 spelled slippery times for America. The fate of the Perkins note was both a symptom and a symbol of the kind of dislocation that occurred as the country was wrenched into the nineteenth century, accompanied by a migration unparalleled since the fall of Rome.

It turned out that Perkins's inimitable note was not quite foolproof after all. It was not his fault: the blame lay with the banks. Perkins had always meant every dollar to look the same, apart from the name of the bank that issued it; that would have made a forgery much easier to spot. His plan had been brushed aside by the banks themselves, who wanted them to look different. They composed a great gallery of Americana, but their security was compromised. Thousands of different notes were being printed and issued by hundreds of state banks. It was hard to know anymore what a dollar ought to look like, and the farther a dollar traveled from the bank that had issued it, the more gingerly it was treated by people who could not be expected to recognize the note or even the bank, let alone assess its reputation.

Miss America: winners and losers.

During the bank freeze in 1815, between the death of the First and the birth of the Second Bank of the United States, when none of the banks in the country were paying gold for bills at all, a Philadelphia bookseller brought out *The History of a Little Frenchman and his Bank Notes*.

> It seems the little man had arrived from Cuba, with about eight thousand dollars in gold, which by way of security he lodged in one of the banks of Savannah. When he came to demand his money, he was told that they did not pay specie, and he must therefore take banknotes or nothing. Being an entire stranger . . . he took the worthless rags and began his Journey northward. Every step he proceeded his money grew worse and worse, and he was now traveling on to Boston with the full conviction that by the time he got there he should be a beggar.

Two years later an English traveler, Henry Bradshaw Fearon,[1] approached the business from the opposite angle. In Washington,

---

1. "Sketches of America," "addressed to the THIRTY NINE ENGLISH FAMILIES by whom the author was deputed, in June 1817, to ascertain whether any, and what part of the United States would be suitable for their residence." He enjoyed his trip but told them not to bother emigrating.

D.C., he went to buy a pair of half-dollar worsted gloves. The price of the gloves was fixed, but they haggled over the discount the shopkeeper wanted to take on the various notes that Fearon found in his wallet. Settling on a Baltimore dollar bill, the storekeeper had to admit that he didn't have change. So he took a pair of scissors and cut the dollar down the middle. "Being previously familiarised with Spanish dollars cut into every variety of size," Fearon was no longer surprised by anything Americans did with their money. He merely inquired laconically "if the half would pass, and being answered in the affirmative, took it without hesitation."

Fearon found that he could buy Cincinnati banknotes at a 5 percent discount in Pittsburgh, and Louisville notes at 7½. "This does not proceed from want of faith in those banks, nor are the latter esteemed less safe than the former," he explained: "the increase in discount arises from Louisville being 150 miles further distant. The same principle applies to every other town, and operates vice versa upon Pittsburgh. Had I sufficiently understood this *trade* when I landed in America, I think I could have nearly paid my expenses by merely buying in one town the notes of that to which I was going. There is no difficulty in obtaining them, as there is always a stock on hand at the shavers [brokers] and lottery offices."

It paid to watch the shavers, all the same. A Rhode Island entrepreneur called Andrew Dexter established the Boston Exchange Office, where he offered to buy, at a profitable discount, unfamiliar banknotes issued by back-country banks, which ordinary traders in Boston were reluctant to accept. So it was a useful service, like a bureau de change. Dexter's profit came from bundling together notes from a particular bank, and then traveling to the bank itself to ask for payment in hard currency.[2] This was the operation known as

---

2. The bundling-up process by a shaver was called "assorting"; it produced an assortment of dollar bills and gave a new word to the language.

"shaving," and shavers' shops were opened in every town, "shaving" the discount from every out-of-town bill. Among the odd consequences of shaving and discounting money were: discounts slyly offered on good notes; banks buying back their own notes at a discount; people warily sizing up a stranger by asking to see the color of his money.

In 1808 Andrew Dexter decided to turn his exchange operation back to front. He homed in on the Farmers' Bank of Glocester, which had been given a charter by Rhode Island just four years before and was run, like many others, for the convenience of its directors, who put up $100,000 in capital. They did not put up real money, but IOUs. On the strength of their promise to pay hard cash, the bank started to issue its notes to borrowers. Some of its biggest borrowers were the bank directors. By 1808 the bank had $22,514 circulating in notes, and $380.50 in hard cash. It was a very confident institution.

Dexter did better. He bought out the eleven directors of the Glocester bank by dividing up its assets between them, returning the IOUs they had lodged with the bank in the first place. Now that he owned a bank, the bank naturally lent him money—as much money as he wanted, for whatever security he chose to offer, at any interest rate he wanted to set, for as long as he liked. He was "not to be called upon to make payment until he thinks proper, he being the principal stockholder and best knowing when it is proper to pay."

He brought the printing plates from Glocester to Boston and had a local printing firm produce the money. Once signed by the Glocester cashier, Dexter sold the notes at a discount in Boston, or made up parcels to send to one or two banks in far-off Ohio with whom he had an understanding. He may have owned them too. The main thing for Andrew Dexter was to issue as much money as he possibly could, sell it for whatever it might fetch, and stop it from returning to the bank.

To push the business, Dexter told the bank's cashier Mr. Colwell, a Quaker, to sign the notes only at night, so that no one would actually see how many were being issued. Colwell's day job was to discourage people from redeeming their notes in hard coin; rather than give cash, he would issue a draft payable at the Exchange Office in Boston in forty days' time. If this failed, he would begin clumsily and with painful slowness to count out money. Often he made mistakes and had to start over again: American coinage was very complicated, after all, and many coins had to be questioned, examined, and compared with each other before the cashier could add them to the count.

The notes were usually small denominations, of a dollar or so, for experience showed that small notes came in for redemption much less often than big ones. This meant more work for Colwell, and Dexter bombarded him with exhortations to sign notes faster. "I wish you to employ yourself constantly in signing bills," Dexter wrote, "except during the time you are naturally in the bank. . . . You might write in the day time as well as night, provided you shut yourself up between the bank hours in your private chamber, letting no-one know or suspect your business."

Mr. Colwell signed and signed. "I think it will be best at present to do it as privately as possible, mostly in the evening. I believe I can finish fifty thousand a week." Dexter snapped back that he expected more like twenty thousand notes a day. "I am sorry you have signed no more bills, and beg you sign at least twice as many more during the next week. I wish you would work day and night."

Colwell—on four hundred dollars a year—did work day and night. A neighbor saw people working in the bank when he went to sleep, arriving back at four and sometimes two in the morning. Dexter presented himself to Colwell as a public benefactor, fighting to give the people currency, straining to beat a parcel of men "perfectly contemptible in their manner and character" who would try to turn

in their Glocester banknotes for hard coin and profit from everyone's distress.

Colwell plowed on through the winter of 1808/9. Dexter shipped
the money to and fro, swapping Glocester notes for notes on a bank
at Pittsfield, Massachusetts. By now, everyone was talking about the
bank: "The discontent and irritation among the people is very
great," Colwell explained. At last, his will snapped. "I do not think it
will be the least injury to the bank to shut it up for a day or two."

When officers of the law turned up to investigate, the Farmers'
Exchange Bank of Glocester had disappeared. Colwell and a director
had removed everything, down to the cash reserve of $86.46. On this
reserve, it was said, the bank had issued $800,000 worth of notes.

WHILE AMERICANS grew increasingly restless and footloose, their
money, paradoxically, seemed to get more and more parochial. They
traveled about; but their encounters with money were as unpredictable as a journey through the highlands of Papua New Guinea,
where every tribesman speaks his own language. You could actually
describe a journey in terms of money, as in a letter to the South Carolina senator John C. Calhoun, offering a condensed journal of a
traveler who recently left Virginia for the West. Here it is:

> Started from Virginia with Virginia money—reached the Ohio
> River—exchanged $20 Virginia note for shin-plasters and a
> $3 note of the Bank of West Union—paid away the $3 note for
> breakfast—reached Tennessee—received a $100 Tennessee
> note—went back to Kentucky—forced there to exchange the
> Tennessee note for $88 of Kentucky money—started home with
> Kentucky money. At Maysville, wanted Virginia money—
> couldn't get it. At Wheeling, exchanged $50 note, Kentucky
> money, for notes of the North Western bank of Virginia—

reached Fredericktown—there neither Virginia or Kentucky
money current—paid a $5 Wheeling note for breakfast and
dinner—received in change two one dollar notes of some Pennsylvania bank, one dollar Baltimore and Ohio Rail Road, and
balance in Good Intent shin-plasters—one hundred yards from
the tavern door, all the notes refused except the Baltimore and
Ohio Rail Road.

Thirty years later a writer in the *Merchant's Magazine* said: "Our
paper money, as it now exists, is an intolerable nuisance, unworthy
of the genius of a people making as high pretensions as Americans."
An Iowa banker recalled, "It was a queer mess of stuff that floated
around as money in that early day."

So it was, bobbing in the current of currency, the flotsam and jetsam of money from failed and ailing banks, from banks that had
never existed and others that planned to disappear. The Perkins system was powerless to prevent it. No one could imagine an alternative either. Coins were more gnarled and harder to recognize than
ever, and the Mint produced almost nothing.

Straight counterfeits were less common under the American System, as Perkins had hoped: there were simply too many expert features on his bills for any one man to reproduce—ornamental lathe
work, detailed vignettes engraved by skilled artists, professional lettering. Otherwise his dollars had become victims of their own success. Hezekiah Niles,[3] whose *Register* was the closest thing America
had to a national weekly in the early nineteenth century, complained
in 1818 that he never went two days without finding himself carrying
a forged note. He blamed the banks, more than the counterfeiters: it
was the banks who created irresistible temptation.

---

3. Hezekiah Niles's father, a carpenter, was killed when the shop sign he had nailed up
over his workshop door fell on his head; the son learned not to trust appearances.

The unexpected result of the Perkins dollar system and the rash of feeble banks that grew up to exploit it was a growing market in old dies and printing plates, produced to the correct standard but now surplus to requirements. It wasn't hard to put together a dummy bill that actually looked better than a counterfeit, using bootleg plates that had been filched from printers, or bought at auction when a bank failed and its assets were sold. These spurious notes might carry the name of a real bank without troubling to be a match for the bank's real notes. Altered bills were printed with real banknote plates, exchanging the name of the issuing bank from the one that had failed—called an exploded or broken bank—for a thriving one: it was more easily done when so many banks were known as the Farmers' Bank of X, or the Commercial Bank of Y. It's not surprising that even in law-abiding Iowa, forged notes supplied jails with a quarter of their population.

Like Niles, the public tended to blame the banks—God made the criminals but the banks gave them opportunity. This was by no means their only failing either. Wily bankers like Andrew Dexter had done nothing to improve people's confidence. A bank in one state would agree to circulate bills from another, faraway bank, in its own district, and vice versa: the local bank would accept these notes at face value, but refuse to redeem them in coin. At the Bank of Darien, in Georgia, anyone who wanted to redeem his notes had to present himself personally at the bank. He was made to swear they were his own property, bill by bill, in the presence of qualified witnesses; they included a justice of the peace, the bank cashier, and five of the bank's directors. The charge was $1.37½ per bill.

Kentucky, which had debts of its own in the 1820s, would have liked to issue paper money. The Constitution prevented it from doing so directly, so the state established a corporation, the Bank of the Commonwealth of Kentucky. Its stock was owned by the state.

It had no reserves, but it issued paper currency down to a 12½-cent bill. Federal law said that no one had to accept these notes, which were not legal tender. Kentucky law, however, was altered to strike at anyone who refused the notes and insisted on hard currency. If he tried to sue his debtor for hard money, the action was automatically suspended for two years. The Supreme Court upheld the legality of the notes.

FINALLY, THERE WERE banks operated by people who didn't seem to understand the fragile skein of confidence on which sound banking had to operate. The Mormon leader Joseph Smith, for example, started a bank for the convenience of the faithful in Kirt-land, Ohio, in 1836. The bills he issued tended to leak out beyond the Mormon community, and the gentiles were annoyed when Smith refused to redeem them for hard cash. When a Pittsburgh banker sent some notes back for redemption, the bank president tartly replied that he had issued notes for the convenience of the people, and to redeem them would defeat the purpose. The bank failed in 1837, with forty thousand dollars in notes outstanding, a major reason for dete-riorating relations between the Mormons and gentiles of Illinois in 1837. Once the faithful had grasped the mechanism, and removed to the Promised Land, Mormon banks proved to be extremely well run, and their dollar bills were universally accepted.

Public opinion was divided on the question of banknotes. Certainly a bank ought to redeem its notes in silver and gold, because that was the promise. Dollar bills were promissory notes. But everyone's local bank was a special case. Locals understood that the more a bank had to redeem its notes, the fewer it had to lend them. These notes might travel miles away, where their value slipped. Far away, through nobody's fault, some sleek speculator—a Dexter, in his earlier incarnation, shaving notes in his exchange office—would start buying up their banknotes at the discounted rate. He would gradually amass a small fortune in bills. One morning he would arrive at the bank's doors, carpetbag in hand, demanding gold and silver to the full value of the notes he presented for payment. The carpetbagger was a figure of American myth long before the Civil War, and he wasn't after southern offices. He was after everyone's hard cash.

So whichever way you looked at it, a stranger could spell trouble. Perhaps you found him making for the bank with his carpetbag. Perhaps you saw him peel a fresh and unfamiliar bill from a wad. He might come to rook or to rob. If only people would use banknotes in the spirit in which they'd been issued, business would jog along nicely for everyone. It was the redemption problem that bedeviled the antebellum dollar bill. A sound bank would redeem its notes at par in gold. But how could you be sure it was sound, unless you tried redeeming its notes? And if everyone tried to redeem its notes, what started as an inquiry would turn into an autopsy when the bank ran out of reserves. If only people could have more confidence.

At Michigan's Bank of Battle Creek the arrival of a state inspector caused no alarm: the bank sent for the box of gold it shared with all the other banks in the neighborhood. But whenever a stranger breezed into Battle Creek the town went into alert. Small boys ran to warn the cashier. The cashier would flee, leaving the bank in the temporary custody of Lou Jackson, Battle Creek's first black man, who was a habitual lounger around the bank. Lou Jackson pottered about with a brush, singing and chattering, telling absolutely nothing.[4]

---

4. During the Civil War, Jackson would sign batches of Battle Creek banknotes and send them to local boys soldiering at the front. One of these soldiers used a bill to buy ten meat pies from a farmer. The first was delicious, but the second was more obviously "rat pie, small care having been taken to remove even the hide or the hair of the rodent," and he never used Battle Creek money again.

IN THE CLASSIC American saga of opportunity, the strains of living with it tend to get forgotten. When people were wound up tight to catch the faintest whiff of a New Thing, they hummed like telegraph wires in a small wind too. Bad news traveled as fast as good, a rumor cut both ways, and the persistent expectation of a bonanza around the corner also honed the sense of envy when it came—as it so often did—to somebody else. The gullible, hog-washed, uprooted, and drifting American public was easily alarmed. A matrix of fears revolved around paper money: fear of the wildcat and the counterfeiter, fear of the newcomer, fear of the distant money power pulling strings, fear of failure. They were the embodiment of the core anxiety Americans felt in a land where everyone had called each other neighbor, and now called each other "stranger" to their faces, like the Chinese.[5] They couldn't help it, the thought buzzed in their heads the moment they saw someone from out of town. People wanted to see the color of the stranger's money before they served him at the bar; and they called nonlocal paper money "foreign notes."

Some of these experiences warred in the public's mind with the message of American optimism trumpeted from dollar bills and tree stumps. It was true that from the 1820s vast and visible progress was being made to "civilize" the country: canals were getting dug, lands were being platted and sold, bridges were being built, turnpikes were cutting through the country, factories were going up. But plenty of people felt left out of it all. It wasn't that they didn't work hard, or failed to seize their chances: they did these things, so it wasn't their own fault.

Nowadays we are incessantly told how hard financiers have to

---

5. "Mister," a railroad steward told Charles Dickens, "in America we are all strangers."

work, with their 6 A.M. breakfast meetings and their legendary burnout rate from weeks and years of constant stress. Jacksonian Democrats were less easily impressed. All they saw was certain people getting fantastically rich without doing very much at all.

To set up a bank, a businessman approached the state legislature for a charter. There was no earthly reason why he should get one: no ordinary workingman ever asked the legislature to drop everything and pass a bill, let alone a bill that operated to his sole benefit, so it was reasonable to assume that he got attention through bribery. From that moment on, the promoter and his stockholders possessed a privilege nobody else enjoyed: a license to print money. Their dollar bills were made legitimate by the state administration agreeing to accept them in payment of dues. They might make a fortune, but if they lost somebody else's they had limited liability.

There seemed to be one set of laws for bankers, and another set for everyone else. For subsistence farmers working dawn till dusk the sums involved seemed obscene, and the principles of banking defied common sense. Armed with a charter, a banker could print money on demand to manufacture, out of thin air, a substance other people would pay him to possess. Yet he didn't own it to begin with: it wasn't anything but a promise, written on paper, to pay gold on demand—and he didn't have the gold. Adam Smith, the Scottish political economist, had calculated that a bank might safely lend out about five times as much cash as it actually possessed in silver or gold. So a bank possessed only twenty cents for every dollar it put into circulation. That was if the bank was safe and prudent. Some were more forward in their policy; some would lend out thirty times as much cash as they really possessed. Some, of course, had almost nothing behind them at all. And they all charged.

As banks proliferated, all their old critics seemed to have been quietly maneuvered out of politics. John Adams, for instance, had never entertained a doubt. "Every dollar of a bank bill that is issued beyond the quantity of gold and silver in the vaults represents nothing and is therefore a cheat upon somebody." That somebody was suitably vague; Jefferson was only faintly more precise. Banks, he said, serve "to enrich swindlers at the expense of the honest and industrious part of the nation." If you were honest and industrious, but never rich, that somebody might as well be you.

In which case, obviously, the republic wasn't panning out the way it was meant to. Banking laws were passed to benefit the money power; nobody else wanted them; therefore the money power must have taken control of the lawmaking process. It was hardly a surprise, for in these times everyone seemed to prey on everyone else. The town booster trying to create a town meant to drive up real estate values on land he owned. People sold sections they knew to be worthless. They paid for things in counterfeits. They sold useless patent medicine, watered-down whiskey, phony lottery tickets, stolen horses. People and dollar bills were hard to trust. The frontier widened, the cities grew, people moved far and moved often; no sooner had they got to know their neighbors than they were replaced by others, or they moved themselves into a new settlement, and started getting to know yet more new neighbors. Not only in the West either. "For eight weary months, I have met in the crowded streets but two faces I have ever seen before," wrote Lydia Maria Childs in New York City. A famous story told of two men who had lived for years in the same apartment block. One day they met in the lobby where they gathered their mail, and realized that they shared the same surname: two long-lost brothers living all those years in the same block! In American literature the experience of alienation could be comic or heroic. Poe made it sinister. Herman Melville pinned it down in a book called *The Confidence-Man,* set on a river steamboat.

By the 1840s, every settlement in the West that was worth its salt had access to a river, however small: it was said that steamboat captains would try to reach them on a heavy dew. The passengers by and large were mutual strangers, whose motives were hard to appraise. Even the reader of Melville's nihilistic comedy can hardly say whether the man who laments the decline of confidence and trust is victim or offender, and the link with money—with paper dollars— is explicit. There was something about all paper money, with its cheerful eagerness to please, entertain, divert, and cozen the multitude that must have reminded Melville of the peculiar anonymity of so many American encounters. Here was the wilderness again, pathless and unknowable. What was a civilization, he seemed to wonder, if it could force an elderly, puzzled, half-blind man to spend hours poring over his dollar bills, checking them point by point against an outdated counterfeit detector?

THE FIRST *Banknote Reporter and Counterfeit Detector* appeared in 1826, rapidly spawning imitators. The detectors were sold by subscription to storekeepers, bankers, and merchants who needed to tell at a glance what sort of money they were taking. It was much too early to describe America as a throwaway culture: but the detectors, and many dollar bills themselves, had a startlingly short shelf life, being printed by the hundred thousand on the cheapest sort of paper and chucked at the end of the week. (They are very rare now.) "BEWARE!—As every number of this publication will contain a description of all NEW COUNTERFEITS, this copy of the 'DETECTOR' will be of no value, and will only calculate to deceive any person who may refer to its pages, after the new number is published," *Thompson's Bank Note Detector* warned.

In cold print, the danger to people's prosperity looked clear and present. A *Counterfeit Detector and Bank Note List* of 1839 lists 54 banks that had failed, though their dollars were still out there, 20 fictitious banks, 43 banks whose notes were valueless, 254 banks whose notes had been widely counterfeited and altered, and 1,395 fake banknotes ranging in value from a dollar to five hundred dollars. The detectors supplied thumbnail descriptions of the genuine and phony notes:

> *North Bank, Rockland: 1s, upper centre, female seated on a bale pouring water into a cup for an eagle . . .*
> *Lumberman's Bank, Oldtown: 2s, upper centre, Santa Claus in a sleigh drawn by eight reindeer above the roof of a house. . . . Right end, drove of cattle, sheep and pigs.*

While saving storekeepers from expensive errors, the detectors also kept everyone in a state of heightened insecurity bordering on hysteria. As a Boston writer put it: "The Counterfeit Detector is like a powerful optical instrument. It reveals to you, through the darkness of human hypocrisy, a dim outline landscape of a great system of counterfeiting, by which, however, you may know with perfect safety that it is nearly as extensive as our vastly ramified system of banks, and may be regarded as an image of that system reflected from the mirror of the depraved classes."

That "perfect safety" is good: the only thing you could know for sure was that nothing was ever quite what it seemed. It colored everyone's reaction to money. The depraved classes, whoever they were, lurked behind their sinister mirror, dressed and speaking like anyone else in a country where snobbery was alive and well but class distinctions were inevitably blurred. Dollar bills were just the same: they looked good even when they were snapped together from a bunch of old dies. They came out in public, crisp and plausible. In an anonymous society they belonged to a code of recognition that didn't work well anymore.

The 1840s marked the heyday of the detectors, but eventually people grew wary of them too, for they grew as lively and unpredictable as the money they patrolled. A popular detector, after all, was a powerful adjudicator, in a unique position to "puff" or to "blow" the credit of a bank. Money changed hands. The newspapers warned against blackmail detectors, published with the sole purpose of wringing money out of sound banks. Detectors devoted pages to detecting their rivals' rackets, and to swearing to their own incorruptibility. But no one could ever be perfectly sure with a detector. No one, as Melville pointed out, had absolute confidence anymore.

Dollar bills were so varied that the public struggled to tell good money from bad. This likely-looking bill is a counterfeit.

AMERICA WAS TO be baffled and haunted by its state banknote system right up to the Civil War. When William Fowler, a Wall Street dealer, took a thousand-dollar promissory note—an IOU—

from an operator who said he was "in deep waters," he received a visit from "a tall, lathy man, with a bilious smile," who offered him 5 percent for the note.

Agreeing to 10 percent, the stranger counted out a hundred dollars in tens and fives on the Bentonville Bank, Illinois. Fowler growled at the "suspiciously new" bills, but his visitor whipped out a *Bank Note Reporter* published only the day before, which quoted those notes at 1 percent discount. Fowler accepted the dollar's loss, "and the tall lathy man and note vanished through the door-way."

Fowler showed the notes to a friend who dealt with western banks. He studied the Bentonville vignettes for a while, "gave a long doubtful whistle," and offered to send the money to a correspondent in Chicago, though he suspected the bank was a wildcat and the notes were "stump-tail and red-dog." The Chicago correspondent wrote back: "I visited Bentonville day before yesterday, and found it a small hamlet, consisting of three houses and a grocery store, situated on a prairie, about ten miles from the railroad. The back part of the grocery was occupied by the bank." But the bank had disappeared. "I saw no safe or other evidences of cash, and so conclude the assets are in the breeches pocket of the President and Cashier."

He offered to buy the notes at 2 percent face value, and enclosed a bill for fifteen dollars for expenses. So much for the lathy man and his counterfeit detector.

Bentonville was a good joke: everyone knew that Senator Thomas Hart "Bullion" Benton of Missouri had been the wildest opponent of paper money in the country. He had been, of course, a Jackson man. Even bankers' talk grated on his nerves. "It is the old worn out, used up, dead and gone, slang upon which every red dog, wild cat, owl creek, coon box, and Cairo swindling shop which has disgraced our Country, obtained their charter," he told the U.S. Senate in 1842. Paper money was "a pestilential compound of lampblack and rags."

In 1834 Congress rearranged the Mint ratio between silver and gold that Hamilton had laid down forty-three years earlier. The old ratio had undervalued the silver in a dollar. The new ratio overvalued it. Benton wrote ecstatically, "Gold began to flow into the country through all the channels of commerce, old chests gave up their hordes, the Mint was busy; and in a few months, as if by magic, a currency banished from the country for thirty years overspread the land and gave joy and confidence to all the pursuits of industry." Gold coins were known as Benton's mint drops or Benton's bullets. For about twelve years the two metals circulated together, gold gradually replacing silver until gold was found in California and Australia, and gold was so cheap that the silver in a silver dollar became worth about $1.03. So silver was melted or exported.

SENATOR BENTON'S language had a peculiarly western vigor, which suited the crazy pace of change and the freedom of the frontier to choose its own metaphors. A wildcat bank was a man who printed money and then did anything in his power to avoid having to redeem the face value of the note in gold. Scattering cash, he sprang into view and then disappeared in a trice. He was one with the quack doctor and the phony land agent, preying on the dreams and anxieties of uprooted people. Sometimes he holed up in such a remote, backwoods place that no one but a trapper or an Indian could ever reach him to present the note for payment. Perhaps that's why he was called a wildcat. Often he skipped state. States appointed bank inspectors to verify the banks' hard currency reserves. By the 1850s the inspectors were a special class of men, like bounty hunters, who forced redemption of notes in gold at the end of lonely mountain trails and needed iron nerve to do it. But banks, like any business, prefer combination to competition. Out-and-out wildcats did not generally succeed long in canny, communicative states like New York, but they infested new states like Michigan. "Yankee wit and western grit" came together to sort out the inspections. The southern Michigan banks clubbed together to raise five thousand dollars in gold, which was circulated in advance of the inspector. Day after day, one old-timer recalled, as the chest moved from Marshall to Battle Creek to Kalamazoo, "the touching intimacy of friendship must have grown up between him and those gold coins." Sometimes there weren't all that many gold coins either: only a thin layer of the right stuff over a chest of broken glass or nails.

Western banks spawned a whole menagerie of money: red dogs, catamounts, bob tails, blue dogs, stump-tails, and blue pups. When the detectors failed, people were left with the money. They checked to see that it looked like money. Then they felt the paper. The more worn and dirty the note, the more likely it was that it had been in circulation: there was a certain safety in crowds. They would hold the note to the light, looking for pinholes made by bank clerks when they bundled notes together: the more holes the better.

An Iowa banker in the 1850s assorted his money into various classes, by origin, with one dubious tray marked "Western Mixed," into which he put "rag tag and bob tail"—"everything . . . resembling a banknote . . . stump-tail . . . red-horse . . . wild-cat . . . brindle-pup." "In future," an Iowa merchant facetiously announced in the papers in 1838, "I will prefer the Sucker, Puke or Hoosier Tame Cat, and occasionally one of the old domestic species of Buckeye or Corncracker.[6] . . . I will never again entrust my person or property to those crazy animalculae imported over the mountains or lakes."

---

6. Translates as: I'll take banknotes from Illinois, Missouri, and Indiana, and also Ohio and Kentucky.

IN 1860 Alexander L. Stimpson, a pioneer express man, told the story of the Morocco Bank, which did business out of a potato barrel.[7]

Stimpson's express firm offered local merchants and brokers in the Midwest a redemption service for private banknotes. Stimpson was the Indianapolis agent, and he ran a team of messengers to track banks and get notes redeemed.

A rich broker had set up twenty wildcats in Indiana. He took a list of "paper towns" from a real estate dealer, towns that existed in the minds of promoters and perhaps on crude plat maps lodged in obscure county courthouses, and proceeded to set up a bank in each one. Morocco was one of these towns.

A thousand dollars on the Bank of Morocco arrived in Stimpson's office. No messengers were available, so Stimpson went himself to the state auditor's office in Indianapolis to find out where Morocco was. All they could tell him was that it lay in Newton County, in northwest Indiana.

Stimpson traveled in that direction as far as the new Indianapolis and Lafayette Railroad could take him, reaching Lafayette by stagecoach. There they told him to take the Rensselaer road through Jasper County. Stimpson rented a horse and reached Rensselaer, where nobody had heard of Morocco. He chose the plainest track he could find on the prairie and started to ride toward Newton County.

Toward dark he saw a couple of cabins up ahead. One was a blacksmith's shop where Stimpson asked for directions to Morocco. The blacksmith said: "You need no direction; you are in the town now."

"Is there a bank in this town?"

The blacksmith looked astonished. "Yes; why do you ask that question?"

---

7. *History of the Express Business* (1881).

"I have some business with the bank," Stimpson replied, "and wish to find it."

After a little hesitation the blacksmith asked: "What is the nature of your business?" Stimpson replied stiffly that he could state his business only to the bank officers, if he could find them.

"Well," said the blacksmith, "hitch your critter in the shade there, and I'll go with you to the bank."

Stimpson followed him across to the other cabin. As he stepped inside, the blacksmith said: "This is the Bank of Morocco; take a seat."

Stimpson asked if he was the cashier.

"I don't know what they call me," he replied, "but I do all the business that is done here."

Stimpson told him about the thousand dollars he wanted in gold.

"Well," said the smith, "it is too late now and you will have to stay overnight; we will transact the bank business tomorrow."

Stimpson had little choice. He staked out his rented horse to graze, and had supper in the bank with the blacksmith, his wife, and their four children. The blacksmith explained he was not equipped for "keeping tavern," and that the two beds were used by his family. He slept on the prairie on these warm nights, and he could offer the agent a blanket and a pillow.

"That will suit me exactly," said Stimpson. The blacksmith saw he was uneasy about sleeping in the open with a thousand dollars in his pocket, so he solemnly said: "If you wish, I will put your money in the bank vault tonight, and give you your gold in the morning." The agent thanked him, and handed over the wad of notes.

The blacksmith took the bundle to the corner of the room and started taking potatoes out of a barrel and putting them into a basket. When the basket was full he put the money in the barrel and put the potatoes back on top.

"That vault is easily unlocked," he explained, "but it is as safe as any they have in Lafayette."

The two men slept well on the prairie, and after an ample breakfast next morning the blacksmith said briskly: "We will open the bank now and proceed to business."

He retrieved the banknotes from the potato barrel, counted them on the breakfast table, and seemed satisfied. He took the rest of the potatoes out of the barrel and brought up a bag lettered "$5,000," from which he counted out fifty gold double eagles. He gave the gold to Stimpson, and put the notes in the bag before returning it to the barrel and covering it with the potatoes.

The agent thanked him, and offered to pay for his food and lodging. The blacksmith refused.

"You are the first man who has ever found the Bank of Morocco," he said. "If you keep the location to yourself you are welcome to all I have done for you."

Stimpson agreed. The bank was never heard of again.

11

KILLING THE BANK

Breaking the Bank—Louis Remme's Ride

In the middle of this uneasy period, General Jackson had put himself forward for president. In 1824 he found plenty of people who identified with his well-known refusal to truck with paper money and admired his determination to stand up for himself. But when his inveterate sense of grievance was sharpened by his failure to win, the identification was complete. Jackson had been sold down the river by Henry Clay, "a trickster who defrauded the people of their choice." Men like Clay, or John Quincy Adams, wanted to "convert our government into a heartless aristocracy, in which the people are to be transferred, cheated, taxed, and oppressed, that a few may revel on the spoils of many." Clay's American System was only cover for the departure of the gravy train: more expenses, more taxes, more dollars for the politicians to squander on themselves. Jackson seemed ready to do something about it.

Americans, Tocqueville said, "owe nothing to any man, they expect nothing from any man." The Democrats who voted for Jackson in 1824, 1828, and 1832 were not all poor men by any means; but most of them lacked the essential American quality the world has come to believe in and admire. They lacked confidence.

As far as Biddle was concerned, Jackson launched his attack out of a blue sky. Biddle ran a tight ship at the Bank of the United States; he had voted for Jackson himself. The new president made no mention of the bank in his inaugural address but waited for his first annual message to Congress, instead, to declare that "both the constitutionality and the expedience of the law creating the bank are well-questioned by a large portion of our fellow citizens, and it must be admitted that it has failed in the great end of establishing a sound and uniform currency."

The facts admitted no such thing. The Supreme Court had upheld the constitutionality of the bank, and various committees that investigated the president's claims found that Biddle's notes "actually furnished a circulating medium more uniform than specie." They were at par all over the country. After a tumultuous decade of boom and bust, the bank presided over a relatively calm, expansive economy. Biddle was surprised and rather hurt by Jackson. "My impression," he wrote to a friend who assured him the president bore him no personal malice, "is that these opinions . . . are entirely and exclusively his own, and that they should be treated as the honest though erroneous notions of one who intends well."

It didn't really do to condescend toward Andrew Jackson. Biddle had the committee reports reprinted and distributed at the bank's expense. Old Hickory ominously observed: "This is intended, no doubt, as the first shot; it will pass without moving me." With the election of 1832 looming, the question of the bank's recharter—not due until 1836—suddenly and unexpectedly shot into prominence when the Whigs, under Henry Clay, pushed a bill through Congress to renew the bank's charter.

Clay's idea was to embarrass the president. If Jackson allowed the bill, he would lose the support of his Democratic riffraff. If he vetoed it, against the wishes of the nation's elected representatives in both House and Senate, he would stand unmasked as a despotic demagogue. The president wasn't an absolute monarch who could do what he liked, claiming some sort of mystic communion with the people right over the Constitution's head. The respectable, Whiggish, professional people in the country would be mobilized to defeat him at the presidential election. Clay thought he had sprung a trap.

Jackson simply charged through it. He vetoed the bill. In a grand, angry, rambling message he set the poor, the West, and democracy against the rich, the East, and the privileged few. Jackson dealt with justice, not economics, and if his veto message was riddled with errors and misapprehensions about the bank's contribution to America's prosperity, it was reinforced by a sublime concern for the principles of fairness and equality. Jackson was determined to make money republican, to make the dollar the very symbol of liberty, and not just a soft, expedient grease to the wheels of industry and commerce. His supporters hailed his veto message as a second Declaration of Independence. Biddle, on the other hand, sensed in it "the fury of a chained panther biting the bars of his cage . . . a manifesto of anarchy." The bank, Jackson warned, was a monopoly—a foreign-owned monopoly. The Supreme Court, it was true, had upheld its constitutionality; but the Supreme Court was not the sole arbiter of republican justice. The system of checks and balances gave the executive—meaning President Jackson—and Congress an equal right to pronounce on constitutional issues. Furthermore, there was every reason to think that the bank had abused its charter.

"It is to be regretted," he concluded, "that the rich and powerful too often bend the acts of government to their selfish purposes. Distinctions in society will always exist under every just government. Equality of talents, of education, or of wealth can not be produced by human institutions. In the full enjoyment of the gifts of Heaven and the fruits of superior industry, economy and virtue, every man is equally entitled to protection by law; but when the laws undertake to add to these natural and just advantages artificial distinctions, to grant titles, gratuities, and exclusive privileges, to make the rich richer and the potent more powerful, the humble members of society—the farmers, mechanics, and laborers—who have neither the time nor the means of securing like favors to themselves, have a right to complain of the injustice of their Government. There are no necessary evils in government. Its evils exist only in its abuses. If it would confine itself to equal protection, and, as Heaven does its rains, shower its favors alike on the high and the low, the rich and the poor, it would be an unqualified blessing."

Of course on one point the president had overstepped the mark: by throwing out a bill on his own authority, he was acting as a tribune of the people; he was claiming a preeminence over Congress and the Supreme Court. But he was also prepared to put this issue to the people.

It was the first presidential election about money, the only election in U.S. history defined by a single issue. Biddle had no intention of letting his bank be killed, unlike the directors of the first Bank of the United States; his tireless campaign for the bank was taken as a political step. But Jackson too was invigorated by the prospect of battle. One of the bullets fired by Jesse Benton, having worked its way slowly down his arm, had emerged near his elbow, close to the skin, and was successfully dug out; now—though still racked by lung congestion and pain—he looked ten years younger. On his way home from Washington he paid all his bills in gold, saying, "No more paper-money, you see, fellow-citizens, if I can only put down this Nicholas Biddle and his monster bank." He won by a landslide. He was still getting votes in 1860, fifteen years after his death.

His plan was simply to withdraw all government deposits from the bank and redistribute them to private banks: the Pennsylvanians would give the Bank of the United States a state charter but it would no longer have national status or branches. Yet even the private banks urged against his scheme. Committees pronounced the bank safe and sound. Jackson's own secretary of the treasury refused to remove the deposits and had to be promoted out of the way. The man chosen to replace him dithered for months. Jackson got rid of him and found Roger B. Taney to do what he asked. His difficulties left him all the more convinced that the bank represented a danger to "the morals of the people, the freedom of the press, and the purity of the elective franchise."

Nicholas Biddle was utterly thrown by the fury of the Jacksonian assault. Like a man who has been mugged on the street and installs new locks in his home, his confidence was shattered. He wildly assumed that Jackson wanted to do more than revoke his national charter: Jackson wanted to break the bank. Taney was supposed to wind down the deposits gradually, in the natural course of business; instead, he began shoveling the money out of the Bank of the United States and into selected state banks, the so-called pet banks. Biddle launched a policy of massive curtailment, pulling in money and loans, for "nothing but the evidence of suffering abroad will produce any effect on Congress." Savage dislocation of the expanding economy would "lead to restoration of the currency and the recharter of the Bank." Biddle meant to do what the War of 1812 had done: convince Americans that a national bank was too vital to be without.

He took a certain satisfaction from seeing the country thrown into a financial crisis. He thought this proof enough that the country needed the bank. Jacksonians took it as proof of the need to get rid of it. The crisis eased only when Biddle, feeling the bank was again secure, relaxed his policy. In the meantime he secured a Pennsylvania charter for the bank that would keep it going as a state institution.

Yet the coming change to the bank's status was sadly felt in Philadelphia. In March 1834 a crowd of fifty thousand people gathered at Independence Square to pray for the return of the deposits. "In all the proceedings of this institution a calm dignity, a moderation of temper, and a regard to the interests of the country are observable, which contrasts admirably with the perturbed and ferocious spirit that seems to animate its persecutors," a commentator wrote. Jackson had long since achieved a Christlike apotheosis in the eyes of his more fervent supporters; now it was the bank's turn. At a sad meeting the stockholders expressed their full approval of the way the bank had been run while "exposed to both persecution and obloquy . . . unmerited and unjust."

Jackson's political machine created the Democratic Party. His idol, Jefferson, would have disapproved, but he would have understood the contradictions of democracy itself: that it was possible to value nothing but hard money, silver and gold, the way Jackson did, and at the same time aim to break the stranglehold a single private institution held over the direction and aims of American energies. For the Jacksonians promised hard money and gave the country easy credit instead. And easy credit, in the form of state banknotes, ruined the very kind of America Jacksonians revered.

No one has ever quite found an explanation for that irony. Some have argued that he was manipulated by a kitchen cabinet of ambitious businessmen, who used his horror of the Bank of the United States to break the shackles of monetary responsibility and usher in the very changes Jackson would have most abhorred: credit, industry, railroads, and corruption. Some think it smacked of a New York plot to seize the lead from Philadelphia: that worked out too. Others discern only an unfinished revolution, supposing that Jackson meant to rein in the state banks and give America the hard currency Jefferson had wanted. But what made Jackson so fascinating was his raw connection to the people's mood. They wanted hard money and less anxiety: Jackson obliged by destroying the monster. But they were Americans, after all: they wanted things fair and equal, and they wanted a chance. So they took easy credit too, supplied by cohorts of little, lesser monsters who allowed them to burst apart the boundaries of old America.

WITH THE BANK of the United States still in its death throes, America's money grew and grew. More silver was circulating in the U.S., with Mexico in revolution and the Chinese starting to take opium, instead of silver, for their teas and silks. The effect, as ever, was a land boom. In 1834, 4,658,000 acres of public land were sold, 12,564,000 acres in 1835, and 20,074,000 acres in 1836. Prices soared, but the money that covered the price was fantastically elastic. The proceeds of a land auction, paid to the Land Office, was put on deposit in the local bank; if there wasn't a local bank before, one sprang up just to receive the money, with a new set of printing plates and a strongbox. Flush with cash reserves, albeit paper cash, the bank printed more dollar bills. Speculators borrowed them. The speculator stopped an auction by making a bid on all the land the government was ready to sell, having prearranged with the hopeful settlers present to sell them the lands they wanted on flat-rate terms, low and easy. Those early birds, in theory, got what they wanted at the opening price; and the speculator sold the remnant at a better price to latecomers. Everyone was a winner, except the federal government; but at least the land got settled.

During the land boom of the 1830s, a huge amount of paper money was issued on the security of land—what Benjamin Franklin had called "coined land." These American Indians seem to be deciding to move along.

Cheap land and easy credit was a hypnotic combination: you could doubt the money, but the land was real, and its value seemed to be rising every month. At least the land that had already been bought was rising in value; it was significant that the government still sold at $1.25 an acre. Cheap land, easy credit, and the price of cotton helped slavery expand into the Southwest. Alabama, Florida, Arkansas, Louisiana, Mississippi, and Tennessee became slave states almost overnight, as planters started to capitalize on rising cotton prices.

This was just the kind of speculative boom Jackson always hated. The number of those banks he loathed and mistrusted more than doubled. Inflation, which struck him as a sinister machination of the money power, ran wild: perhaps it was the worst inflation in American history. By 1833 the national debt had been paid off and income was stacking up in the government coffers. Jackson, who was naturally opposed to federal government spending the money, preferred giving it back to the states, to spend as they saw fit. (It was called a loan, but it was really a gift.) Most states, in anticipation, launched a huge program of borrowing and spending on the American System.

IN THE MID-THIRTIES, an imaginative armchair traveler on a western tour could stay at some of the best hotels, travel by the most convenient and modern routes, and enjoy healthful air and delightful society in dozens of towns all around the states. He might raise an eyebrow over Kankakee City in Illinois: no one could really want to spend much time in a place called Kankakee City; but its urban lots were going for thousands of dollars, and it presumably possessed some of the raw charm that was later to define Chicago. Fort Sheldon sounded more the place, 124 city blocks on the river in Michigan. It had a lovely harbor, it was about to get a railroad, shipping was protected by a lighthouse, and visitors were accommodated in a splendid hotel that had cost some forty thousand dollars to build. It had a mill too—sawing was the first way to wealth out West. At the height of its prospective prosperity, there were at least fifteen rather small houses there in Fort Sheldon.

Or what about High Bluffs, promoted by a French Canadian, on the eastern banks of the Kaskaskia? "The plan was drawn by a skilled draftsman at St. Louis, and represented the city as standing in the most beautiful natural surroundings, on high ground naturally declining in grade to the river. The lots were numbered far into the hundreds, with finely embellished parts, and here and there a graceful church edifice. On two corner lots were pictured solid-looking bank buildings of Gothic architecture, and on others were schoolhouses, colleges, hotels, and hospitals. Near the river were shown great warehouses, two mills, and various factories. A heavily laden steamboat was depicted approaching the wharf from below; other boats were at the landing." The whole prospect "was lithographed on large sheets of heavy paper in the highest style of art. Supplied with a number of copies, the promoter left for the eastern cities in the fall. He returned in early spring by way of New Orleans and the Mississippi, with an immense stock of miscellaneous merchandise he had received in exchange for his city lots, which he converted into cash as speedily as possible. He was not at home when agents of eastern mercantile houses came West to look up their city property."[1] Perhaps it was like Marion City, Missouri, another well-mapped town, whose lots sold for between two hundred and a thousand dollars back East. It proved to stand just six feet out of the water.

HAVING GOT RID of the Bank of the United States, still Jackson found the money went around and around, out of the banks, into the land offices, and back into the banks, all the time treated as if it were gold and silver, instead of paper. A lot of the federal government's revenue from land sales was on deposit in western banks, not in gold or silver, but in notes issued by the local banks themselves, who lent them to settlers to buy land. Jackson fretted that those deposits might turn out to be much bigger than all the hard money in the West.

On the verge of his retirement, Jackson ordered that public lands be sold only for gold and silver coin, technically referred to as specie, not banknotes: western feelings were running high against speculation, because the scramble for land was driving paper prices up too high for local farmers to compete. It was called the Specie Circular,

---

1. Reginald Charles MacGrane, *The Panic of 1837: Some financial problems of the Jacksonian era* (Chicago, 1924).

and Jackson issued it in July 1836. Jackson hoped for three things: to make the gamblers pay up, give local banks the specie they would need for the government rebate, and damp down the paper money mania.

Within a year, three things happened: the land boom collapsed, banks called in their loans to find the money that Jackson himself had planned to hand over to the states, and the Bank of England, alarmed by the rage for American speculations, raised its interest rate.

Money flows went into reverse. Silver and gold was sucked from the busy cities of the East, where it was needed most, and sent bowling West, where it wasn't needed at all. Two months after Jackson left office, every bank in America had stopped redeeming its notes in silver and gold. Defaulted loans left them with acres of ground. British investors were hit; some British banks collapsed; a British wag wrote a bitter ditty on American attitudes to debt, set to the tune of "Yankee Doodle." The federal government, in the process of shifting specie about, found itself unable to pay wages. The Fort Sheldon hotel, with thirty lots, was sold off for less than the cost of the paint and glass.

Yet by 1838 the crisis seemed to have passed. New York banks resumed gold and silver payments. Philadelphia banks followed. Biddle's bank, on a charter from Pennsylvania, carried on in a national manner, to help southern banks resume in 1838. Its portfolio swelled with southern bank stock and state bonds. Then the 1838 revival turned out to be the lull before the storm. The price of state bonds collapsed. Banks had used them as collateral, and they suspended all over again. The Bank of the United States was out of cash. Forced by law to resume in 1841, it suffered a run on its silver deposits and closed for good. For Jacksonians it was a little ray of sunshine, for the bank's failure simply proved what Jackson had been saying all along.

Philadelphia lost more than the bank. America lost more than the money—it lost the only safe national currency the U.S. had handled in decades. Never again would there be a central bank in America. Never again was Philadelphia to be the city par excellence. When Wall Street banks gave the signal for Philadelphia banks to resume payments in 1838, the crown of supremacy had passed from the city of brotherly love. Philadelphia's shipping business had been quietly slipping away. In 1825, New York handled almost five times as much shipping as Philadelphia, and her population, already bigger than Pennsylvania's, grew twice as fast in the 1820s. New York got its first Cunard Line connection to Europe in 1848. A Liverpool merchant began a Philadelphia steam line, and the *City of Glasgow* entered the Delaware to the cheers of the populace, but she disappeared in 1854 with the loss of all five hundred passengers. The same line's *City of Pittsburgh* was burned out in 1852, and the *City of Philadelphia* sank without ever reaching Philadelphia at all. Within a decade the line had moved its offices and its operations to New York.[2]

Jackson retired to the Hermitage, Biddle to Andalusia. Jackson's successor, Martin Van Buren, said of Biddle, "It is due to truth to say that his private and personal character has never, to my knowledge, been successfully impeached." But Biddle died a bitter man in 1844. Jackson died much adored in 1845. In 1924 a Committee of the Bureau of Engraving and Printing agreed to put Andrew Jackson, looking rather mad, on the back of the twenty-dollar bill.

2. After 1844, too late for George Washington, Philadelphia became known for producing, among a myriad of first-class industrial products, the world's finest and most realistic false teeth: by odd coincidence, Jacob Perkins used his steel process for Charles Willson Peale who, when not painting his miniatures or running the natural history museum, used it to turn out gold dentures.

IT WAS RARELY, though, that a man got the better of the banks. One was Louis Remme, whose story was a legend of early Oregon.

Louis Remme was a French Canadian who came west as a cattle rancher. It was a curious fact that of all the huddled peoples hoping to breathe free, the French—who were no less huddled or more free than, say, the English—never took up the invitation to immigrate to the U.S. except after the California gold strikes of 1848. Then they made up almost a quarter of the hundred thousand or so people who raced to the goldfields, becoming known as the Keskerdees because they eagerly hung around the edge of miners' conversations (hoping, like everyone else, to get early news of a fresh strike), at the first opportunity tugging on a neighbor's sleeve to ask anxiously: *"Qu'est ce qu'il dit?"*

But Remme, hailing from British-ruled Canada, was always at home. He ranged in the Rogue River country of Oregon and in northern California in the fifties. In 1855 he finished a long winter drive of cattle down the Sacramento River, selling cattle for gold as he went along, ending in Sacramento with $12,500 in gold. He promptly banked the money with Adams and Company, a western outfit like Wells Fargo that combined express services with banking. Remme took a certificate of deposit for the money and checked into the Orleans Hotel. It was February and snow lay on the ground; for the first time in weeks he slept in a soft bed and took a long breakfast in the neighboring restaurant run by Marius Bremond.

He took the next boat to San Francisco, where he spent about a week winding down after the long, hard ride. The S.S. *Oregon* arrived, bringing news of the failure of Page, Bacon, and Co., a St. Louis bank with a daughter bank in California. Remme did not think the news affected him until the next day, when the banks in town were surrounded by milling crowds. Remme was not unduly anxious, but he decided to return to Sacramento nonetheless, and retrieve his gold.

He took the night boat and walked straight to the offices of Adams and Co., which were surrounded by a crowd. The cashier looked at his certificate and told him to "see Cohen," the receiver. Things were looking bad. For reasons no longer certain, the public had made an association between the failed St. Louis bank and Adams and Co. The lines at the bank were growing longer; there seemed little point in standing around hopelessly, waiting for the worst.

Remme thought immediately of the branch office at Marysville— but if the news was out at Sacramento it would have reached Marysville too and every other town where the express company had an office. It was then that he remembered that Adams and Co. had a company office in Portland, Oregon, around five hundred miles due north: it would be days, he reckoned, before the news reached Portland. If he could get there first, he might still manage to get his money out in time.

The Pacific mail steamer *Columbia* was preparing to leave San Francisco for Portland soon—but taking the steamer would be futile. News of the bust would go with him. Even if, by some legerdemain, he managed to be first off the boat, racing to the Adams and Co. office, the cashier would know that the steamer was carrying news and instructions from San Francisco, and become suspicious. And the boat might dock after hours, and news would be all around the town by morning. The steamer idea was a nonstarter. There was no stagecoach service. If he was to stand any chance of getting his money, he would have to reach Portland himself, before the steamer docked.

Without a moment's hesitation, Remme pushed through the crowds and barely made it to the riverboat station, where a stern-wheel steamer was just starting for Knight's Landing, about forty miles upstream. There he was on home ground. He bought a horse, headed for Grant Island, and traded there with Judge Diefendorf for a fresh horse. Now he was close to Marysville. He made another change of horses nearby, but he had no friends there and had to pay a "boot" of five dollars. At ten at night he made Red Bluff, where he stopped a few minutes to eat and rest his mount. Twenty miles farther north, he encountered a campfire: the ranchers sprang up and demanded to know his business. He said he was a stockman, after a horse thief, and he needed a fresh horse.

The men in camp were sympathetic. They gave him a new mount and helped him shift his saddle over. Remme rode on. At dawn he took breakfast at Tower House on Clear Creek. It was lucky for him he reached the Trinity Mountains by daylight: the ground was rocky and he had to pick his way with care. But the high country started here, and the icy mountain winds cut through the canyons bringing a swirl of snow. Mountain headlands obstructed his progress; often he had to wind east or west along the canyons, traveling miles to make a mile north. Easier ground was to be had a little farther east, but 1855 was a year of Indian troubles and Remme probably figured he was safer in the highlands. At nightfall he traded his tired horse for another at Trinity Creek and pushed on until sunrise, in Scott Valley, below Shasta Mountain. Here he stopped and slept until noon.

From Callahan's the going improved: now he could ride. In Yreka he found a fresh horse with Horsley and Brastow's Mountain Express, and four hours later he made the Oregon state line. In the mining town of Jacksonville he ate and found some sleep. Two changes of horse brought him to the next mountain range, where he was warned against the threat of Indian attack. Near Wolf Creek he was fired on, but the Indians missed their mark and he spurred his horse through a narrow pass to safety in Winchester village, where he ate at the tavern of Joe Knott and slept a few more hours.

The dangers were behind him, but the winter rains made the going muddy: Pass Creek was almost impassable under deep mud, and it was hard to see his way in the night and the rain. Shortly before dawn he galloped through Eugene City and on to John Milliron's farm, a dozen miles away, where he found a fresh horse and a snatched breakfast.

This was the fifth day of his trail. The rain stopped, and the air was sunny and crisp; away to the east stood the snowy Cascades. He rode a day and a night, and had breakfast with some Hudson Bay trappers at French Prairie, near the present Salem. He paid five dollars and got a fresh mount. By half past ten he reached Oregon City; at noon he crossed the Willamette by ferry; he reached Portland at one o'clock on the sixth day. Leaving his horse at Stewart's stable, he asked whether the California steamer had come in yet. He was told it was expected later that afternoon and given directions to the Adams and Co. office.

There he found Dr. Steinberger, the agent, just back from lunch. Remme waited easily while the doctor opened up the office and unhurriedly inquired if he could cash a certificate of deposit on the Sacramento office here. "Well," said Dr. Steinberger, "it will cost you one half of one percent for all amounts over a thousand dollars."

"That's all right," replied Remme, "I'm a cattle buyer and I need the money."

Steinberger took the certificate and slowly counted out the gold coin, carefully reserving his $62.50 commission. Relieved and exhausted, Remme took the money to a hotel and saw the gold secured in the safe. With a receipt in his pocket he sauntered out into the street to see what would happen next.

There are several versions. In one, the steamer docked almost straightaway. Ralph Mead, the *Columbia*'s purser, was on the dock before the skipper had his lines ashore, and managed to retrieve $950

from the bank before news of the suspension reached Dr. Steinberger. In another, the boat arrived at nine at night, and the news of
the busted bank flooded Portland before the night was out. However
magnificent Remme's ride, he should not, by rights, have beat the
steamship at all: because of the Indian troubles, it had made stops at
Humboldt Bay and at the mouth of the Rogue River to put ashore
soldiers.

Whatever the exact details, the story of the crazy Keskerdee's wild
ride to beat the banks appealed to settlers on the Long Tom or the
Umpqua. Louis Remme enjoyed four years of notoriety. In the winter of 1859 he got caught in the Siskiyou Mountains, driving a herd
from the Rogue River down to Yreka. Again, he made a quick decision to push on. The snow deepened. Icy winds gusted down from
Mount Shasta. Remme never came through.

· 12 ·

THE SPY

**On Paying for a War—Greenbacks—The Secret Agent—
The Hydrostatic Press Scam—Working Women**

Three generations had passed since the nation's sleepy capital was founded on a spur of the Potomac River. Washington was still a small town. Huge boulevards between the White House and the Capitol existed only as thoughts, between grassy open fields. When war broke out in April 1861, it became a frontline city, and half its better buildings, including the Church of the Virgin and the Patent Office, were turned into hospitals. Mortars would sometimes land in the streets. In the old days some ironist had dubbed Washington the "city of magnificent views," because the streets were so wide and there was so little on them; in the early months of the war the Stars and Bars of the rebel army could be seen flying from Virginia Heights across the Potomac.

The city took three months to turn into a dust bowl. Mules and horses ate all the grass down to the roots, the sun dried the earth, and the wind came and blew it all over. Real estate's high, they joked. Soldiers tramped up the dust from unpaved streets. Gun carriages cracked the cobbles. The flies had never had such a summer, what with the animals and the provender wagons and the effluent of a quarter million men that mostly found its way into the lake at the back of the White House. Anything that didn't move was speckled with fly dirt.

Six months after that, Washington turned into a swamp. The streets were slimy and black. The sewage lake seeped. The rains came and washed the mud off the bare fields. Boots and hooves poached the ground. On overcast days, yellow soot hung in the air from thousands of stoves and fireplaces burning soft Virginia coal, and the empty space beneath the boardwalks gurgled and sucked. Then people flailed along like drunks, lurching from one rail to another, sometimes grabbing each other for support. They crossed the street knee-deep in the mire and lost their boots and tempers.

The war made Washington filthy.

SMOOTH LITTLE TEN-CENT bills, crackly dollars, a wad of tens in the wallet like sheets on a newly made bed: federal government money slips persuasively across the bar under the sign NO LIQUOR SOLD TO SOLDIERS; goes folded in a little wad in the breast pocket of a gunner's tunic, promising a new dress or a stiff drink or a rollover at Ma Applebaum's; whispers visions, settles rows. Spencer Morton Clark is the man everyone has to thank for it, acting engineer in charge of the Treasury's new currency operations, supervising the cutting and trimming of finished notes, which were delivered in sheets by private banknote companies.

Fifty-two, maybe fifty-three, he lives with Mrs. Clark in a clapboard walk-up in the third district, sleeps in a second-floor room at the back of the house, and employs a black servant. Each morning, in a shiny new top hat, a clerkish coat, swell boots, and side-whiskers, he makes his way without haste along Y Street. Mr. Clark has a nasal voice, and his accent is not Virginian, but he's been in Washington long enough to remember when all the cobbles on Pennsylvania Avenue were laid straight and the street was bordered by fields. Two years. Now the avenue is lined with tenements and wooden shacks and the cobbles are all askew, sinking in ruts into the mud beneath. The crowds swirl around him as he walks—men in blue, a Confederate officer with white gloves on, an anxious civilian asking directions to a hospital, a chain of invalids, soot-blackened and bandaged, wearily stumbling toward their billet, a barefoot Negro. Whips a-cracking, an artillery train pulls up the road, shouts from the leading men smothered in the groan of the wheels.

Over Y Street Clark passes through a small city of tents, pitched on the Parade by men of the Sixteenth Infantry on furlough. They are digging latrines, or sitting with outstretched legs at the flaps of their tents, cobbling boots, sewing buttons, or dismantling and reassembling their Martini rifles. They all know the names of their commander, their generals, and their president by now. Some have heard of Salmon P. Chase, Lincoln's treasury secretary. But the name of the man who feeds them, billets them, and gives them something to send home to their families escapes them. Really they don't even see S. M. Clark—the nuts and bolts man, the moneymaker—walking with renewed purpose toward the gleaming behemoth of the U.S. Treasury.

The doorman sees him. The doorman tips his hat, with a cheery "Good morning, Mr. Clark." Clark gives him a hard look and a grunt, continues through the brass gates, and walks with a measured pace across the terrazzo floor to the stairs, his heels clicking.

It's one of the biggest buildings in the United States, taking up the side of Fifteenth Street between Pennsylvania Avenue and G

Street, almost four hundred feet long, roped in colonnades, slapped down where it had no business to be so that it blocks the view from the White House to the Capitol.[1] Three of the best porticoes overlook the president's kitchen garden. Clark likes going into it. He reaches the Currency Bureau by a staircase that grows meaner as it climbs.

On his way to his office he looks in at the sorting room, where seventy young women are hard at work with shears cutting up sheets of printed dollar bills. First they examine the sheets for errors and irregularities, then they cut and stack the bills. When a stack reaches a thousand dollars, it is taken away to be stitched into a muslin bag. These women, thanks to Spencer Morton Clark, are the first in America to work for the government. He says their work is neater than men's, they are less boisterous. A century later he will be remembered as an emancipator.

Mr. Clark walks solemnly down the line of cutting tables. Mrs. Brown is humming to herself. One of the new girls looks half asleep. The shears go snip, snip, snip. Pretty Ella stretches and waggles her fingers over her head. She looks at Clark and her eyes go wide. Mr. Clark smiles back.

THE UNION ENTERED the war with two hundred thousand dollars in its coffers, but the treasury secretary, Salmon P. Chase, remained cool until the Battle of Bull Run in July 1861 upset all hopes of an easy victory over the South. The army was now looking at a long campaign, and soldiers needed to be paid. Chase borrowed

---

1. Nicholas Biddle helped with Strickland's design, amused to think his influence would be felt here in Washington, right under Jackson's nose.

from the northern banks, sold war bonds to patriotic investors, and finally, sorrowfully (for he was a hard-money man) he turned to the option of printing money. In April 1862 Chase issued $150 million on the credit of the United States. Five months later he ordered a second round of $150 million, and another $150 million the next year. The second issue included the first government-issued one-dollar bills. They were nothing like the dollar bills Americans already knew, with pictures of "Indians, steamboats, trains, settlers, frontiersmen, buffalo, Liberty, Justice and historical statesmen like Washington and Jefferson." They actually bore a portrait of Salmon P. Chase himself, and were printed in black ink on the front but in green on their backs.

Like the revolutionary Continentals, the greenbacks were supported by promises only. The solidity of the promise was measured in depreciation: when the Union was winning, greenbacks rose in gold value—in August 1863, after Gettysburg and Vicksburg, they hit eighty-two cents a dollar. But by June the next year a greenback dollar was valued at thirty-five cents. A new word then entered the language via a pamphlet called "A Warning to the People: The Paper Bubble," which described the rise in prices in terms of "inflation." By May 1865 greenbacks had recovered to seventy-eight cents.

Salmon P. Chase now appears on the ten-thousand-dollar bill,[2] a clear case of inflation; he also had an inflated sense of his own worth. As governor of Ohio he had contested the leadership of the Republican Party with Lincoln in 1860. Lincoln won and brought him into government, where he grew famous for appointing his own creatures to every office that conceivably fell under his jurisdiction and to several that did not. Whenever he felt crossed by the president he

---

2. The world's largest collection of ten-thousand-dollar bills, with a face value of a million dollars, was on display at Binion's Horseshoe Casino in Vegas until January 2000.

would pompously tender his resignation. Fourteen times between 1861 and January 3, 1864, Lincoln had to cajole his secretary of the treasury into staying on, despite his flagrant misuse of power and his undisguised desire to have Lincoln's new job himself. After these interviews, Lincoln used to lie down and make faces.

Chase was also a man of deep and imposing piety—he naturally saw himself in a client/patron relationship with the Almighty—so he was touched to get an anxious letter from a Rev. M. R. Watkinson, of Ridleyville, Pennsylvania, early in the war. "You are probably a Christian," the reverend wrote. "What if our nation were now shattered beyond reconstruction? Would not the antiquaries of succeeding centuries rightly reason from our past that we were a heathen nation?" The reverend was talking about coins: he had a morbid fancy, in which he saw the pious archaeologists of the future pondering the fact that U.S. coinage celebrated only the Goddess of Liberty, "the ignominy of heathenism." To put them right he proposed a design of flags, all-seeing eyes, stars, rings of unity, and the words "God, liberty, law."

Chase instinctively snuggled up to the idea: by then the pared-down rationalism of the men who had made the Constitution a century before had succumbed to the earthier realization that no one ever lost votes by invoking God.

"No nation can be strong except in the strength of God, or safe except in his defense," Chase wrote to the director of the Philadelphia Mint. "The trust of our people in God should be declared on our national coins." The Mint hastened to oblige, and suggested "Our country; our God" and "God, our Trust," but Chase hit on the final wording himself. From 1864, *In God We Trust* was to be reproduced on every coin where it could be made to fit.

Almost a century passed before the motto appeared on dollar bills. President Lincoln, instead, teased Chase by asking him whether issuing greenbacks would mean he would be expected to sign them all by hand. Chase—who took it for granted that Lincoln was the wrong man for the job—spent a week agonizing over how to explain paper money to the president. In the meantime he established a team of seventy clerks on twelve hundred dollars a year to sign the money out. This went on for six months before Spencer Morton Clark pointed out that the signature could be printed. He had the signature engraved on the plates and saved the government thousands of dollars. Maybe it was this that gave him a sense of entitlement.

IN JULY 1862, Clark demonstrated to Treasury Secretary Chase that the banknote companies were overcharging on the greenbacks. His solution was to produce them all in-house, putting an engraver to work on the design of new dollar and two-dollar notes and getting a plate printer, Charles Neale, to set up a full-blown printing operation, with paper, ink, machinery, and workmen. Neale took over three months to find printers prepared to work for the department: nobody believed the government project would last very long.

But demand for money was rising in the meantime. With the value of greenback dollars sinking fast, people preferred spending paper to spending silver, obedient to Gresham's law that the existence of bad money always drives out good. In one week, in Boston as in New York, as June turned into July, 1862, all the silver quarters, dimes, and three-cent bits that oiled the machinery of daily life simply disappeared. Most wound up in Canada, which had adopted its neighbor's decimal system and the dollar in 1858. Not a pocketful of coins jingled any longer in the city streets, not a single barman stood you change. Nobody could take the omnibus or ferry to work because there was no money between a cent and a five-dollar note:

public transport ran empty while thousands of its recent fares walked grumpily alongside.

If you wanted a button sewn on your jacket or a two-cent cigar, you had to buy in bulk, or barter like your grandfather did when he was a boy in the penniless young republic. The match sellers presented you with a filthy little scrap of paper in lieu of change, on which was written, "good for so many boxes of matches." Try to use it, though, and they'd pretend to be someone else. Big stores issued tokens. Communities printed their own ten-cent notes. "The saloon-keeper, the cigar-dealer, and the barber have turned banker," said a New York paper. The traditional word for all this stuff was shinplaster. Chase's first idea was to shrink the coinage, to save on silver, but there was no time to do so. Some very old and worn Spanish silver emerged from hiding and started to circulate, until the fall of the greenback made this, too, disappear.

Faced with the possibility that daily life in America would simply grind to a halt for lack of small change, Chase suggested that everyone could use postage stamps instead. The law was amended without consulting Montgomery Blair, the postmaster general, who went ballistic with fury when the post offices were besieged with people trying to break their five-dollar bills. New York post offices normally sold around three thousand dollars' worth of stamps a day. On July 18 they sold ten thousand dollars' worth, sixteen thousand dollars' the day after, and twenty-four thousand dollars' at the start of the new week. The New York postmaster cabled Washington urgently for more stamps.

Montgomery Blair, who came from an old political family, saw that his fief had been invaded. Never mind the threat of real invasion from the South: he sent a brisk telegram to New York that ran: "Restrict sales of postage stamps to former customary amount per diem, as this Department is not to furnish stamps for currency." The public was told that the Post Office was not selling stamps for currency, nor accepting dirty stamps for payments, and that anyone buying stamps at the counter would have to swear, in an echo of the wildcat days, that they were going to use the stamps only for their mail.

A mediator from the Internal Revenue Department finally persuaded Blair to issue special postage stamps, which the Treasury, not the post office, would pay for. By the spring of 1863 more than $20 million of stamp currency had been issued, though soldiers stuffed the little notes into their boots, or crumpled them up in their trouser pockets with the jackknife and the plug of tobacco, and barely half of it was ever redeemed. The life span of a modern dollar bill is eighteen months: after six months the non–postage stamps, passing much more frequently from one sweaty hand to another, had all but disintegrated. Blair now argued that post offices had no duty to redeem unused stamps, but there was a public outcry and post offices were overwhelmed with sticky messes of colored paper. The New York post office alone paid out three hundred thousand dollars of these disgusting little squares, and everyone suspected widescale petty fraud.

The ever-helpful Spencer Clark delighted Chase by offering to temporarily drop his work on full-scale dollar bills and work up a series of smaller notes to replace the stamp money, and in March 1863 his newly hired engravers produced designs for a "fractional" currency—five-, ten-, twenty-five-, and fifty-cent notes, bearing the heads of Washington, Lincoln, Jefferson, and Grant. By then Clark was employing 237 men and 288 women who, among other things, cut out all the greenbacks in America. He was also in some respects a figure of notoriety.

IN 1861 Lafayette Baker, America's first secret agent, went into action against the secessionist states. Frequently working under-cover, he created a skeleton organization that developed after the war into the U.S. Secret Service, officially founded in 1865 to protect the body of the president and the integrity of the dollar. Baker was a fine horseman and, according to friends, the best shot in the North. He arrived at the house of General Winfield Scott, springing up the steps two at a time, dust flying from his riding boots; a Negro atten-dant with bare feet ushered him into the general's study. Outside, the dust drifted above the boards, then settled.

"Young man," General Scott had said, thumbing gold double eagles from his waistcoat pocket, "if you have judgment and discre-tion, you can be of great service to the country." One month later, Lafayette Baker lay motionless in the sweet dust of the Union, the lazy gurgle of water at his feet. His limbs felt empty and his mind was blank. In Baker's pocket as he lay on the riverbank were his hard-won assessments of southern army strengths.

Baker had been captured fifty miles behind rebel lines. He was delivered to the "rebel chief" himself, Jefferson Davis, president of the Confederacy, in Richmond. Baker's alias was the name of some-one he'd met in California, Samuel Munson of Knoxville, Tennessee, with a business engagement in the South. Jeff Davis sent his aides to find someone from Knoxville.

He was bent over some papers at his desk when an orderly entered bearing a calling card on a tray. Baker gestured to the orderly, read the name on the card, and replaced it on the tray. A moment later Davis looked up to receive the card and asked the gentleman to be shown in.

A flash of well-timed recognition lit up Baker's face.

"Why, how do you do, Brock?" he cried, leaping from his chair and pumping the fellow's hand. Brock looked surprised, but he soon thought he did remember young Munson, changed, for sure, by those California years.

Lafayette Baker *had* been west, like Munson. One of his ancestors was Remember Baker, one of the Green Mountain Boys, who made Vermont ungovernable in the last years of colonial rule. Lafayette's father, another Remember, took the family to Michigan in the early twenties, where Lafayette was raised knowing right from wrong (the difference was marked in Michigan). He pushed on farther west in turn, following the trail to California. A big man among those stunted European innocents and the lean-eyed sharps and vagabonds who accompanied them, Baker was always swift—perhaps too swift—to champion natural justice. They looked surprised when he broke their noses, bloodied their chins: almost as surprised as their victims. Weary Irishmen, the prim and desperate Yankees, foreigners from deep inside Europe chattering in their own babble, black runaways: all the same biped, hopeful, helpless lot. Once a ferryman threatened to throw a baby overboard unless the passengers paid double. Baker simply killed the ferryman.

In California Baker joined the Vigilantes, self-appointed guardians of the peace who administered rough justice on the frontier. Baker went into business too, and he was on the East Coast when the war broke out. He had promptly reported for duty. "Judgment and discretion," old General Scott had said. "God Speed in Dixie, young man."

WINFIELD SCOTT was notoriously slow and incompetent, so it's surprising he used a newfangled word like *Dixie* at all. "To all men whose desire only is to be rich, and to live a short life but a merry one, I have no hesitation in recommending New Orleans," wrote Fearon in 1819. The produce of the whole American West came rolling down the

Mississippi to New Orleans, and money oozed through this city, curling like ornamental ironwork around the houses in the old French quarter, flowing like molasses, dissipating itself in the noonday heat. In 1816 a Frenchman had found the city "flooded with paper notes so dirty and so disgusting that one can hardly bear to touch them. The notes for one, two, or four escalins hardly show their printing; and their decrepitude makes it necessary to stitch them together out of three or four scraps. Often it seems like a poor joke to be offered these miserable rags for a piece of money." He blamed the appearance of paper money here on the Americans who "have built some miserably red houses, with windows like guillotines."

The Americans with their miserable red houses had made the place work. They started the Citizens Bank of Louisiana, La Banque des Citoyens de la Louisiane, in 1833. It issued notes up to a thousand dollars, which stood at par all the way up to Pittsburgh, all the way down through St. Paul and St. Louis to the gulf. Shavers got nothing from a bill on the Citizen's Bank. Steamboat captains, facing enough uncertainty on the maundering river, took them like gold. They were easy to recognize, with their bilingual denominations: even an illiterate steamboat worker could tell where they came from. Ten-dollar bills were favorites among the river people and travelers, easily broken for change, still convenient for fares, remarkable for the prominent *Ten—Dix* printed on their face. And people liked the word *Dix,* the look of it, the American way they pronounced it. They called the note a dix, and steamboat men in the North would say they were running "South after dixes." They were going, they said, to Dixie-land.

The song "Dixie" was written in 1859 by a northerner who had spent a happy summer in New Orleans, and the original first line ran, "Wish I wuz in the land of the dixes." It premiered at the Mechanics Hall, New York, but a year later New Orleans picked it up with enthusiasm. It was left to General Albert Pike of the

The dollar bill that named the South: these bilingual bills were known as "dixes," making the deep southern states where they mostly circulated the land of the dixes, or Dixie-land.

Confederacy to alter the words and turn it into a battle hymn and marching song.

SO HERE WAS Baker in the Confederate president's office, learning his answers from Brock's prattle, drawing the man along. The ruse was eminently successful: Brock confirmed that he knew him and Jefferson Davis let him go. He had scarcely reached the street before a hand came down on his shoulder. "Why! Baker!" cried a voice.

Turning thunderously, he found himself staring at a man he would never forget: the father of the child he had saved on the ferryboat twelve years before. It wasn't the moment for a joyous reunion. Baker cut him, saying he had the wrong man, leaving him perplexed on the sidewalk as he made his escape.

He walked. He had a pass for Fredericksburg, a hundred miles from the Potomac and safety. He dodged arrest twice, but found nothing to eat. Hunger and the question of a boat drove him to approach a tent by a creek that opened into the great river. Jammed between two suspicious Dutchmen in their tent, he had waited all night for an opportunity to escape. Dawn brought his chance. He slipped into the boat and pushed off.

Splash!

Lafayette Baker, not a cursing man, mutters a prayer. Holding a revolver in his right hand, with his left hand he plies a single moldy oar. He makes such slow progress that he has barely escaped the tree canopy that leans out over the creek when his captors come running down to the bank, wide awake and shouting.

"Come pack mit dat poat!"

One of them lifts a shotgun, and Lafayette Baker, steadying his right hand, drops him instantly with the revolver. His companion takes to his heels, crying for help. Baker pulls hard on the oar, and begins to inch out of the creek when a party of soldiers appears in the trees and opens fire. Bullets whack the water and splinter the sides of the boat, but now the current is drawing him steadily down-river and away from the southern bank. The river here is four miles wide. A gust of wind flips his hat into the water and lifts his coat off the stern plank, but he does not stop sculling for two and a half hours, when the keel grates on the northern shore. More exhausted than he ever felt in his life he flings himself onto the grass. The boat drifts away, following his coat and hat.

Over the next three years, Baker developed his detective skills. The war was no cleaner than any civil war, and as it boiled, so Baker raked off the scum—secretly, sometimes in disguise, infiltrating, keeping rendezvous, picking up rumors, and following them to the hilt. He could tell a deserter just by glancing at his hands. He learned to recognize all the symptoms of guilt, all its faces: blustery, violent, outraged, amused. Lafayette Baker could follow the byways of secession and treason as if they were lines drawn on a map.

He had power. Early in the war, Lincoln gave the State Department permission to "arrest and detain without the ordinary process of law such individuals as they might deem dangerous to the public safety." The War Department put Baker in charge of a new "National Detective Police." Habeas corpus was suspended. A fiat currency was introduced. The spirit of the Constitution was broken in defense of the Union.

THERE WERE PLENTY of bad places in Civil War Washington, from Camp Convalescent with its malingering bums and hoods and the shantytown bars and gruesome little shacks for getting clap, to swankier bordellos that Lafayette Baker—now a colonel at the War Department—used to raid, half for the pleasure of seeing senators and generals jump naked out of the windows. There were places of low entertainment, the best being the Canterbury, along with the first of those big, anonymous American hotels where you could get a room with no questions asked. And there was, as everyone liked to joke, the Treasury Department.

By the autumn of 1863 even Mrs. Clark was telling her husband that the Treasury Department was said to be a house of ill-fame. Newspapers were beginning to make sly allusions to the Treasury.

Secretary Chase questioned Clark as delicately as he dared, but Clark stuck stubbornly to the story he was giving his wife. The gossip made Salmon P. Chase feel ridiculous. If Clark said everything was proper and above board then so it was, and certainly Chase believed him. But right now he needed a little proof.

Chase had met Lafayette Baker only once, when on December 20, 1863, he personally summoned Baker to the Treasury.

The meeting was founded on a misunderstanding. Baker thought himself a champion of rectitude. He worshiped honor, gloried in success. Had Baker been less mesmerized by his sense of honor, he might have seen as much and perhaps evaded the events that ultimately secured his downfall and disgrace. His model was the French detective François Eugène Vidocq, who had more or less single-handedly invented detective police work in Paris earlier that century. Vidocq came from the criminal underworld; when he turned policeman, he used every trick in the book—disguises, informers, agents provocateurs, blackmail, and psychology—to worm his way back into the criminal mind, and the criminal world. He had laid down the principle, long held by continental European policemen, that it is better to punish the innocent than let one wrongdoer escape. Baker followed the principle minutely, sternly excusing his enthusiasm for making arrests by pointing out that there was a war on. Anyone who found this explanation insufficient was branded as a copperhead, or southern sympathizer.

Chase's mistake was to think of Lafayette Baker as a poodle. Americans, who preferred that justice, like government, be open and above board, viewed spying as low. The story of Civil War espionage is brief. Neither side started with any sort of machinery for gathering or digesting information, and both would have considered it rather beneath their dignity to have done so. Baker broke the mold, but when he rowed the Potomac with a pocketbook of observations nothing shows General Scott knew what to do with it—military leaders on both sides got perfectly satisfactory reports of enemy troop strengths and aims by reading each other's newspapers.

Self-belief was Baker's tragic flaw. The detective in him had few illusions, but he had too much energy to be a pessimist, and too much faith in himself to grow cynical. He had whistled down the California trail like an avenging angel, smacking bullies high and low, and as long as the world had Lafayette Baker, he supposed there was still hope. Six years lay between Baker swinging up the steps of General Scott's office and Baker's ultimate disgrace. Two years later came the private printing of *A History of the United States Secret Service,* starring Lafayette Baker on every page.

In action he was as quick-witted as he was brave. Milder men might have given themselves up in situations where Baker determined to rescue Baker for the world, and his best stories, when all is said and done, involve ingenious methods for saving Baker's hide. He once had half the Confederate army at his tail and clawed his way to freedom. He made forays across the border, and night escapes, and formed a mounted brigade in D.C. called Baker's Dozen, dedicated to bringing Mosby's Rangers to book. Mosby's achievements, coincidentally, included a raid on an excursion ferry that ended in the death of one of Clark's most promising engravers.

Everywhere Baker found himself he spotted terrible wrongdoing, and did something about it. A teetotaler, he was convinced that an end to drunkenness in the army would see the war brought to a successful conclusion in no time at all, and so he set about confiscating supplies of liquor to the troops, and more particularly the brandy and wines ordered up by officers. There was no end of angry generals and fuming subalterns once Baker had unearthed their scams. Dealing swift impartial justice as he went, his passage was marked by a stream of unfortunates diverted through the gates of Washington's horrible Old Capitol Prison. It was inevitable that when Baker, at

Chase's special request, left the War Office for the Treasury to peer into the activities of Clark and his colleagues on the fifth floor of the Treasury Building, he recoiled in open-eyed stupefaction. It seemed to him—because he was there—that he had seen the foundations of civilization in America shake.

WAR OR NO war, forgery was a never-ending menace. A rural occupation in days when American cities were places too small to hide in, "coneymen" were now part of the big-city underworld. Even before the federal government solidified its money power in Washington, the forgers had centralized theirs in New York City.

Concentrated in Lower Manhattan, the ordinary printing trade was going through a bad patch. The small jobbing printer Franklin would have recognized as a fellow spirit was not in such demand, and others who depended on his work—suppliers of ink and paper, type foundries, and press makers—were feeling the pinch. The area was changing too. By 1860 a warren of tightly packed houses reached up to Forty-second Street: no longer elegant, they were partitioned into slum dwellings for day workers on the waterfront, garment workers, petty shopkeepers. Hustling was a way of life for people who slipped between legitimate work and crime as opportunities arose. As the port grew, there was more to steal, and a rash of little stores provided somewhere to fence the goods. Crowds of shoppers on Broadway made fertile ground for pickpockets. Big-city stews no more cared where the money came from than their tiny colonial forebears, who had snaffled greedily at pirate gold, and in the dark, mean, crooked streets where drop-offs could be made without attracting much attention, the saloon bars were ideal for forging connections and making the deals that pushed the money out into the streets.

Most of the forgers were American-born. English immigrants were too flighty and inexperienced. The Irish preferred horses, and ran the faro and betting industry. Jews didn't do much counterfeiting. The Italians took to it as craftsmen; if they didn't have the right skills themselves, they sent to Italy. They were craftsmen of a more volatile temper though: perhaps they found the language hard. Congregating on the East Side, they brought a new level of violence to the easygoing rhythms of American criminal life. The English and Irish relied on blarney and bluster, and their fists; the Italians were always quick with a knife.

In the underworld, the greatest risks came from other criminals. Passing nightwatchmen posed little danger to burglars; constables existed only to help the courts serve papers. In big cities the arrival of a police force made the shovers, the small fry who actually took delivery of the "boodle" from retailers, more wary, but detective work was unpaid and had to be done on the policeman's own time. Rewards sometimes spurred them to this effort but so did the possibility of using information to extort money from a suspect. Police detectives were not held in very high regard.

Counterfeiters had a healthy market for their product, if they could reach it. It was the perfect victimless crime. Counterfeiters marketed their notes quietly to thieves and merchants, to saloon keepers, hoteliers, country store keepers, and peddlers. One New York dealer who bought "queer" off local wholesalers paid monthly visits to northern Pennsylvania, and sold to four regular customers including an attorney, a doctor, and a hotelier. Three wholesalers who served North Carolina and Tennessee in the 1870s put together a network of retailers and shovers who included a former Tennessee attorney general, a county commissioner, a deputy U.S. marshal, a county sheriff, eleven merchants, and twelve farmers. Shovers, at the bottom of the pile, often carried the highest risks, but they could do well in their humble way, working down a street and making small purchases in each store for change. In the summer of 1893 a New York lemon peddler who shoved five-dollar notes was banking as much as thirty-five dollars a day, and traveling shovers could do better still. When a New Orleans group hit Louisiana in 1866, they passed off twenty-three thousand dollars in fake greenbacks.

Some didn't even go to the trouble of counterfeiting. They ran the so-called green-goods game, running an advertisement with a price list, inviting prospective customers to write in for specimens "for their own advantage." With the list they got a genuine five-dollar bill. In 1893 the records of a major green-goods operation showed a profit of $40,185 in one month.

The counterfeit industry was naturally rather fluid. It took dedicated work, by several partners and experts, to make a decent counterfeit, and the business risk was high. Once a note was widely known to be counterfeit, the bottom dropped out of the market. Good new counterfeits retailed at anything up to thirty-five cents on the dollar; poor-quality notes, or known counterfeits, were to be had for half as much. Secrecy was paramount, of course, which caused supply problems—sometimes an active retailer missed the boat when a new set of counterfeit notes was distributed by the wholesaler. Sometimes the notes entered the market when prospective buyers, ironically, were running short of cash to pay for them. It was a difficult market to gauge.

Few partnerships endured. Drink and sudden giddy sprees soaked up the profits. Each successful partnership had to be built slowly and cautiously from scratch, assembling the right people to provide capital, supplies, potential customers, and technical skills. It was, all the way down the line, a question of knowing the right people.

NO SOONER HAD Spencer Morton Clark persuaded the treasury secretary to cut out the private banknote companies than an ambitious inventor approached him with a new kind of banknote paper that was bound to stop the counterfeiters in their tracks. The inventor was a small-time bankrupt called Stuart Gwynn, with an amazingly stiff and shiny paper unlike any ever made before. It was also very cheap, being produced at an ordinary mill and finished off in great secrecy by Stuart Gwynn himself. He called it "membrane paper"; but once he had the contract, and had installed himself in some style in the Treasury Building as the new "volunteer consulting engineer and chemist to the National Note Bureau," with his own paper-making rooms, laboratory, and offices, he preferred calling it "national paper." "Volunteer" meant he wasn't being paid directly, still "free to come and go as I pleased with my assistants and operatives." His profit came from his contract to supply the membrane paper.

Clark was delighted with his new discovery, and understandably put out to learn that the detective Baker had arrived with special instructions to look into Gwynn and his operations. The inventor, he pointed out, was not a Treasury employee, but was working in the building under secure conditions to apply the secret finish to his banknote paper. So secure were his premises, and so sensitive his secret, that not even the comptroller of the currency himself had any right to look at them. Standing with Baker in front of the locked door to Gwynn's workshop, he informed the irritated detective that it was perfectly impossible to let him in.

Baker wasn't a detective for nothing. Pulling open the door to an adjacent furnace room, he made for a door on the opposite side and stepped straight into Gwynn's impregnable stronghold. The workshop was stacked with paper. It was also full of people coming and going through the main door at the far end, which was open to the courtyard; through it he could see a gang of workmen relaying a pavement. A cheerful young operative who seemed to be in charge met Baker without surprise or alarm and answered his brief questions easily. What methods, for instance, did he use to stop people stealing the paper?

"None whatever, except we count the sheets at night."

Baker's response was to order the room cleared and locked.

More surprises were in store for the investigator when he started making inquiries in the printing rooms. Mr. Gwynn's remarkable membrane paper, it seemed, came as a surprise to the experienced men who worked the roller presses. To take a good impression and pass easily through the rollers, ordinary banknote paper had to be first lightly damped; damping was not a very scientific process but a good printer would know just how the paper should feel as it was laid on the printing bed. The new membrane paper needed no damping, according to its inventor. In fact, it couldn't take it: at the slightest touch of moisture, membrane paper grew hopelessly wrinkled. Left dry, on the other hand, it proved so hard and shiny that the ink refused to stick, and the impression just smeared off. The printers found themselves at a loss, but Gwynn and Clark saw this bothersome quality as the ultimate guarantee of security: if the government printers could do nothing with the paper then neither could counterfeiters. A new type of press, meanwhile, would have to be devised.

Dry printing was the philosopher's stone of the trade. It had been sought without success for years in Europe and America: a method of printing that did away with all need for dampening the paper first. To Baker's utter astonishment an unknown inventor and a relatively minor government functionary had chosen a moment in the middle of a desperate war, when demand for paper money was at its height, to relaunch the quest for printing's Holy Grail. Behind Baker stood his new friend Charles Neale, the bureau's chief printer and a troubled and unhappy man.

When Gwynn was installed in the spring of 1863, Neale was supplying the Union's acute demand for cash with fifty roller presses worked day and night by a team of around one hundred men, each machine rolling off about eight hundred impressions a day on standard banknote paper. For the sake of his new contract, Gwynn was designing a new sort of press that would bring an inked plate down flat on a dry sheet of his membrane paper with enough force to leave an impression, and the first of these revolutionary presses was delivered to the Treasury in May. It was worked by a handwheel, and within three hours it had broken down. Another five machines were ordered from a company in Baltimore and manhandled upstairs to the printing rooms, where they promptly exploded.

But Gwynn wasn't interested in the fate of the machines. What troubled him was their print quality. However hard a man dragged on the wheel, the plate could not quite leave a steady impression on his paper. Neale, the orthodox craftsman, pointed out that Gwynn's method was doomed to fail, for however hard the printing plate came down on the paper it was bound to leave air bubbles trapped beneath: with roller printing, bubbles were expelled as the paper slid between the rollers. Nothing in Gwynn's system could get rid of them, and air bubbles in the meantime kept the ink off the paper. Yet Gwynn was convinced that he only needed more power: a hydraulically operated press, squeezing down with astonishing force. He ordered another batch of machines from a firm in Pittsburgh, which soon joined the original six, damaged beyond repair, on the top floor of the Treasury Building. One after another the new machines broke down.

Gwynn was now a man possessed. As the machines exploded, he ordered others; eventually there were seventy-six of them crammed into Neale's attic, and the girders of the building started to bend under the weight. Gwynn's determination to press down harder on his dry printing plates peaked when he suspended a system of cranes and pulleys from the decorative cornice of the building to support a series of weights amounting to one hundred tons running down the side. The weights were to be ratcheted upward by a steam engine and then dropped; the force of the drop was to be transmitted via oil-filled hydraulic cylinders to the printing machinery under the roof. No doubt everyone was anxiously watching the presses to see them explode but as luck would have it the cylinders outside ruptured first. The second test brought the same result. This particular contraption, Baker later noted, was inherently unsafe, pointless, and created at a cost of twenty thousand dollars.

What had begun with the introduction of a cheap new type of paper had unaccountably ballooned into a potentially lethal experiment that threatened to bring the world's first office block down on the heads of anyone in it, or even just close. The costs were ridiculous—every one of Gwynn's exploding presses cost $1,700 (compared with a mere $120 for the reliable workhorse Neale and his printers were used to), and the roller presses worked seven times faster. Even the paper was liable to be filched from the supposedly secure workshop. According to Neale, Gwynn had boasted of making "such arrangements with the government that if the secretary of the treasury himself were to come in here, it would be only as a matter of courtesy." A day after he shut down Gwynn's paper rooms, Baker had him arrested and taken to the Old Capitol Prison, a rickety old building that had been hastily converted into Washington's newest and most overcrowded jail.

There Gwynn rotted. Baker's report was delayed by "the apparent indisposition of parties fully cognizant of the facts to testify in such a manner as to compromise Gwynn." The inventor appeared to have drawn $35,000 from the Treasury to pay for his paper works, and had held on to the money; meanwhile he owed money everywhere.

Yet the firms that had supplied machinery to the Treasury were coy about testifying. They had supplied thousands of dollars' worth of machinery under the impression that Gwynn was a fully representative agent of the Treasury Department, placing orders with the backing of the government, and nobody wanted him to go down with their debts still unpaid. Gwynn had been full of plausible explanations. The owner of one machine firm actually came down to Washington to check on Gwynn's credentials and was so thrown by the magnificence of Gwynn's establishment in the Treasury Building that he slipped away without bothering to trouble anyone at all, let alone Clark or Chase, whose continued goodwill he valued highly.

Baker was an expert in matters of fraud: despite his man-of-action tag, he did most of his work slogging through records of dodgy deals, blockade-running, smuggling, and false accounting. Everyone in Baker's world was on the take. Bounty hunters enlisted men for a fee, then sprang them from the recruiting yards and enlisted them all over again; merchants smuggled war matériel into Dixie under licenses to export ladies' millinery; dealers smuggled cotton back; quartermasters left whole armies underfed and pocketed the difference. Baker reckoned that Gwynn had not yet paid a single invoice, beyond a sum of $800 toward a claim of $34,000.

The more Baker thought about Gwynn, festering sadly in the Old Capitol Prison, the more bizarre he found him. Gwynn, he decided, was "a monomaniac on the subject of inventions," all of which seemed to involve the outlay of huge sums of other people's money. Going through Gwynn's papers, he found that he'd tried a new process of iron-plating ships, invented a new sort of insulatory telegraph wire, come up with a way to bore the Hoosic tunnel, tried to sell the government a steamer called the *Nephon,* and invented a new propeller and a heavy gun. The paper didn't even seem to be his own invention—a man called Hart in Boston had done all the experiments. Yet there was something tireless about Gwynn that Baker found disturbing, a kind of self-propelling confidence he dimly recognized.

Eventually Mrs. Gwynn arrived in Washington to try to get her husband out of jail, confessing to Baker that he had at one time been confined to a lunatic asylum. So much for him, the detective thought. Yet Baker was amazed to find workmen still busily tearing down a wall to put up two more of Gwynn's hydraulic contraptions. He was less surprised to discover that the order had been given in Gwynn's absence by Spencer Morton Clark.

AT THE OUTSET of the investigation, Chase had confessed to Baker that there seemed to be something wrong with Spencer Clark. Just what that was became familiar barroom gossip all over Washington. It had nothing to do with Stuart Gwynn, although Baker was already convinced that Clark's otherwise inexplicable dealings with Gwynn hid criminal motives of some sort. The vulgar multitude were not interested in Clark's attitude to membrane paper, after all. What intrigued them was Clark's attitude to the women he employed.

Washington has never been a salubrious city. British diplomats posted there used to get a hardship allowance to make up for the sultry summers and freezing winters, which made the city as uncomfortable as Calcutta or Rangoon; in the days before air-conditioning, the city was tolerable for less than three months in the year. At the time of the Civil War there was still malaria about, borne by mosquitoes that bred in the greasy waters of the Potomac. The infant drainage system provided for cholera and typhus to break out with monotonous regularity in August and September, sweeping through the slums of Murder Mile and sometimes creeping, via nuns and do-gooders with unwashed hands, into the more glittering purlieus of the place.

Buttons were undone, cravats loosened, starched collars unstiff-ened by sweating fingers. There were no fans or punkahs, just vene-tian blinds and the prayer of a breeze through an open window. In the Currency Bureau the heat in summer was especially infernal. The Treasury was one of the world's earliest office buildings, but nobody had yet dreamed up mass methods of sanitation or ventila-tion. When winter came, seven hundred coal fires were lit through-out the building. In summer, the banknotes stuck to the fingers and the rooms were dredged in dust. There were forty washrooms, but water had to be carried in by hand. Steam engines, dampened paper, gas lamps, and the quantity of human flesh rendered the atmo-sphere, already sultry, suffocating. Columns of paper dust rose up from the sorting office and stuck to the skin. Coal in the yards below sent dust aloft at the slightest breeze, and soot had already begun to stain the white stucco. Even the inks that were ground and mixed in the basement "permeated the building, fouling the air and discolor-ing the ceilings."

Just outside the Treasury Building stood a small shack, or kiosk, where a crippled Hungarian boy sold soda water. His father had come across with Kossuth in 1854, too young to accept defeat and eager to make a new life in the United States. He had six children in all, five boys and a pretty daughter, and one by one he set about find-ing them positions—draper's assistant, secretary, cashier, he ranged them around the city and its trades.

In 1862 he had petitioned the secretary of the treasury for permis-sion to erect the soda water stall for the benefit of his crippled son. Laslo managed the stall from eight in the morning until eight at night; one of his brothers would arrive with him to help him set up and fetch him again in the evening. Laslo soon knew the bureau women—they used to reel out of the Treasury Building at twelve o'clock and buy his water at fifteen cents a bottle, complaining of the heat and dust. In a short time he knew that the department was on the lookout for new girls, and that the wages were good. He passed the news on to his father, who was looking for a position for his daughter.

She stood the job for three weeks. Halfway through her fourth week she was sacked.

Her father was perplexed and furious; Laslo, meanwhile, had been watching people come and go: women from the bureau, he reported, often worked late at the office, and were regaled with more than soda water; some of them left positively drunk, and several had gone along with Clark or one of his male subordinates to the notorious Canterbury Hotel.

The next time a man from the bureau took a party of lady friends to the Canterbury in a closed carriage he was surprised and alarmed to see a brougham pull away from the curb behind him and keep up a measured distance to his rear. A few days later, the old Hungarian appeared at the office and spoke to Clark in private. His daughter returned to work, but the father had made sure she never worked late.

Several women who worked for Mr. Clark in the Currency Bureau had apartments at 276 Pennsylvania Avenue: they took home fifty dollars a week of their own money and paid their own bills.

They also kept love letters. Ella Jackson wrote a journal that Baker found in a search of her room. Ella was young—barely eighteen—and she lived in a state of independence that seemed to heighten her dependence on the men who came to pay her court. She slept with some of them, sometimes for money, and fell in love.

When her lover went out of town she wondered if he would come back. Sometimes she seemed overcome with remorse. "Oh ma, why did you ever leave me?"

Her diary, and various letters discovered in her rooms, opened the way to Clark's secret life. Baker brought Ella Jackson in for questioning and extracted a surprisingly frank statement about her relationship with Clark.

But even as Baker set about uncovering Clark's immoralities, Clark was preparing to launch a new five-cent note. Technically there was nothing wrong with it—a scythe leaned against the right-hand corner, and on the left a winged staff with a serpent coiled around it. The vignette was a portrait of some bearded worthy and the words *Fractional Currency* were draped tidily overhead. The bearded worthy, unfortunately, was Spencer Morton Clark.

When Spencer Morton Clark put himself on the five-cent note he was already under investigation for embezzlement, fraud, and sexual harassment. Congress immediately ruled that no one living could be represented on the currency of the United States.

This note caused a sensation. Queer things had turned up on dollar bills in the past, from Santa Claus to the Delaware rat, but nothing to match the appearance, on a U.S. note, of a bankrupt sex pest under investigation for embezzlement and fraud. Nineteen days after the new notes went into circulation, Congress passed a law forbidding the likeness of anyone living to be used on U.S. currency, stamps, or coins. The fact that Mr. Spalding, the inoffensive comptroller of the currency, appeared on the fifty-cent note was quietly ignored, while the five-cents were pulped. Clark was not the whit discouraged.

BAKER, NOT CLARK, suffered by his thorough investigation. A congressional committee offered two reports. One, it is true, spoke of "a mass of immorality and profligacy, the more atrocious as these women were employees of Clark, hired . . . for their youth and personal attractions. Neither the laws of God nor man, the institution of Sabbath, nor the common decencies of life, seem to have been respected by Clark in his conduct with these women. A Treasury Bureau, where is printed the money representative or expressive of all the property and all the industry of the country—there where the wages of labor are, more or less, regulated and upon the faith and good conduct of which depends, more or less, every man's prosperity—is converted into a place for debauchery and drinking, the very recital of which is impossible without violating decency." But this was the minority report, and it wasted no praise on Baker either, merely observing that he possessed the "unlimited confidence" of the secretary of war and that Chase himself "had such confidence in this officer, and in the value of his services, that he 'confidentially' requested the use of these services in the Treasury Department."

The officially accepted report was purest whitewash. General Grant had at last taken over the Union forces and was leading the army south to smash Lee: the public had already lost interest, though they might have heard Baker dismissed as a conspirator and a cheat, the women in the Treasury described as "wives or sisters of soldiers who had fallen in the field," and Spencer Clark as a man who had "conducted the affairs of his department with great energy and skill, and has made its operations successful against formidable obstacles and discouragements."

Freud thought that everyone was impelled by sex. Cynics think it is done for money. Historians see people go for glory, fame, a good name. Spencer Clark, with his finger in the till, his pants down, and his face on the five-cent note, was apparently impelled by all three at once. Clark was not removed from office. "Treasury woman" became a snickering euphemism for prostitute. The inventor Gwynn—whose own strange life had been marked by tragedy—launched a salvo of legal assaults on everyone. Even so, Salmon Chase, the vain and slippery treasury secretary, escaped censure, free to concentrate on his career ambitions, though the presidency eluded him.

As for Baker, he was instrumental in capturing Lincoln's assassin, John Wilkes Booth, but his card was marked. His enemies waited for him to slip—a secret agent without a handler, loose in the moral maze of Washington corruption and cronyism. When he ran up against the Washington establishment again over the impeachment of President Johnson, his enemies threw the book at him. Hauled into court, he was convicted of a rights violation. His enemies crowed, and the judgment finished his career. But the jury fined him one paper dollar.

His account of his Civil War role, which he wrote in 1867, is a cri de coeur from a man who felt himself sadly wronged. Scarcely had it appeared, in all its sensational detail, than he contracted meningitis and died.

· 13 ·

THE COUNTERFEITERS

A Chapter on the Secret Service—
Toy Money—An Almost Perfect Crime

Baker's successor at the "National Detective Force" (not a euphemism he ever accepted—he called it the Secret Service and its motto was *Death To Traitors*)—was his comrade-in-arms James Wood, who ran the Old Capitol Prison. The outfit he took over was a roughriding collection of rogues and ne'er-do-wells—almost half of them had done time in jail, and some were actually convicted murderers. Together they were rather successful. In 1865 they made a sweep of western counterfeiters and secured two hundred convictions. But their powers were irregular, their methods flamboyantly so, and as the mood of emergency eased after the war, Wood found himself replaced. The service was reformed to act as the guardian of America's sovereignty, protecting the president and the currency. It sought out a more middle-class type of officer, and as they wrote out their expenditure accounts and filed their unimpeachable reports, the Secret Service became less quixotic and more orderly. The new Secret Servicemen were less pally with the criminals, who they did not know socially. Agents began to infiltrate the gangs. Shovers who were caught stayed caught. Confessions were welcome, but agents gave no guarantees. Fake bills were detected more quickly and, when detected, publicized to the world. For the first time, the counterfeiters began losing confidence.

The Secret Service's metamorphosis was a symptom of Washington's rising influence in all spheres of American life. The federal government had increased its powers through the Civil War—it had been easier to do so when the most unruly or disobedient states were in secession—and most notably its control over money. The National Bank Act of 1863 exploited the wartime emergency to make every bank that wished to issue currency hold its charter from the federal government; a tax was levied on state banknotes to kill them off and drive the latecomers into the system; and the dollars they issued were exactly alike, except for the name and place of the bank, just as Jacob Perkins had suggested sixty years before. No one could simply turn banker with "a furioso plate—flaming with cupids, locomotives, rural scenery, and Hercules kicking the world over." Gone were the riotous raw times when one impudent counterfeiter made spurious notes on the so-called Ohio River Bank (the Ohio River had two banks, neither of which issued dollar bills).

Now the dollar was an affair of state. It was no longer acceptable, for instance, for businessmen to print so-called flash notes, advertisements rigged up to look like dollar bills—nothing grabbed people's attention quite like a dollar. State banknotes, after all, had not been so very different: apart from serving as money, they also publicized a bank or a project of the bank. But the dollar now represented the sovereign majesty of the United States. Congress ruled flash notes illegal in 1867, and the Secret Service enforced the law. Respectable businessmen were astonished to find themselves suddenly ordered to surrender their advertising copy, dies, and plates, or face arrest. In August 1881 the Secret Service turned on a Manhattan toy shop and demanded a list of all the games manufacturers who supplied the trade with play money. Agents swooped, confiscated their supplies and equipment, and concluded the operation in November 1881, when R. H. Macy solemnly surrendered 160 boxes of toy money for destruction.

In 1883 the Secret Service was outsmarted by a deaf-mute hustler from Boston called Josh Tatum. The Mint had just produced its first copper-nickel coin, a five-cent piece with a big V on the back. Various mottoes were on the coin but not the word "cents." Some people thought it looked quite like the five-dollar half eagle. Tatum operated on this theory. He gold-plated a thousand nickels and set out to buy five-cent cigars. Being a deaf-mute, he pointed to the cigar, laid a plated nickel on the counter, and waited to see what happened. If the clerk dropped the coin into his cash desk, Tatum walked out with a cigar. More often, though, he walked out with a cigar and $4.95 in change.

So he had five thousand nickels plated, and started traveling between New York and Boston. He spent around three thousand of his coins, always on a five-cent item, and received thousands of dollars in change. When the Secret Service brought him to trial, the judge reluctantly let him off: poor Josh Tatum, said his attorney, couldn't say that his five dollars was only a nickel, so he took the change. Even gold-plating a nickel wasn't strictly illegal: it was still a nickel.

The last great counterfeit operation of the nineteenth century was put together by two cigar makers, Jacobs and Kendig, whose first idea was to forge the excise label put on cigar boxes after duty was paid and so skip the tax. To work the scam, they pulled in two young engravers with experience in securities and banknotes: Taylor—short, fat, and blond; Brendell—a tall, dark, studious fellow who could copy machinery "just by looking at it." Jacobs set them up in their own print shop on Walnut Street in Philadelphia.

Excise labels were printed on paper with the watermark USIR for U.S. Internal Revenue. So Kendig ran off a letterhead for the Indian Rheumatic Ulmer Syrup Company of Lancaster, and got an old German paper maker in Chambersburg to make him ten tons of wrapping paper with a watermark bearing the company initials repeated across the paper. IRUS became USIR. Taylor and Brendell did the engraving, and the phony labels saved Jacobs so much duty that he doubled his output of cigars, to 45 million a year.

Early in 1896, the cigar men drew their engravers toward higher things: $10 million in perfect counterfeit $100 bills. Taylor got down to an engraving of James Madison, and Kendig took Brendell to Massachusetts to see how government banknote paper was made at the Crane Paper Mill. Progress was slow, but sure. At last, in June 1897, Taylor and Brendell carried out early trials. They printed onto paper that Brendell had prepared by splitting some dollar bills in half, bleaching off the ink, then pasting them back together with a silk thread in between the halves.

Altogether they do ninety-seven trial $100 bills. The quality is excellent. In July and August, saying nothing to Kendig and Jacobs, the engravers pass a few of the trial notes in Philadelphia with absolute success. Taylor takes the rest on a trip south, and soon they have about $8,000 in legitimate cash, which they split, and get back to work.

It is late December before a sharp-eyed teller at the U.S. Sub-Treasury in Philadelphia notices that a vermilion Treasury seal on a $100 bill in his pile is less gorgeous than usual. Colleagues conclude that the Treasury's inking machinery must have misfired momentarily, until four more bills with the same lightly inked seal turn up that week. On January 3, 1898, the teller takes all five with him on a routine trip to Washington. Apart from the color of the seal, the bills appear to be genuine. Treasury experts agree that the notes are the result of a mechanical fault, although some wonder if the notes could have been stolen from the bureau or the Treasury before the seal was placed on them. What nobody really dares contemplate is the possibility that they are counterfeit through and through.

So the notes are taken later that day to the Secret Service offices where the country's leading expert on counterfeits finds nothing wrong with them either, except for the pale seal. Perhaps the paper feels a trifle thick. On a hunch he puts one note in a pan of hot water and in twenty minutes—to general dismay—the two halves separate, and the silk thread floats free.

He then begins to scan the notes line by line, identifying half a dozen minuscule variations—like a missing crosshatch on Monroe's buttons—simply too slight for adequate description. The next day, the *New York Times* informs its readers:

> TREASURY OFFICERS FOOLED BY A BOGUS ONE-HUNDRED-DOLLAR SILVER CERTIFICATE. In view of the dangerous character of the counterfeit, Secretary Gage today decided to stop issuing and call in all one-hundred-dollar silver certificates of which there are about twenty-six million dollars outstanding.

The news brought the cigar men racing to the printing shop. Frightened and ashamed, the hapless engravers admitted that they had pulled off the eight-thousand-dollar scam that had led the government to withdraw the design they had so ably counterfeited. Ten million dollars lost for the sake of a few thousand! It was a tense moment: Jacobs snatched the printing plates and stormed out of their shop. Later he cooled down. After all, the Treasury had never pulled an issue of bills before: Brendell and Taylor were obviously better than he had ever imagined. Kendig was sent to soothe their feelings, and present them with a yet bigger plan to do a whole range of bills, from ten dollars to one hundred dollars. The shamed engravers hastily agreed.

In the meantime Secret Service chief John Elbert Wilkie, former city editor of the *Chicago Tribune,* had drawn up a profile of the counterfeiter: a young man who had never gone on the records before, perhaps living in Philadelphia where the first forgeries had appeared. He had agents onto every decent engraver in the country, wherever they were employed, looking for signs of sudden affluence. He wanted to know who sounded busy. In Philadelphia an agent posing as a western printer advertised for talented engravers who could handle photoengraving.

Taylor and Brendell answered the ad. The agent soon found that they fitted his brief: diamond rings, fur coats for their wives, a vacation trip to the South. Surveillance was increased. The houseboy at the printing premises was induced by the promise of a theater career to change into a rented masquerade costume, while another agent searched his knickerbockers for the shop key and made a copy, all in the time it took to give the boy an "audition" (they told him to keep the day job).

Waiting until the counterfeiters had shut up shop and gone home for the night, the agents let themselves in and found enough work in progress to know they had their men. Still they bided their time, and they got their break when they followed Taylor to Jacobs's cigar factory. On a hunch, Wilkie had the cigars' revenue stamps examined, and they proved to be false. Soon twenty-eight Secret Servicemen were snooping around the town.

Kendig and Jacobs buried the cigar plates and persuaded a member of an eminent law firm to offer the Secret Service a bribe. The screws were tightened. On April 18, 1899, Brendell and Taylor were arrested at their shop. Kendig and Jacobs were picked up the next day. The lawyer was reeled in. After a further attempt was made to bribe jurors, the lawyer got thirty months; Kendig and Jacobs went down for twelve years apiece, with five-thousand-dollar fines. Taylor and Brendell trembled in their cells.

Their attorney told them of a notorious counterfeiter who had bargained his freedom in return for handing over the actual printing plates, which the government considered too dangerous to lose. Unfortunately, in their eagerness to cooperate Taylor and Brendell had already turned their plates over to the Secret Service. The attorney mused on this, and wondered if they had actually turned over *all* the plates. The hapless engravers cottoned on. If they could only secretly turn out a new counterfeiting plate, they would be in a position to bargain with the authorities. In a cell nine by six, using smuggled tools, Brendell and Taylor set about manufacturing a whole new counterfeit plate, one of them working at night under a blanket in the corner while the other slept. They split a one-dollar bill, oiled it transparent, and concocted a photographic emulsion from the kitchen. They developed the photographs in the light of their barred four-inch window, moving the plate slowly to and fro so that the bars would leave no shadow. With two plates, one for the back and one for the front, they began etching. They bleached 150 new dollar bills with a solution they boiled up from the prison food.

Taylor's brother provided black and green ink. Brendell told his father that he had invented a new kind of ironer for French cuffs, and that he wanted a prototype made so he could tinker with it in prison. Brendell's brother smuggled it in: it fitted into a cigar box. The cuff iron operated as a miniature printing press, and for several nights Taylor and Brendell took turns to print the notes. When they had used up all the paper, the materials were smuggled out again.

In May 1900 Taylor's brother began to pass the bills. On the thirty-second pass the bill was questioned. The rest he burned. Interviewed by the Secret Service chief, he explained, as arranged, that Taylor and Brendell had left the equipment behind when they were imprisoned. The two counterfeiters told the same story. Yet as fate would have it the bill they had copied had in fact been issued after they went to prison, as a routine check on the serial number now revealed. Taylor's brother was arrested for conspiracy. For his sake Brendell and Taylor surrendered their plates and agreed to testify against their attorney.

He walked free. He produced expert testimony to show that the prison counterfeit could only have been made with an eight-ton press, four assistants, a five-hundred-dollar camera, and a twenty-by-twenty workroom. Even when Taylor and Brendell were obliged to demonstrate their tiny apparatus the jury remained unconvinced.

Taylor and Brendell got seven years each. They came out in March 1905. Brendell set up an engraving firm, keeping his old friend in work until Taylor died in the mid-twenties. He became head of an engraving department in a Philadelphia publishing house until 1934, when he started the Girard Bank Note Company, probably to tease the Secret Service. They were in the habit of visiting Brendell whenever a clever counterfeit appeared on the streets, and in 1938 they finally gave the Girard Bank Note Company the once-over. Nothing untoward was found. The Secret Service concluded that none of the counterfeits in circulation was up to Brendell's standard anyway. He died in 1956.

· 14 ·

THE GREAT CONSPIRACY

Federal Dollars—Silver and Gold—The Crime of '73—
Cataline Assemblages—Coin Harvey—
The Wizard of Oz—Almighty Dollar or Almighty God—
The Boy Orator—A Cross of Gold

Looking back on the Civil War, Congressman James G. Blaine recalled that paper money had been a jolly experience for almost everyone. "As trade revived under the stimulus of an expanding circulation, as the market for every species of product was constantly enlarging and prices were steadily rising, the support of the war policy became a far more cheerful duty to the mass of our people," he intoned. "The engagement of the people in schemes of money-making proved a great support to the war policy of the government. Money was superabundant; speculation was rife; the Government was a lavish buyer, a prodigal consumer. Every man who could work was employed at high wages; every man who had commodities to sell was assured of high prices."

The prices, however, went higher than the wages: the soldiers got a three-dollar hike to their basic thirteen dollars a month in 1864, but prices meanwhile doubled. When the war ended the government stopped buying, and prices declined by 15 percent; wages sank faster as men were discharged from the army. Salmon P. Chase, who had sanctioned the issue of $450 million in greenbacks in wartime, now fretted that they were unconstitutional: no wonder that a greenback dollar was worth only half as much as its gold equivalent. He wore a gold dollar on his watch chain, "intending to keep it there till the greenback was as good as it was," and in 1864 left the Treasury Department to become chief justice of the Supreme Court.

Congress now ordered the gradual withdrawal of the government paper currency, at a rate of $10 million a month. This move to shrink the money supply aroused vigorous opposition in the midst of a postwar slump. Congress nervously agreed to a halt to the withdrawals. They even issued a few more. A decade later a compromise froze the value of greenbacks in circulation at $375 million, a sum that remained technically unchanged until 1986.

Chase got his chance to settle a money case in 1870 when a creditor who had lent gold dollars refused to accept payment in depreciated greenbacks and went to court. Chase ruled that the greenbacks he had invented, and which bore his own image, were not constitutional. Even Congress could not force a creditor to take back paper for the gold he had lent. Greenbacks existed as currency, certainly, but they were not actually legal tender. They were rather like wampum two hundred years before.

The words "legal tender for all debts, public and private" still appear on the face of every dollar bill because a shuffle of judges and a new case allowed the Supreme Court to overturn Chase's ruling the next year. The court decided that the government was entitled to issue legal-tender paper money because that power was latent and implicit in the right of sovereignty, not itself expressly withheld from the Congress.

Commenting on the national banknotes, Senator John Sherman had meanwhile predicted that a uniform currency would make "every stockholder, every mechanic, every laborer who holds one of these notes . . . interested in the Government." His grim prophecy proved correct. Americans rose to the challenge in legions. Anything about the dollar that had ever interested them, or antagonized them, or encouraged or bamboozled them, was now a government responsibility, and they could even do something about it. Before they had grumbling and unease. For the next thirty years different interest groups would drive the dollar into the footlights of politics and attempt to cudgel it into submission in full view of the whole nation. In 1875 a Greenback Party entered American politics, polling a million votes in the congressional elections of 1878. Greenbackers wanted greenbacks to circulate forever; and they wanted more of them. They sang:

> *Thou, Greenback, 'tis of thee,*
> *Fair money of the free,*
> *Of thee we sing.*
> *And through all coming time*
> *Great bards in every clime*
> *Will sing with joyful rhyme,*
> *Gold is not king.*

> *Then smash old Shylock's bonds,*
> *With all his gold coupons,*
> *The banks and rings.*
> *Monopolies must fail,*
> *Rich paupers work in jail,*
> *The right will then prevail,*
> *Not money kings.*

They were against banks and hard money, and believed that the government should have the right to issue its own currency on their behalf.

IN 1875 THE outgoing Republican Congress settled the greenback question—and passed trouble on to its successors—when it bound the country to redeem its greenback dollars in gold and at face value on January 1, 1879. The doomsayers predicted that on that day a rush on government gold stocks would bankrupt the nation. They were wrong. Without a murmur the public turned "the grandest page in the history of the United States," as the *New York Daily Tribune* called it. Flags were flying on Wall Street. The greenbacks turned out to be quite as much in demand as gold and silver, because the nation's economy had simply grown up to the extra money. The value of a paper dollar had been rising cent by cent until, two weeks before the great redemption date, greenbacks were on par with gold dollars. An anxious treasury secretary telegraphed from Washington to find out what was happening. The answer was nothing. A mere $135,000 in greenbacks had been presented for gold, while the same day $400,000 in gold had been changed into the more convenient paper money.

Even Spencer Clark's fractional currency had finally disappeared, as dog-eared and disgusting as the long-lost *picaillons* of New Orleans. In the winter of 1877 all the little silver coins that had vanished when the first greenbacks were issued came flooding home. Hundreds of millions of three cents, five cents, dimes, quarters, and half-dollars mysteriously bubbled back into the channels of trade. Many had spent the last fifteen years in Canada, but others had gone to South America where they had formed an entirely new local currency. Few people wondered why they came; everyone was simply glad to have their coins again.

THE UNITED STATES became a major producer of the world's silver around the time of the Civil War. Output doubled between 1870 and 1873, and by 1893 it had doubled again, making the United States the world's biggest silver producer after Mexico. Most American silver was coming from states that hadn't been states at all until silver came. But by the 1890s Nebraska, Nevada, Montana, and Colorado had sprung from the desert, boasting capitols, boom towns, hog roasts, railroads, street lighting, churches, bums, museums, do-gooders, and, not least, senators and representatives in Washington who owed everything to the fair metal. Their populations were small, but not their political clout. There was only one thing that bothered the silver miners. The faster they turned out the precious metal, the less the world seemed to want it.

Gold was still in demand. All across Europe countries were following Britain's lead of 1821, abandoning silver and going over to the gold standard.[1] They could see that Victorian Britain was richer and more successful than any other nation. In 1821 she had decided to stick, through thick and thin, to the principle that every note issued by the Bank of England would be honored on demand in the world's scarcest precious metal. Britain's commercial supremacy—from which flowed her naval supremacy and her empire—seemed to have followed as a direct result: it took a Disraeli to suggest that the gold standard was the effect, not the cause, of British prosperity.

---

1. They were also following in the footsteps of Jefferson and decimalizing their coinage: Italy in 1861 and Germany in 1871, when each country was unified; Austria in 1873; Russia in 1900.

The French had inevitably caviled. In 1867 Napoleon III had held a conference in Paris to urge the nations of the world to agree to a standard that would admit both gold and silver as money. France had two coins worth five francs, one a very small coin of gold and the other of silver. Switzerland, Belgium, Italy, and Greece had used the five-franc piece as a model for identical coins, an early dream of world money. The American delegation doubted that their country would accept a new dollar that looked like the French five-franc coin; the Germans disagreed with the whole project; the British did not bother to attend; and the conference broke up. The last conference on the subject was called in 1892 by the United States, eager to the last to find some role for silver in international trade and finance. By then, though, nobody else on the international scene shared the U.S.'s difficulties: every European country had adopted the gold standard.

"We chose gold, not because gold is gold, but because Britain is Britain," explained one German politician. When they attacked and beat the French in 1871, the Germans hoped that the "reparations" they imposed in return for peace would give them the money they needed to switch to gold. The French turned to gold to spite the Germans: they not only refused to buy Germany's silver but started to sell their own in 1873. With both countries selling silver, others began to join them in panic. The price of silver fell again.

America's silver-mine owners felt the blast. For years, as fast as they had the precious metal hacked from the seam, buyers had stood poised to whisk it all away and make them rich. For years they'd enjoyed fancy prices in Europe and the Far East. Silver was far too valuable to make into dollars: it was worth more as bullion than as money. In other words, while a silver dollar in coin was worth only a dollar, the same amount of silver, melted down and turned into gold, gave you enough gold to buy more than a dollar's worth of goods. But the balance was changing. The silver men were down to a dollar for a dollar, and praised God for Hamilton, who had declared a silver dollar as good as a gold one. Senator Benton, of course, had slightly tilted the balance against them—thanks to him, it took sixteen parts of silver to make one part of gold—but that silver all the same was gushing from the mines.

But when the mine owners cast about for the buyer from the Mint, they discovered that the U.S. had silently dropped her commitment to silver herself. They called it the Crime of 1873, but it was really a quagmire of doubt, theory, and politics into which all America stumbled and floundered for the next quarter of a century.

With hindsight, it made no difference whether dollars were gold, silver, paper, or bank credits. In practice they were generally credits—the country was moving on to the use of checks, whose modern equivalents are our plastic cards. Nothing tangible, not even paper, secures our wealth: money is numbers, plus regulations, plus belief. By the late nineteenth century, four out of five dollars existed only in bank ledgers. Why didn't people see that it no longer much mattered what sort of currency they used, provided the numbers moved about? Why didn't Americans, experimenters, above all, see that?

The numbers didn't move as quickly as they do now: money, in the jargon, was inelastic. Based on precious metal, and on reserves, it wasn't always in the right place at the right time. Industry—packed around a town—grew its own money centers; agriculture—spread over thousands of square miles—didn't. Someone in New York or Chicago with money to lend found it hard to connect with a farmer in the middle of nowhere who wanted to borrow.

The money in New York or Chicago was connected to money abroad. As long as money was backed by a metal, the farmer's demand for money might have to be answered, ultimately, somewhere in Europe where the metal was idle and waiting for the call. The farmer's weak signal took a long time to filter through the layers of middlemen who each helped decide where money ought to go.

So one response to the periodic crisis—when the money simply wasn't there, and needy people went bankrupt while money was stashed uselessly away elsewhere—was to demand more money. If local banks could create and lend more, the squeeze would pass. If money were cheaper—if it were more plentiful—there wouldn't have to be a squeeze at all. Classical economists called this a confusion between capital and currency. But many contemporaries pointed out that the squeeze paid the squeezer. The banker got a better rate for tight money. He was on the East Coast; he was way across the Atlantic. He fixed it that money was scarce by wrecking any attempt to make more money.

AMERICANS FROM Jefferson on had been remarkably watchful of British efforts to rearrange America's finances to their own advantage. They never doubted that the attempt would be made. Britain was rich and had an empire, but she could be expected to see the United States as the one that got away. America was largely built on British capital, for sure, but the British were always complaining about the risk. The dollar was unstable and returns did not always match expectations. Sometimes debts had been scandalously repudiated: "Yankee Doodle borrows cash, / Yankee Doodle spends it," crowed an infuriated English poet in the 1840s. "And then he snaps his fingers at / The jolly flat who lends it." (How deeply involved the English must have been, when even their poets held American securities!) Some Americans went in dread of an "attack" from Lombard Street, or so they later said.

Of course Americans had missed it when it came, they explained. For the impact of the Civil War was still sending ripples across America when English capitalists seized a fugitive opportunity to transform America's monetary landscape in a manner so innocent that almost nobody would realize what was happening. The British used the stiletto, and America went on walking for several years before the lifeblood of the republic was found to be draining through the concealed wound.

In the winter of 1872 Sir Ernest Seyd, a British financier and monetary theorist, arrived quietly in New York and took the train for Washington. According to the story Seyd was a regular and respectable visitor to America. He had a bag containing a hundred thousand pounds in cash, and a mission to put an end to America's financial independence. The Rothschilds had advanced him the money. Congress had given him the pretext. Silver dollars were his target.

Congress was about to consider a dull technical bill for "revising and amending the laws relative to the Mints, assay offices and coinage of the United States." Nobody—not even legislators—had given much attention to the bill; they gathered that it would help the Mint and the Treasury sort things out internally after the dislocation of the Civil War, which was perfectly true. The bill contained a list of all the coins that the Mint could produce as legal tender—cents, dimes, eagles, and so on.

All Seyd had to do was to get the silver dollar dropped from the sacred list. No one was going to pay much attention to a routine bill like this. Seyd sailed for England, as quietly as he had come. The 1873 act made no mention of the silver dollar as legal tender. Hamilton's bimetallism was finished.

✌

AGAIN AND AGAIN, the "silverites" who peddled this story were reminded that the real reason no one had attacked the coinage bill was not, as they claimed, because it had been whistled through Congress in secret, but because silver's market value in 1873 had been so high that a silver dollar of 371 grains, set down by Hamilton, was actually worth $1.03.

No mining outfit was going to lose three cents on the dollar by bringing its silver to the mint for coining. No one in 1873 cared whether the silver dollar lived or died—it was only a legal fiction, not a real coin. Senator Sherman of Ohio assured the Senate that in all his years in business he had never clapped eyes on a silver dollar. Striking the coin from the list in 1873 merely recognized a situation that had prevailed for more than half a century. The silver lobby talked about conspiracy, but the coinage bill got full debates in both houses, and explicit reference had been made to the demonetization of silver. Several representatives who later claimed it had been "stolen through Congress" were on record approving it. It had been before Congress for three years before it went to a vote, with a paragraph captioned in capital letters, SILVER DOLLAR—ITS DISCONTINUATION AS A STANDARD. It had received thirteen printings. It got 144 columns in the *Congressional Globe*. One insider said it was given "as careful attention as I have ever known a committee to bestow on any measure."[2]

There was, as it happened, conspiracy of a sort. Various leading Republicans already foresaw that the value of silver was set to fall. They were afraid that if the U.S. supported its dollar in silver as well as gold, gold would disappear as its value rose, and the country would be left operating on a silver standard, which would create

---

2. The same man later claimed he "did not know that the bill omitted the silver dollar."

inflation and, more worryingly, a barrier between a silver America and a golden world. Above all, it would be harder to raise money in London, the center of international capital.

But the silverites could never resist the spicier embellishments to the story, and never wavered from their conviction that for a hundred thousand pounds or less, the British financial establishment and its Wall Street dependents had shackled the freedom of the United States and reduced its people to the status of colonial dependents.

By "demonetizing" silver, the silverites argued, half the money available to Americans—the silver half, the old money of the poor and the respectable—was withdrawn from circulation. Gold's monopoly would slash prices and wages as money grew scarce, but the rich would do very well. They had been craftily saddling debt onto the United States ever since Hamilton first found a way of funding it. Now the rich had stopped the United States using its large and adequate supplies of silver to pay the debt as God and nature had decreed. They had shrunk down the money supply and wanted solid gold. All the silver in America—including the silver dollar, the old dollar of Jefferson and Hamilton, what people now called affectionately and regretfully "the dollar of the daddies"—was to be turned into making the silver spoons that lackeys of British economic imperialism had in their mouths at birth.

"These conspirators have kept up their Cataline assemblages ever since," wrote E. J. Farmer in 1886 in *The Conspiracy Against Silver or a Plea for Bimetallism in the United States,* "and, backed by England, have their daggers ever ready to strike down the silver dollar. No statement is too false for them to make; no scheme too dastardly to attempt—the exaltation of their golden idol is their one song, and as priests do to the golden Juggernaut, they smile to see the wreck and ruin its gilded wheels have wrought; while around this car may be seen the bloody footprints of the British lion."

Sir Ernest Seyd appears to have been an inoffensive, studious family man who had made a name for himself in the City and wrote dull books on finance; his family were at first exasperated and finally patiently amused by the furor that surrounded him on the other side of the Atlantic. Sarah E. V. Emery released her book *Seven Financial Conspiracies which have Enslaved the American People* in 1887. Their efforts to salvage his reputation went unrewarded among people who insisted that choosing Seyd as a go-between had been the cleverest—most chillingly ruthless—part of the whole plot.

The damning of Seyd's soul was in full swing when someone owlishly observed that Sir Ernest Seyd had never been a "gold bug" at all. Rather the opposite: he had been a proponent of a combined gold and silver standard all his life, and had written a major study on bimetallism. The gold bugs crowed with happy relief, but the silverites merely digested this new fact and promptly turned it to their own advantage: it only went to show just how powerful and cunning the money power really was. Far from being abashed when their opponents brandished Seyd's book, *Bimetallism,* under their noses, the silverites read the book, agreed with most of its contents, and followed Gordon Clark, author of the 1896 *Handbook of Money,* in explaining that Seyd was under *normal* circumstances a bimetallist, but "as 'adviser of the Bank of England,' [he] was forced to postpone his theories, when that huge octopus came to see its fat prey in the United States. He was in a difficult position. For the time, he was serving his country, his friends and his blood, as against a country that England, at heart, still regards as a rebel to her throne and policy. . . . Though untrue to his deepest convictions, he is to be blamed somewhat as Americans blame the unfortunate Major Andre, whom Washington hanged with heart-felt sorrow. Andre was a true Englishman; and so, by position, was Seyd."

Clark's identification of Seyd as a dandy, a Jew, and an Englishman just about settled his case. So it could hardly be shaken by evidence that Sir Ernest Seyd had spent the spring of 1873 in London, had never been to Washington, had not, in fact, visited the United States at all since 1856. These were details. "When I was a boy," said the arch-silverite William Harvey, "I heard a lawyer say 'When a crime is committed and you want to detect the criminal, look for the man that is benefited by the crime.' Reasoning by induction will more invariably locate the criminal than any uncertain human testimony." To the immense frustration of establishment propagandists, the U.S. Treasury really had sent Seyd a draft of the bill for comment in 1872. Thereafter the plot was quite apparent. Seyd had left blank sheets of paper, signed by him, in London: they were filled in while he was away, to give the impression that he had stayed in London. His name was carefully kept out of Washington hotel registers, ship's passenger lists, and even local newspapers; for proof, one had only to consult the registers and lists for the period to see how his name never appeared, although the *National Republican,* a Washington paper, had almost given the game away with its mention of "an eminent foreign banker" in connection with the coinage bill.

The conspiracy theory behind the Crime of 1873 had an enduring appeal. It was still news as late as 1946, when Olive Cushing Dwinell published *The Story of Our Money,* all in quotes interspersed with semaphoric captions "couched," as the introduction put it, "in a language which is nothing if not vigorous." She could turn the volume up and down. In 1878 Senator Voorhees had this to say on the crime:

> The 12th day of February, 1873, approached, *the day of doom* to the American (silver dollar, the dollar of our fathers, *how silent was the working of the enemy!*). Not a sound, not a word, not a word of warning to the American people *that their favourite*

coin was about to be destroyed; THAT THE GREATEST FINANCIAL
REVOLUTION OF MODERN TIMES WAS IN CONTEMPLATION,
AND ABOUT TO BE ACCOMPLISHED AGAINST THEIR DEAREST
RIGHTS!

In *The Story of Our Money,* President Grant is quoted as saying, "I
did not know that the Act of 1873 demonetized silver. I was deceived in
the matter." And a host of notable Americans—senators, representatives, even economists—line up behind him to deliver their terrible,
italicized, and capitalized Götterdämmerung on the Crime of 1873.

Silver had a tireless advocate in William "Coin" Harvey. Harvey
had worked in a silver mine, the Silver Bell in Colorado. He slept in
the engine house, ready to dash out at any second if he heard the
bucket winches stop. Later he blamed his rheumatism on his habit
of running down the shaft in his nightdress that year. Mining
seemed a sure thing until the price of silver started falling—from
$1.32 an ounce in 1872 to $1.11 in 1884 and a paltry 63 cents in 1894.
In three years Harvey was down to selling real estate and an elixir of
life: he sometimes claimed to be a Scottish descendant of Sir
William Harvey, who discovered blood circulation. He had a mineral palace erected in Pueblo, Colorado, which featured a one-and-a-
half-ton block of coal carved into a massive figure, King Coal.
Moving to Utah, he organized the biggest promotional carnival in
the West for Ogden, bringing the real Mardi Gras king and queen
up from New Orleans for the event. The carnival was a total loss and
Harvey was broke. He went to Chicago and set up the Coin Publishing Company, dedicated to the cause of his western friends, free
coinage of silver at a ratio of sixteen to one.

One of his jaunty publications ran a poem that, like much of the
free silver propaganda, is irritating to read, but curiously difficult to
forget:

The prise uv wheet wuz fawling fast
As up wall street a banker past
His kloze perfumed and smellin nise
While threw hiz hed ran this devise
Sownd munney

From albion's shores heed just arrived
With plans mature & well contrived
& softly in the kokney tung
he warbled owt with hiz wun lung
sownd munney.

O stay thy hand the widow kride
Evikt not those so harshly tride
He simply sed economize
& then thay herd abuv her krys
sownd munney.

William Harvey's little book, *Coin's Financial School,* was a best-seller when it appeared in 1894, the publishing phenomenon of the age, "sold on every railroad train by the newsboys and at every cigar store . . . read by almost everybody." Mrs. Harvey thought it must have sold a million copies. Harvey himself guessed a million and a half, with four hundred thousand shifting in the first eleven months. It was a frisky little book that pitted living American experts in banking and economics, one after another, against a rather preco-cious child, who trounced them on the silver question. Some experts wrote their own bitter ripostes—*Coin's Financial Fool* was one of them, and *Coin at School in Finance;* they lacked Harvey's relent-less style and weren't so successful. None of these debates had ever taken place, and "Coin" was full of nonsense—bogus assumptions, misapplied analogies, false history, and general windbaggery—but it was a compulsively readable explanation for the state of affairs plenty of Americans found themselves in, commanding territory Americans were deeply familiar with.

Americans had joined in battles for and against a Bank of the United States, a uniform currency, free banking, no banking, private money, government money. They had experience of Continentals, shaver's shops, rampant counterfeits, scrip and shinplasters, convertible notes, bills of credit, foreign coins, and mint ratios. "Easy money" was an American coinage; so was "currency," "inflation," and "depression." Nobody shied from the argument as too arcane. People had identified a problem—falling prices—and recognized a solution—more money. Descendants of the people who had invented modern money saw no reason why they should not continue to experiment. Money was not a dark art, nor yet a dismal science. It was something that Americans had always felt competent to agitate about, in a way Europeans had never, ever understood.

Despite their air of perpetual grievance, the silverites often got what they wanted. In 1877 they had managed to have a bill passed that obliged the Treasury to buy in, every month, between $2 million and $4 million's worth of silver and turn it into coin. Over the next thirteen years the government coined 378 million silver dollars, at a cost of $308 million. For all that talk about the dollar of the daddies, nobody actually wanted to use the coins, and they were very hard to get into circulation. The banks saw no need to use an overvalued coin when they could use gold instead. The people found them heavy and awkward. The Treasury shipped them out, as far away as they could get: but the coins kept coming back.

The situation was growing impossible. The government faced the possibility of running out of gold altogether. Foreign investors worried that if the country moved onto a silver standard they would be repaid in a dollar worth only eighty cents. But the silverites and inflationists split Congress. In 1890 a new act committed the government to buy in silver in exchange for silver certificates, which were to be legal tender. This injected $156 million into the economy; rates were easy; gold tended to drain away to London, where the rates were higher. But when Grover Cleveland came into office in March 1893 he was faced immediately with a money panic that was to bring on one of the most far-reaching depressions in American history.

The country simply couldn't carry on exchanging silver for gold: but it did, for another seven years. In May 1893 banks began refusing to redeem notes and the president demanded an emergency act to repeal the silver purchases. But it was not enough. Foreign investors sold their U.S. securities for gold while they could still get it. The government began to sell bonds to get hold of gold; each time the reserves were replenished, they soon drained away again. By 1895 the government was operating in an atmosphere of crisis—reserves were down from the safety limit of $100 million to a mere $40 million, and $2 million was leaving the Treasury every day. The financier J. P. Morgan patched together a European syndicate with the Rothschilds to buy government bonds for gold, but when the deal was announced, members of the syndicate were denounced in the papers as "blood-sucking Jews and aliens." Cleveland seemed to have turned into a Republican. He was a hard-money conservative. He later took his place on the thousand-dollar bill. Democrats looked elsewhere.

THE LAST GREAT wave of American migrants descended on the so-called Great American Desert after the Civil War. They had good rainfall, new railroads, and easy credit as eastern money came flooding in to invest in fine cattle and farm mortgages. Then came the terrible snows of 1886, the droughts of 1887, a flight of eastern capital, and an ever-declining spiral of wheat and cotton prices too. As the bankers foreclosed on the mortgaged farms, the pioneers discovered that for the first time in American history there was nowhere else to go. The 1892 census announced the final closure of the frontier. *In Kansas We Trusted, In Kansas We Busted* ran the motto on hundreds of wagons rolling back east.

There industry was in full swing. The Civil War had turned the Northeast into a behemoth of production, setting the U.S. on course to become the world's largest manufacturer a generation later. New factories were mopping up spare hands, soaking up spare money. Fortunes were being built, and the beginnings of America's productive, competitive, dollar-driven economy were being laid. American industry was set to drive countless products into American homes, from fridges to sewing machines[3]; fierce competition drove down prices across the board and increased sales; more money was changing hands faster than ever before. Once it had been land, now it was industry that drove the economy. America's industrial wage bill had been $28 million in 1800; it was $2.4 billion by 1900. Week after week, millions of families were being fed a drip of cash.

But not farmers. Farmers saw cash in an annual lump sum whose size depended on the weather, the market, and the price of railroads. Year after year they went into debt to buy seed, barbed wire, or fresh stock. But prices were falling, and money was frequently tight. Wheat sank from $1.37 a bushel in 1870 to 56 cents in 1894; cotton from 23 cents a pound to just 7 cents. With the frontier closed, the republic could no longer offer its farmers the bittersweet consolation of fresh new land to the west. The farmers began to organize themselves.

---

3. During that period the organ in my tiny village church in Sussex was made by Estey Organ Company in Brattleboro, Vermont.

What they wanted seemed then like a socialist extension of government power: income tax, a postal savings bank to free them from banks proper, nationalization of the railroads, the telegraph and telephone system, secret ballots, immigration control. Above all, of course, they wanted a reform of the dollar. They fell on the currency question because it touched so many others central to their difficulties—the problem of managing accounts, the difficulty of predicting cash flow, the indifference of the easterners, who lost interest and withdrew their capital, the rapacity of the railroads, who cornered them with exorbitant charges for freighting their grain—and because it was something they could deal with, unlike the weather. Farmers' parties, calling themselves independents or people's parties, fought state elections in 1888, and by 1892 they formed a grand coalition under the banner of Populism.

The Populists' plan for the dollar went far beyond the silverites' demands. Purists in the party wanted to escape the tyranny of precious metals, serving a class of mine owners, traders, bankers, and speculators. Silver and gold might be rare, but that did not make them into money. Money was only an idea, but as long as it was controlled by a pyramid of private finance, and backed by gold, it would always grow tight when the need for borrowing arose in the fall, when farmers needed to hire machinery and hands, pay freight, and get money for their produce. Every year, America's creaking and fragmented money supply system found itself dangerously overstretched by the call for money from the West and South. All too often the system snapped; banks unable to cover their loans went bust, and money disappeared faster than ever.

The Populists argued that the government should step in to create an "elastic" money supply that would stretch to meet emergencies and contract again when the need passed. It could be founded on a commodity that existed on the spot and belonged to every farmer: grain. Grain was not rare, but it was necessary in a way gold and silver were not. It rotted: but every year it grew again. The farmer's grain, stored in a federal grain elevator, would serve as the collateral for a low-interest loan in the form of greenbacks issued by the government, allowing the farmer to buy seed and such for the next year. When the farmer sold his grain and repaid the loan, the dollars the government had created would be retired, ready for the next harvest. The money supply would expand or contract depending on the state of the harvest, but in the meantime it would circulate just like any money. The difference was that instead of money being created by banks, who took advantage of the annual squeeze to levy interest rates at 30, 40, or 100 percent, it would be provided at cost by the government for the benefit of the citizen majority.

The People's Party held its Omaha convention in 1892, and the old Greenback Party chief, Ignatius Donnelly, wrote the opening address. Between his disappearance as a Greenbacker, and his reemergence as a Populist éminence grise, Donnelly had become America's most characteristic—and successful—visionary. His book *Atlantis: The Antediluvian World* argued, from Plato, that a lost continent had once stood in the Atlantic, opposite the mouth of the Mediterranean. There were echoes of the discovery of America in his notions of Atlantis, which was "the true Antediluvian world; the Garden of Eden; the Garden of the Hesperides," with fertile plains and richly forested mountains.

Decadence and corruption had overwhelmed Atlantis, and Donnelly—whose book was a sellout around the world—gave the Populists a vision of their own nation tottering toward its fall. "The newspapers are largely subsidized or muzzled," he told them, "public opinion silenced; business prostrated; our homes covered with mortgages; labor impoverished; and the land concentrated in the hands of the capitalists. . . . The fruits of toil of millions are boldly stolen to build up colossal fortunes for a few, unprecedented in the history of mankind; and the possessors of these, in turn, despise the republic and endanger liberty. From the same prolific womb of governmental injustice we breed the two great classes—tramps and millionaires."

But third parties never succeed in America. Significant parts of the Populist agenda were taken over by the Democrats, who were also providing the silverites with an umbrella. The Populists' ideas for a grain currency backed by nothing more than government credit didn't survive the fatal glitter of silver: prosilver Democrats captured the party at the 1896 convention. Many people who had never approved of the greenbacks saw nothing wrong in pushing for the free and unlimited coinage of silver—though cheap paper and cheap silver came to the same thing.

HE CAME FROM the West, and he was young, only thirty-six when he took the Democratic presidential nomination in 1896. They called him the Boy Orator from the Platte. His name was William Jennings Bryan. He talked farms and herds and English poetry and the King James Bible, and they made him a representative at Washington. He spoke against falling prices. He said: "They call that man a statesman whose ear is tuned to catch the slightest pulsations of a pocketbook, and denounce as a demagogue any one who dares to listen to the heartbeat of humanity." Everyone loved his oratory, though one critic "discovered that one could drive a prairie schooner through any part of his argument and never scrape against a fact or a sound statement."

In Congress Bryan met a Texan who liked the way he talked. The Texan showed him pamphlets put out by the Bimetallic League. He got him to read the report of the Royal Commission on Currency, and the works of leading European bimetallists: Cernuschi, Bonamy Price, Gibbs, and De Laveleye.

After that he talked only money, only silver, only the money of the poor. Three times he ran for president on the Democratic ticket, always for the free coinage of silver at sixteen to one. A British journalist who traveled the country came back with a book he called *In the Land of the Dollar,* because everyone from sharecropper to shareholder talked of nothing but money. Silverite Republicans absconded to the opposition. "Every crank in the country is loose," admitted a Kansas editor, while in Illinois, politicians found good, intelligent people "utterly wild on the money question. You can't do anything with them—just got to let them go."

Bryan spoke for farmers, for laborers, for the West and South. It was purely mystical. "My boy, I was brought up from my mother's knee on silver and I can't discuss that with you any more than you can discuss your religion with me," an Arizona senator lied innocently to a member of the administration. Once they gave Bryan "the foot of a rabbit killed at midnight in a churchyard at the dark of the moon," and this started a kind of votive frenzy. Thousands of rabbits' feet, a stuffed alligator, four live eagles, a mule, a pair of suspenders, Jefferson's *Works,* an ostrich egg, and dozens and dozens of horseshoes, canes, and sticks were sent to his house. There were canes made from antelope horn and fish vertebrae, from macerated newspaper editorials, lacquered, from Andrew Jackson's hickory, from George Washington's cherry tree, with silver knobs—one with sixteen silver petals and a single gold one. He received a mushroom that resembled him, and an egg with his initials on it.

He seemed to exude an aura of the miraculous. He was asked for money, for a bicycle, for a wheelchair. Hundreds of people named their children after him, including several sets of triplets called

Bryan, Jennings, and William. Many of them hoped for a photo; sometimes more. "We are the only democrat there in our naiber-hood thay are all republican thay say you not send any thing there was one of our nabores sent to makindly and he sent them 25 dollars thay are lifted up big." A boy from Japan even wrote to ask if the Bryans would adopt him. Bryan wrote back a kindly letter explaining that he had three children already and couldn't take care of another. A few weeks later Yamashita rang Bryan's doorbell in Lincoln, Nebraska. He stayed five and a half years. The Bryans sent him to school and Nebraska University.

Not everyone thought Bryan was a miracle worker. In Madison Square Garden the newspapermen turned up in force to disparage him. The respectable classes derided his logic, but they were also afraid of his eloquence and of his communion with the farmers.

He didn't drink or smoke or swear. He felt sorry that other people did; reporters who followed his speaking tours appreciated his solicitude and saw that he used alcohol rubs to keep up his energy. He spoke to vast crowds and stank like a distillery. In 1896 he made the speech that gave him immortality.

"You come to us and tell us that the great cities are in favor of the gold standard; we reply that the great cities rest on our broad and fertile prairies. Burn down your cities and leave our farms, and your cities will spring up again as if by magic; but destroy our farms and the grass will grow in the streets of every city in the country. . . . If they say that bimetallism is good, but we cannot have it until other nations help us, we reply, that instead of having a gold standard because England has, we will restore bimetallism, and then let England have bimetallism because the United States has it. If they dare to come out in the open field and defend the gold standard as a good thing, we will fight them to the uttermost. Having behind us the producing masses of this nation and the world, supported by the commercial interests, the laboring interests and the toilers everywhere, we will answer their demand for a gold standard by saying to them: You shall not press down upon the brow of labor this crown of thorns, you shall not crucify mankind upon a cross of gold."

The Populists sang an operetta chorus:

> Chink! Chink! Chink! No crown of thorns for labor's brow!
> Chink! Chink! Chink! No cross of gold for mankind now!
> Chink! Chink! Chink! We'll not to single standard bow!
> Chink! Chink! Chink! We'll vote for freedom now!

The Silver Party nominated Bryan too. "The time has come to determine whether this country is ruled by an Almighty Dollar or by an Almighty God," they said.

The Republican contender William McKinley came out directly for the gold standard in July—for which he was to be immortalized on the face of the five-hundred-dollar bill. He sat on his porch at home in Ohio while Mark Hanna ran his campaign. He sent out 120 million pamphlets, in all major languages, mostly arguing against free silver. One of them was titled *How McKinley Is Hated in England.* Bryan traveled eighteen thousand miles by train, made six hundred speeches, and was heard by 5 million people. Not enough of them backed him. McKinley carried twenty-three states and Bryan twenty-two: 271 electoral votes to 176. Bryan, exhausted, was sorry to lose. He wrote up the election story in *The First Battle,* but reruns of the election, in 1900 and 1908, produced the same results and made it seem, really, like the last. Free silver might have set the West alight, but it was cold water to the furnace of eastern industry.

Bryan's last election was 1908, when he lost to Teddy Roosevelt's nominee William Howard Taft—hardly a disgrace, for Roosevelt was the consummate politician. When the Democrat Wilson took the presidency in 1912, he made Bryan secretary of state—only for Bryan to resign when it seemed America would enter World War I. He became—like Roosevelt too—supernumerary, a grand old man reliving yesterday's battles. In 1925 he found himself drawn into a legal battle in Tennessee, which put him and Tennessee under the spotlight again. Tennessee wanted its children shielded from evolutionary theory: a teacher who disagreed was reluctantly prosecuted. It was known around the world as the Monkey Trial.

Bryan stood up to the evolutionists partly because their evidence didn't seem very convincing, partly because he believed in the Bible, and essentially because he felt that Darwinism stripped men and women of their dignity. He didn't care about the apes, but he preferred the angels: evolutionary theory meant consigning American farmers to their fate. It gave people the right to ignore him. Weakness would always be a signal for redundancy, although the Bible said the meek would inherit the earth. Darwinism suggested they would be torn apart. Bryan died there, in Dayton, Tennessee, still angry.

After 1896 the Republicans controlled Congress. A foreign diversion was found—or made—in a war with Spain, which freed Cuba and the Philippines from Spanish rule: that was the end of the Spanish dollar. In 1900 they won another election. McKinley was shot dead by an anarchist, and Teddy Roosevelt—a Republican populist of a broader stripe—stepped up from the vice presidency (one of his ambitions was to make America's coins beautiful).

It had been a time of political ballads, glees, anthems, and parades. Everyone had had an opinion. Even the "Wholesale Dry Goods Republicans" had sung an anti-Bryan song of their own. But Vachel Lindsay years later wrote a poem called "Bryan, Bryan, Bryan, Bryan."

Election night at midnight:
Boy Bryan's defeat.
Defeat of western silver.
Defeat of western wheat.
Victory of letterfiles
And plutocrats in miles
With dollar signs upon their coats,
Diamond watchchains on their vests
And spats on their feet.
Victory of custodians, Plymouth rock,
And all that inbred-landlord stock.
Victory of the neat.
Defeat of the aspen groves of Colorado valleys,
The bluebells of the Rockies,
And blue bonnets of old Texas,
By the Pittsburgh alleys.
Defeat of alfalfa and the Mariposa lily.
Defeat of the Pacific and the long Mississippi.
Defeat of the young by the old and silly.
Defeat of tornadoes by the poison vats supreme.
Defeat of my boyhood, defeat of my dream.

As for the best-seller that emerged from the currency imbroglio
of the late 1890s, it was not *Coin's Financial School* but L. Frank
Baum's bizarre children's classic *The Wonderful Wizard of Oz.* Baum
was a midwestern journalist who in 1900 decided he wanted to write
an all-American fairy tale. Thanks to the 1939 musical with Judy
Garland, everyone knows the story of how Dorothy and her little
dog, Toto, were gathered up by a huge Kansas whirlwind and rushed
to Oz, where they land on top of the Wicked Witch of the East and
follow the yellow brick road to meet the Wizard who will send

Dorothy home, cure the Lion of cowardice, give the Tin Woodman a heart, and the Scarecrow brains.

In 1964 Henry M. Littlefield wrote a delightful essay[4] that pointed up some entertaining parallels between Baum's fairy story and the political situation of the 1890s. Oz, it turned out, was a roman à clef, and the business of decoding *The Wizard of Oz* became a minor academic industry, spurred on by history teachers desperate to engage the interest of their listless students in the 1960s.

More and more parallels were uncovered. The Scarecrow stood for the farmer, the Tin Woodman for the factory worker, and William Jennings Bryan himself was the Cowardly Lion. Mark Hanna, the Republican Party guru, was the Wizard found by the travelers in the Emerald City, where everyone wears green glasses fastened with a golden buckle. He turns out to be a tiny shrunken little fraud, working a system of huge levers and gears to convince the people of his omnipotence. Oz was his power base, gold itself, measured in ounces. Meanwhile the Wicked Witch of the West who enslaves the Yellow Winkies was imperialist America, which had lately captured the Philippines from Spain and was refusing, like George III, to give them independence.

Toto the dog—from his name, his nobility, and his natural ability to function without strong liquor—was found to stand for the teetotal faction among the Populists. Dorothy was a young Mary Lease, the Populist firebrand from Kansas, whose slogan for farmers was "raise less corn and more hell!" (and whose complete prescription for world justice included a global segregation of the races: the Populists weren't all about post office savings and a minimum wage). The Deadly Poppy Field where the Cowardly Lion was lulled asleep

---

4. Henry M. Littlefield, "*The Wizard of Oz:* A Parable on Populism." *American Quarterly* 16 (1964).

was anti-imperialism itself, a plank of the Populist coalition that threatened to make Bryan forget the main issue of silver at sixteen to one. Even the Crime of '73 got a mention: in the Emerald Palace, Dorothy passes through seven halls and climbs three flights of stairs.

The four friends of course discover their real strengths in exposing the Wizard's wicked pretense and the Tin Woodman, armed with a silver oil can against rust, goes back to work wielding a golden ax with a silver blade. Bimetallism triumphs. Dorothy, with a click of her silver slippers, returns to Kansas.

Plenty of people remain justifiably suspicious of the Oz theories: after all, they can't all be right, and either the Wicked Witch of the East is Grover Cleveland or industrial capitalism, and the Wicked Witch of the West either imperialism, McKinley, or the Populists. A reader would do well to go back to Littlefield's charmingly diffident essay, which merely browses on possibilities.

One interesting new angle from William R. Leach doesn't at all see Oz as parading the values of down-home country America so dear to the Populists. His *Wizard of Oz* reads as a wacky celebration of the wonderful rejuvenating power of city life, as rich and magical as life in the Emerald City, with its echoes of the amazingly clean and efficient "White City" that went up for Chicago's World Fair in 1893. A drop of voguish theosophy in a tincture of traditional American boosterism produces an "optimistic secular therapeutic" story in which people get what they want by taking an upbeat attitude. *The Wizard of Oz* doesn't push for a return to an older, gentler, bimetallist America, but helps Americans feel good about the way the new industrial economy gives everyone leisure, wealth, and consumer goods.

Baum certainly had no trouble with big cities and visited the World Fair several times. He may even have sung anti-Bryan songs with those Wholesale Dry Goods Republicans, for in the same year as *Oz* he published his less celebrated work on *The Art of Decorating Dry Goods Windows and Interiors*. Baum was a Republican hard-money man, writing an American fairy tale. There was no La-la land like the one the silverites inhabited: the story almost wrote itself.

The wind was already flapping in the silverites' sails when William Jennings Bryan lost his second election battle with McKinley in 1900. Huge new gold strikes were made in Australia, South Africa, and the Klondike, which, along with the invention of the cyanide process for extracting gold from ores, boosted the world stock of gold and lowered its price. There would be more dollars, after all. The farmers found less to grumble about; prices were rising again. In March 1900 the U.S. moved definitively onto a gold standard. As the tumult died, it was found that nobody much wanted a silver dollar anyway.

COIN HARVEY KEPT on working. He discovered that wherever British investors owned land in America, statistics revealed rising levels of suicide, insanity, and crime. He supported the Boers in South Africa against the British, and the Filipinos, maybe Baum's Yellow Winkies, against an American imperialism that would try to saddle America with a monarchical system, including standing armies. He had evidence that the attempt would be made: it included the chilling fact that one of the beds in the White House was "patterned after the style of the bed the Queen of England sleeps in."

In 1900, after Bryan's second defeat, Harvey left Chicago, bought a tract near the Ozark Mountain town of Rogers in Arkansas, and opened a hotel. It had Venetian gondolas, fiddlers, a private railroad, and its own bank. He was hardly surprised when the enterprise collapsed. In 1920 he started to build a vast obelisk, 40 feet square at the base and 130 feet high. In it he intended to put all the books he had written, along with various twentieth-century artifacts. On the apex he would fix a plaque with the words: When this can be read go below and find the cause of the death of a former Civilization.

He had the footings excavated, and by the time he had built what he called the foyer, "an asymmetrical mass of concrete and stone in the form of seats, but without any semblance of regular order," as one local reporter described it, he had run out of money. The foyer was taken up as an attraction, and people came to gaze, for a fee, on his folly. The experience seemed to revive his energy, and in 1932, four years before he died at eighty-four, he did what he always should have done and ran for president.

· 15 ·

WORKING FOR
THE YANKEE DOLLAR

**Power—Modesty—"Stored Possibility"—
Englishmen—No Money—Ultimate Money**

The myth of the Anglomen died hard in America, but it had to die eventually if the country was ever to grow easy in itself. And in spite of Bryan's fears, the gold standard of 1900 signaled the full flowering of U.S. independence, not its end. The country had put itself on an equal footing with the other nations of the world. In little more than a generation, it would dominate them all.

Of course the process was not exact, rather a series of little steps, each one drawing the country closer to the point of real independence. Perhaps it began at the moment that the frontier closed, and America stood revealed as an empire unto herself. It crept on when the old tug-of-war in American life between Anglophobes and Anglophiles was revealed to be irrelevant: the voices had grown shrill in the closing years of the nineteenth century, but when the U.S. adopted gold as her standard, and abandoned a centuries-old affair with silver, she arrived as a world power. Not that gold could achieve everything: another money panic in 1907 showed that the banks themselves were too weak to support the economy and Congress established the Federal Reserve.

Either way America no longer stood at the world's edge. By the end of World War I the U.S. had turned from a mammoth debtor into a gigantic creditor: it no longer needed to import capital. It no longer needed to import ideas either: President Wilson delivered his famous Fourteen Points at Versailles in 1919, and America found herself in the position of instructing Europe. In the years that followed, America's position in the world only strengthened. Britain struggled to maintain a currency convertible into gold—it was actually Winston Churchill who was responsible for renewing the old pledge after the ravages of World War I. "If the English pound is not to be the standard which everyone knows and can trust," he told the Commons in 1925, "the business not only of the British Empire but of Europe as well might have to be transacted in dollars instead of pounds sterling." The *Times* thought it time "to face the dollar in the eye."

One by one, countries dropped off the gold standard. The U.S. was one of the last to abandon gold, in the face of the Great Depression, but the benchmark price of gold for settling international accounts was set in dollars and by 1940 many of the world's leading nations had placed their gold reserves in New York for safekeeping. Fifty years earlier they would have rather died.

EXPRESSIONS OF POWER can be magnificent displays of gaudery that may or may not mask hollowness and uncertainty: pomp and circumstance often mark an empire at the moment of its turn. Or they can, perhaps with greater effect, dispense with show altogether.

Dollars in the 1880s and 1890s had been triumphalist. Trumbull's famous painting *The Declaration of Independence* graced the back of the bills, or Greek goddesses with progressive names: Steam, Electricity, or History. Sometimes they were in battle mode: one glorious design of the 1890s showed a bevy of American Amazons hurtling out of the dome of the Capitol on a flash of wings and a swirl of loose robes, trumpets tooting, torches blazing, flanked by a chariot dragged by stamping, snorting horses harnessed to a thunderbolt. They were plainly bringing the light of America to the world—or rather the light of Washington to America. They were crusaders for sure; but they too, beneath the bombast, struck a hollow note. They were too fierce for their own good.

But by the late 1920s the U.S. no longer struggled to make its way in the world, and dollar bills became less strident and more lapidary. Dollars no longer had to toot and trumpet: America *was* the future. Skyscrapers, bootleg gin, easy money, jazz; Harlem was a Parisian arrondissement—or perhaps it was the other way around. Some months before the great stock market collapse of 1929, the dollar took its near-final form. The bills were shrunk to their current size to save money. The images portrayed on them were—and still are—unabashedly American, reflecting the point where history and myth collide. A myth of the West was caught in those familiar laurel swags and that unmistakable lettering; each bill figured one of the Great Men, who had all—one way or another—played their parts in the drama of the nation's birth.

Uniform across America, the dollar was the perfect ingredient in the corporation paycheck. Rackety dollars spun out of log cabins and potato barrels belonged to another era altogether, when people had to make their own decisions and their own entertainment. Money was something they arranged to suit their interests. The dollar issued by the Federal Reserve was like an elegant well-paid lawyer, an indispensable partner to Big Business. It was a kind of Big Business itself: like a Model T or a Hollywood movie, a dollar was something you could have confidence in wherever you were, a reassuringly familiar quantity from coast to coast, a brand like the other brands already beginning to conquer and even define aspects of the nation. The dollar helped this happen. Uniformity drove down price: a clear price fostered uniformity.

Jefferson had wanted land and the dollar to run together. When industrial America discovered and encouraged the limitless appetite of the consumer, consumer goods became what unlimited land had been to an earlier generation: Henry Ford paid his workers well so that they would be able to buy his cars, rather as frontier America had offered its land cheap to generate its own expansion. That, after all, was the ultimate logic of democracy: a joyous entitlement, whether to new farms in new territories or to new cars to drive on new roads provided by the government.

EDMUND WILSON wrote in *Europe without Baedecker:*

> We find making money exhilarating, but we also find it exhilarating to spend it. Money for us is a medium, a condition of life, like air. But with the English it means always property. A dollar is something you multiply—something that causes an expansion of your house and your mechanical equipment, something that accelerates like speed; and that may also be slowed up and deflated. It is a value that may be totally imaginary, yet can for a time provide half-realised dreams. But pounds, shillings and pence are tangible, solid, heavy; they are objects one gains and possesses.

Old World money meant hanging on: the dollar was about contingency. "The use of money is all the advantage there is in having money," Ben Franklin wrote. Nelson W. Aldrich has called it "stored possibility," a medium in which the entrepreneurial spirit moves, "fluid, buoyant, and powerful, but otherwise as susceptible as water to whatever desire may dictate."

Europeans have often complained that Americans are obsessed with money, and that dollars take the place of culture in American society. Some Americans think so, too, and outside Europe the view is almost universal. Like any generalization it contains a germ of truth: you can find Americans at every level of society indulging in rituals of spending and display, as the American sociologist Thorstein Veblen pointed out when he coined the phrase "conspicuous consumption." On my first visit to the U.S. I was amazed to hear the announcer on NPR beg his listeners to send in money, or to see the list of donors plainly chiseled into the marble of foyers of libraries and museums.

But since fairly indifferent aspects of American culture, like the Big Mac or Hollywood, do so well abroad, it rather seems that wily birds of the Old World have forgotten the irony game they so relentlessly played against the Americans. In spite of Big Macs and all that Hollywood agenda-grabbing, star-making, storytelling gumbo, you don't, actually, have to eat rubbish, or watch it. You never have to buy, but the old rule applies: caveat emptor.

Old World money found the dollar fascinating. "There's no doubt but money is to the fore now," wrote William Dean Howells in *The Rise of Silas Lapham* (1885). "It is the romance, the poetry of our age. It's the thing that chiefly strikes the imagination. The Englishmen who come here are more curious about the great new millionaires than about any one else, and they respect them more."

Scott Fitzgerald heard the Englishmen himself, eighty years ago: "all well dressed, all looking a little hungry, and all talking in low, earnest voices to solid and prosperous Americans. I was sure they were selling something: bonds or insurance or automobiles. They were at least agonizingly aware of the easy money in the vicinity and convinced it was theirs for a few words in the right key." P. G. Wodehouse heard them too, liner-loads of Pongos and Bertrams just bright enough to cross the Pond and check on their investments. Since the days of Sir Walter Raleigh the English have always had hopes of America, and have never lost the old habit of equating America with money. "Why, man," says a character in a Ben Jonson play, "their very chamber pots are gold," and thousands of English, Scots, Welsh, Ulstermen, and Irish believed him. Penniless Victorian earls married American heiresses, and the trade of cash and title used to be a stock joke on both sides of the Atlantic. (President Lincoln was enjoying it in the form of a popular play, *Our American Cousin,* laughing heartily, before Booth shot him in Ford's Theater.) From computers to the Net to *Masterpiece Theater,* the English have been selling things to solid and prosperous Americans forever. They can't get enough of those dollars.

And if, sometimes, the money hunger presents itself as a morose neurosis, or in a flickering, Gatsbyesque sadness around the edges of American civilization, on the whole, Americans have, it seems to me, a fair degree of innocent enjoyment from their money. The antics of the very rich, for instance, entertain millions. The Almighty Dollar is unquestionably their God; but it is a pagan deity of a Mount Olympus kind who intervenes almost merrily in their affairs. There is a particular brand of hubris that the dollar gods tend to punish in spectacular ways: Masters of the Universe striding from their penthouses to jail cells, Howard Hughes hiding from germs in a cellophane-wrapped Vegas hotel room, firework bankruptcies, divorce spectaculars, the icy fear of Andrew Carnegie, who said that a man who dies rich dies disgraced and proceeded to give away $350 million.

Plenty of Americans have treated dollars with disdain. "It would be very gratifying for us to see the Yankee dollar disappear altogether and forever from our vocabulary," sniffed an editorial in the *Richmond Whig*, a southern paper, during the Civil War. Mark Twain treated sudden wealth as a glorious joke in *Roughing It*. Lucius Beebe called money stuff that is good for throwing off the back of a moving train. Americans coined "too much too young" and "poor little rich girl" as well as "easy come, easy go": rags to riches is one story, but rags to riches to rags and back up is almost equally familiar. Many American fortunes have been made by men who weren't very interested in money: what interested them was the process. In the early 1930s an incorrigible gangster, who took a percentage on every liquor sale in the country and was perhaps one of the richest men on earth, liked nothing better than to loaf around in his vest, eating his mother's meatballs. Like Carnegie, many people who amassed a fortune worked almost as hard giving it away. Or else they spent it— which might amount to the same thing. Indeed, the persistent refusal of the public to rise up in bloody revolution against the superrich stems from an attitude that sees money in meteorological terms, falling like rain, flowing here and there, now pooling and now draining. When it comes down to it, Americans are surprisingly philosophical about money.

There has always been a counterstrain, too, of people who wanted nothing to do with money in the first place, including a variety of visionary and utopian communities who tried to abolish money and think of something else (slavery came to mind, perhaps). Roger Williams, who arrived in Massachusetts in 1637 and founded Rhode Island, immediately saw the absurdity of America belonging in any sense to the king; he despised the moneygrubbing colonists and thought that Indians, with their shells, were closer to God. Generations of frontiersmen went cheerfully penniless, living on tick and barter. Self-reliant, self-sufficient, and sometimes plain lost to the world, country people had little use for money before the invention of the Sears, Roebuck catalog. Frederick Law Olmsted, traveling in the South in 1854, heard of people who had never used money at all. And the pioneer constitutions of several midwestern states actually outlawed banks.

The visionaries shared this much with the Huckleberry Finns, who simply fled "sivilization" like a tight collar. Huck Finn sped away from home on the Mississippi, but forty years later the wandering way of life depended on the railroads, which at one end made some men fabulously rich—Jay Cooke, Cornelius Vanderbilt, Andrew Carnegie (who supplied the steel), Jim Fisk—and at the other allowed the hobos to travel free on and under and sometimes in boxcars the length and breadth of the United States, cadging work, tips, meals, beer, shoes, and meeting up again far away and by chance. Perhaps they were "the two great classes—tramps and millionaires" that Ignatius Donnelly's Populist manifesto spoke about.

Hobos left minor monuments to their culture: a mended gate, a painted barn. The word *punk* is a hobo word. "The Big Rock Candy Mountain" was dreamed up by a hobo frightened by the attentions of older, tougher hobos in the boxcars. But there was also "Hallelujah! I'm a Bum" in celebration of the simple life. Money creates desire, and desire creates headache: better, the hobos thought (and sang), to give up money and property altogether and live like the lilies of the field—traveling lilies, of course, because that is the continental imperative.

Hobos tended to flourish on the generosity of their fellow citizens. But sometimes a hobo would take a nickel and carve something new on its face—a self-portrait, a jackass. The nickel was a godsend, being cheap at five cents, big and soft: a nicely made object, especially the old Indian-head nickel the hobos liked best, with a buffalo on the reverse. It came to them looking like a million other nickels. They killed it as money—who'd take a disfigured nickel?—and reinvented it as art. They obliterated its conventional value and found it another one.[1]

AFTER 1929 the dollar was immutable, the canon fixed and sealed. Only in America can anyone still use money made 150 years ago. Nobody's currency looks the same now as it did eighty years ago: the Bank of England pound note changed six times after 1914 and eventually disappeared altogether. Nobody else has bills showing a vintage motorcar driving past a public building, like the old upright with running boards chugging by the Treasury Building on the ten-dollar bill. None of the other rich countries has an equivalent to the one-dollar bill, only coins.

If there was one wobble, one giveaway anxiety, it was in 1956, at the height of the Cold War, when the rubric *In God We Trust* was put onto the dollar bill. It was meant to please the people who took their dollar bills seriously, like their flag and their oath of allegiance. They liked the way that nothing about them changed, too, so that when someone in 1957 compared two bills reading *In God We Trust* on one but on the other nothing at all, they jumped for joy. This was the

---

1. The sixties impresario Andy Warhol did just the same; the difference is that he liked money, respected it, and wanted to keep it by him; several people who felt the same way were reassured into giving him a whole lot more than anyone ever gave the hobos (much paper: he folded it lengthwise, which he claimed was what the Rothschilds did, and kept it in carrier bags).

evidence they needed to start a full-blown Red scare: the motto must have been removed.

Reds under the beds, or rather the specter of Koreans at the photocopying machine, impelled the Secret Service to push for a currency overhaul in the early 1980s. They came up with three prototype twenty-dollar bills that incorporated about a dozen modern devices to bust counterfeits, including chemical markers, holograms, microprinting, an embedded polymer strip, and the use of more colors, to upset photocopy machines. The prototypes reached the White House, where the treasury secretary found that "they didn't float." Tinkering with the dollar, in the eyes of many politicians, was akin to redesigning the flag. The bills were slightly altered in the 1990s, but the greenback stayed. Mary Ellen Withrow, the treasurer, told the *New Yorker*: "Green is the color of prosperity, and black is a good thing, too—it shows we're sound and solid and in the black." And I thought prosperity was mauve!

The public were money conservatives. They turned down a coin, and made it hard to put two-dollar bills into circulation—perhaps because of an old superstition linking a two-dollar bill with twins, or even a traditional memory that made it the price of prostitution. When the dollars did begin to change, for the first time in seventy years, public reaction was cool.

In 1966 the Australians finally abandoned the pound sterling. They launched a campaign to find a name for a new, decimal currency. The treasurer proposed the auster. The public came up with berra, victa, tasma, newal, quee, cook, smithie, alp, brumbie, anzac, melba, magpie, camber, regal, eureka, billy, pacific, and noodle. Government ministers soberly drew up a shortlist, including royal, crown, dollar, pound, and sovereign.

The Australian Council of Retailers said that its members, for their part, hoped to see an Australian dollar, but the government's position had hardened. The ten-shilling unit would be the royal, it announced; a fifty-cent piece would be called a crown, twenty cents a florin, and ten cents a shilling. The public were still full of ideas—ausdol, dauler, dolaroo, ducat, noble unite, and wollar, dinkum, fiddely, spin, and spondu—and the royal met with stiff popular resistance. The Labour opposition sneered at the government's "quaint terminology," and threatened to reverse it when they came to power. The *Melbourne Age* disliked "royal" because it converted an adjective into a noun: English gossip columnists might talk about "the royals," but "citizens in the more rugged outposts of the Commonwealth, with more respect, call them members of the Royal family." The government caved in, protesting that it "did not select dollar in the first place [because] it would not be a distinctive Australian name."

The British decimalized their currency in 1971, dropping shillings much faster than Americans had done in 1776. European integrationists worked toward their ultimate goal, a single currency for Europe.

The dollar isn't all it seems. Perhaps, after all, there's a whiff of the cathouse in those nineteenth-century swags; a glimpse of western vulgarity in the burly type; a touch of dubious decorum in the mottoes and symbols, like the instant ancestors of the nouveaux riches. It's so terribly busy that it gets the brains of paranoiacs humming in busy sympathy too. Why are all bills the same size? What make of car is that—a Ford? What is the meaning of number thirteen? Is the seal a coded reference to the New Age?

You find these people writing on the Internet: where the forces of propriety—the U.S. Treasury, the Bureau of Printing and Engraving, the U.S. Secret Service—come out to meet them. Perhaps the Internet points to the dollar's ultimate destination. When the whole country is webbed with electronic money—cash cards, credit cards, smart cards, direct debits, automatic transfers—cash will be for paupers only. The grandeur and majesty of the dollar bill will be revealed for a sham, rather more circuses than bread: tawdry glamour for the poor and very old. For the rest of us shall be like the queen of England, who famously never has to handle money at all.

Bibliography

Two general American histories by Brits: Hugh Brogan's *The Penguin History of the United States* (London, 1990) and Paul Johnson's *A History of the American People* (London, 1997). Daniel J. Boorstin's three-volume social history *The Americans* (New York, 1958–1973).

On money in general, *The Oxford Book of Money*, edited by Kevin Jackson (Oxford, 1995), and Norman Angell's *Story of Money* (London, 1930). James Buchan's *Frozen Desire* and Nelson Aldrich's *Old Money* show how money ought to be written about. Paul L. Bernstein's *The Power of Gold* (New York, 2000), Glyn Davies's *A History of Money* (Cardiff, 1994), and of course J. K. Galbraith's *Money: Whence It Came and Where It Went* (London, 1975). *The History of Money from Sandstone to Cyberspace* by Jack Weatherford (New York, 1997).

On American money in particular, Bray Hammond's *Banks and Politics in America from the Revolution to the Civil War* (Princeton, N.J., 1957), Arthur Nussbaum's *A History of the Dollar* (New York, 1957), William Greider's *Secrets of the Temple: How the Federal Reserve Runs the Country* (New York, 1989). Joseph Dorfman's *The Economic Mind in American Civilisation* (London, 1947). Ted Schwartz's thoroughgoing *A History of United States Coinage* (San Diego, 1980).

Cultural factors shaping the American landscape are brilliantly explored in *Common Landscape of America 1580 to 1845*, by John R. Stilgoe (New Haven, 1982). Also in Gunther Barth's *Fleeting Moments: Nature and Culture in American History* (New York, 1990). The artistic response is outlined in Robert Hughes, *American Visions: The Epic History of Art in America* (London, 1997), and was given magnificent treatment in the London Tate exhibition, *American Sublime* (catalogue by Andrew Wilton and Tim Barringer, London, 2002).

On colonial America, Kenneth Silverman's *The Life and Times of Cotton Mather* (New York, 1985), Carl Van Doren's *Benjamin Franklin,* and Franklin's own *Autobiography. The New England Knight: Sir William Phips, 1651–95* by Emerson W. Baker and John G. Reid (Toronto, 1998).

American Sphinx, The Character of Thomas Jefferson by Joseph J. Ellis (New York, 1997); *Understanding Thomas Jefferson* by E. M. Halliday (New York, 2001). Forrest McDonald's *Alexander Hamilton* (New York, 1979).

G. and D. Bathe's *Jacob Perkins* in the Historical Society of Pennsylvania, 1943. *Early Engineering Reminiscences (1815–40) of George Escol Sellers,* edited by Eugene S. Ferguson (Washington, D.C., 1965).

Colonel Baker wrote the *History of the United States Secret Service* (Philadelphia, 1867); Jacob Mogelever wrote about him in his *Death to Traitors* (New York, 1960). The Bureau of Printing and Engraving's *History 1862–1962* (New York, 1978).

Richard Hofstadter's "Free Silver and the Mind of 'Coin' Harvey" in his *The Paranoid Style in American Politics and Other Essays* (London, 1966). James H. Hutson's essay "Public Jealousy from the Age of Walpole to the Age of Jackson" in *Saints and Revolutionaries: Essays on Early American History* (New York, 1984) and *The Politics of Individualism: Parties and the American Character in the Jacksonian Era* by Lawrence Frederick Kohl (New York and Oxford, 1989).

The Dixie story is explored in an essay by W. A. Philpott, Jr. One of the best accounts of the silver conspiracy is given in Robert R. Van Ryzin, *Crime of 1873: The Comstock Connection; A Tale of Mines, Trade and Morgan Dollars* (Iola, Wisc., 2001).

Lewis H. Lapham's *Money and Class in America: Notes and Observations on Our Civil Religion* (New York, 1988). In line with my debt of gratitude to the American Numismatic Association, I should mention their journal, *The Numismatist.* I've ransacked the works of professional and amateur scholars of numismatics; highlights include:

Georgius Agricola, *De Re Metallica,* trans. and ed. by Herbert Clark Hoover and Lou Henry Hoover (London, 1912).

America's Currency 1789–1866, papers delivered to the American Numismatic Society in New York City in 1985.

R. A. Billington, *Western Expansion: History of American Frontier* (New York, 1949).

O. K. Burrell, *Gold in the Woodpile: An Informal History of Banking in Oregon* (University of Oregon, 1967).

Bibliography

Lendol Calder, *Financing the American Dream: A Cultural History of Consumer Credit* (Princeton, N.J., 1999).

Joseph Coffin, *Our American Money: A Collector's Story* (New York, 1940).

William H. Dillistin, *Bank Note Reporters and Counterfeit Detectors, 1826–1866* (New York, 1949).

D. W. Garber, *Wildcat Banks on the Mohican Frontier* (privately printed, 1975).

William H. Griffiths, *The Story of American Bank Note Company* (New York, 1959).

Albert B. Hart, *American History told by Contemporaries, 1897–1904.* Four volumes. (New York, 1897–1925).

Richard Hildreth, *Banks, Banking and Paper Currencies* (1840).

Basil Hunnisett, *Engraved on Steel* (London, 1998).

David R. Johnson, *Illegal Tender: Counterfeiting and the Secret Service in Nineteenth-Century America* (Washington, D.C., 1995).

John Jay Knox, *United States Notes* (London, 1885).

George L. Mckay, *Early American Currency* (New York, 1944).

Eric P. Newman, *The Early Paper Money of America* (Racine, Wisc., 1967).

Eric P. Newman and Richard G. Doty, ed., *Studies on Money in Early America* (New York, 1976).

Waterman Lily Ormsby, *Bank-Note Engraving* (New York, 1852).

Richard S. Patterson and Richardson Dougall, *The Eagle and the Shield: A History of the Great Seal of the United States* (Washington, D.C., 1976).

Henry Phillips, Jr., *Historical Sketches of the Paper Currency.* Two volumes. (Roxbury, Mass., 1865–66).

C. Raguet, *Currency and Banking* (Philadelphia, 1839).

Irwin Unger, *The Greenback Era* (Princeton, N.J., 1964).

Thomas Wilson, *The Power "To Coin Money": The Exercise of Monetary Powers by the Congress* (New York, 1992).

Lawrence C. Wroth, *The Colonial Printer* (New York, 1931).

Acknowledgments

Acknowledgments, or debts public and private, are due to my father, Richard, who sparked off this inquiry by discovering that the green in the greenback came from a beetle that lives in French Guyana (and if only it were true); to Sarah Chalfant, my agent, for her enthusiasm and clarity; to my editor Jack Macrae, for good-humored criticism and many kindnesses; to Katy Hope at Holt who managed so many bits in between. Jane Colville, from the library of the American Numismatic Association in Colorado Springs, went far beyond the call of duty in pointing me toward the right books and, later, on tracking down so many of the illustrations. Thanks to Richard Doty in Washington, D.C.; IOUs to Tom Molner and Andy Brimmer in New York; to Ben Macyntire and Kate Muir all over the place.

Kate and our boys, Izzy, Walter, and Harry, put up with the Monster in the same house. Nothing can repay them for their forbearance, or anything else.

Index

Entries in *italics* refer to captions.

Adams, Abigail, 60, 106

Adams, John, 60, 61, 100, 106–7, 161n, 188–89

Adams, John Quincy, 171, 171n, 199

Adams and Company bank, 211–15

Agricola, Georgius (Georg Bauer), 13–15

Alabama, 143, 206

Albemarle, duke of, 35–36

alchemists, 13–14, 28n, 62

Aldrich, Nelson W., 289

Allen, William, 22

American Accomptant, The (Lee), 121–22

American colonies
counterfeiting and, 130
Franklin and, 50–55
money issued by, 60–61
origin of paper money in, 40–49
paper money in, banned by
Britain, 56–58

Rhode Island paper money, 55–56

silver money in, 28–31

varying legal tender in, 27–28

wampum in, 20–25

American Negotiator, The, 61

American Philosophical Society, 159, 162

American Revolution (War of Independence), 81, *135*, 171
debts of, 101–2
financed by paper money, 59–61

American System (money policy), 175, 199, 207

American System (steel engraving and printing)
adoption of, *137*, 138–40, 145–46, *147*
Bank of England and, 148–50
counterfeiting despite, 183–85
landscape art and, 153–56, 158

Andre, Major, 266

boom of 1834–36, 205–9
Jefferson and, 76–81
-money correspondence, 53, 55
Land Office, 205
Land Ordinance (1785), 78–81
Lavien, Johan, 95
Lavien, Peter, 96
Lawrence, D. H., 54
Leach, William R., 282
Lease, Mary, 281
Lee, Chauncey, 121–22
Lee, Gen. Robert E., 245
legal tender
foreign coins as, 128
greenbacks and, 256
silver dollar dropped as, 263–71
L'Enfant, Pierre, 66, 77
Lewis and Clark, 160, 163
Life and Memorable Actions of George Washington, The (Weems), 161
Life of Washington (Marshall), 161
Lincoln, Abraham, 218, 220–22, 230
assassination of, 127, 246, 290
portrait of, on currency, 224
Lindsay, Vachel, 279
Littlefield, Henry M., 281, 282
Locke, John, 20, 49
Louisiana, 101, 123, 143, 206
Louisiana Purchase, 117–18, 123, 142–43, 165

McKinley, William, 127, 278, 282, 283
Macy, R. H., 249
Madison, James, 98, 111, 250
Manhattan Company scandal, 115–16

Manhattan Wampum, 25–26
Marshall, (biographer), 161
Marshall, Chief Justice John, 166–67
Marx, Karl, 172
Maryland, 60, 124, 166–67
Masons, 3, 63–65
Massachusetts, 26, 28, 33–34, 36, 39–41, 99–100, 141
Mather, Cotton, 43–49, 50
Mead, Ralph, 214
Melville, Herman, 32, 189–90, 192
membrane or national paper, 236–41
Memorial de la politica necesaria y util a la republica de Espana (González de Cellorigo), 11
Merchant's Magazine, 183
Mexican pillar dollar, 31
Michigan, 143, 195
million-dollar notes, 4
"Million Pound Note, The" (Twain), 5
Milliron, John, 214
Mint, U.S., 159, 183, 221, 249
drops commitment to silver, 261
established, in Philadelphia, 106, 125–28
mint ratio
under Hamilton, 125–26
rearranged, in 1834, 194
Mississippi, 143, 206
Missouri, 143, 154–55
"Modest Enquiry into the Nature and Necessity of a Paper-Currency, A" (Franklin), 50, 51
money. *See also* currency; hard currency; paper money
America born of, in Spanish search for gold, 9–12